Briefcase on

CRIMINAL LAW

Third Edition

Julia Fionda, LLB, PhD
Senior Lecturer in Law, University of Southampton
Michael Bryant, MMP, LLB, BA, MA, LLM
Attorney General of Ontario, Canada

Cavendish
Publishing
Limited

London • Sydney • Portland, Oregon

Third edition first published in Great Britain 2004 by
Cavendish Publishing Limited, The Glass House,
Wharton Street, London WC1X 9PX, United Kingdom
Telephone: + 44 (0)20 7278 8000   Facsimile: + 44 (0)20 7278 8080
Email: info@cavendishpublishing.com
Website: www.cavendishpublishing.com

Published in the United States by Cavendish Publishing
c/o International Specialized Book Services,
5824 NE Hassalo Street, Portland,
Oregon 97213-3644, USA

Published in Australia by Cavendish Publishing (Australia) Pty Ltd
3/303 Barrenjoey Road, Newport, NSW 2106, Australia

British Library Cataloguing in Publication Data
Fionda, Julia –
Briefcase on criminal law – 3rd ed – (Cavendish briefcase)
1 Criminal law – England 2 Criminal law – Wales
I Title II Bryant, Michael J
345.4'2

Library of Congress Cataloguing in Publication Data
Data available

ISBN 1-85941-762-0
ISBN 978-1-859-417621
1 3 5 7 9 10 8 6 4 2

Printed and bound in Great Britain by Biddles Ltd, Kings Lynn, Norfolk

For Rob

With love and thanks

CONTENTS

TABLE OF CASES

TABLE OF STATUTES

CHAPTER 1

MURDER AND INTENTION

Introduction

Murder, a common law offence, is defined as the 'unlawful killing of a reasonable person in being'. The *mens rea* of the offence is intention to kill or cause grievous bodily harm. The *actus reus* is reasonably straightforward. Questions have been raised in the courts regarding where a person's life begins in the case of a foetus. The Court of Appeal also had to consider this issue in trying to tackle the very difficult moral dilemma of whether to override the parents' strong objections to a surgical operation to separate their conjoined twins. This case cannot be viewed as a precedent given its highly extraordinary circumstances, but it is interesting that the court decided that the operation should go ahead, notwithstanding that this would immediately cause the death of the weaker twin. Their comment that she could not sustain life on her own suggests that she might not be considered a 'person in being' were a doctor performing the operation charged with causing her death.

The other *actus reus* to note is that Parliament has now abolished the ancient 'year and a day rule' so that murder charges may be brought long after the defendant's act which ultimately caused the victim's death. This was a development designed to bring the law up to date with developments in medical science and technological advancements which mean that an injured victim may be kept alive for many months or even years before death finally occurs.

The larger part of the case law here has discussed the precise meaning of intention and the meaning of the grievous bodily harm intended to suffice for the *mens rea* of murder. Intention has, through the years, been considered to include foresight of highly probable consequences as well as wilfulness or deliberation. This has weakened the notion of intention but the courts have been keen to point out that the line between recklessness and intention has not been blurred – the probability of the risk being the key differentiating factor.

1.1   *Actus reus* of homicide

1.1.1   Death of a person 'in being'

Poulton (1832): Is a foetus a human being for the purposes of murder?

Facts

D gave birth to a child; its body was later found with a ligature around its neck. Evidence established that the child had breathed, but not whether the breathing took place during or after birth.

Decision

D was not guilty of murder. 'With respect to birth, the being born must mean that the whole body is brought into the world, and it is not sufficient that the child respires in the progress of birth' (*per* Littledale J).

Comments

A foetus is not a human being for the purposes of the law of homicide. However, an intentionally procured miscarriage that contravenes the Abortion Act 1967 may incur felonious criminal liability under the Offences Against the Person Act 1861. Terminating a foetus that is capable of being born may also incur liability under the Infant Life (Preservation) Act 1929.

AG's Reference (No 3 of 1994) (1997): Is a foetus a 'person in being'?

Facts

D stabbed a pregnant woman with the intention of harming her alone. She then went into premature labour, her child being born alive. D pleaded guilty to wounding the woman with intent. Subsequently her child died owing to its prematurity and D was charged with the murder of the child.

Decision

The House of Lords stated that D could be guilty of manslaughter but not murder. The requisite intent to be proved in the case of murder was an intention to kill or cause really serious injury to the mother, the foetus before birth being an integral part of the mother. Such intention was appropriately modified in the case of murder. The fact that the death of the child was caused solely in consequence of injury to the mother rather than injury to the foetus did not negate any liability for murder or manslaughter, provided that the jury were satisfied that causation was proved. *Per* Lord Mustill: 'The mother and the foetus were two distinct organisms living symbiotically, not a single organism with two aspects. The mother's leg was part of the mother; the foetus was not.' Nor is the foetus a 'person'. Rather, 'it is a unique organism'. *Per* Lord Hope:

> So far as *mens rea* for the common law crime of manslaughter is concerned, I consider that it is sufficient that, at the time of the stabbing, the defendant had the *mens rea* which was needed to convict him of an assault on the child's mother ... The child in this case, when she became a living person, [should be regarded] within the scope of the *mens rea* which the defendant had when he stabbed her mother before she was born.

Re A (Children) (Conjoined Twins: Surgical Separation) (2001): Is one conjoined twin dependent on the other a person in being?

Facts

J and M were conjoined twins born to devout Roman Catholic parents. The twins were joined at the pelvis but each had their own brain, heart, lungs and limbs. Medical evidence established that J was the stronger twin and was sustaining the life of M. If not separated both twins would die within a few months, but if they were separated J was likely to live a worthwhile life although M would die immediately. The parents refused to consent to the surgical separation on religious grounds and the hospital sought the court's permission to override that refusal. At first instance the judge overruled the parents' wishes and the parents appealed.

Decision

The Court of Appeal argued that the proposed operation was an act of necessity to preserve the life of J and therefore a positive act. It was not the negative act of terminating the life of M. It was inappropriate in these extraordinary circumstances to characterise the foresight of M's death as criminal intention on the part of the doctors. Further, the balance between preserving J's life though accelerating M's death on the one hand and allowing both twins' lives to end naturally on the other was, in the view of the court, heavily weighted in favour of the former. That decision gave the chance of life to the twin whose body was capable of sustaining it, even though that was at the cost of the sacrifice of the life of M which was so unnaturally supported and could not sustain life.

1.1.2   Death following within a year and a day

Section 1 of the Law Reform (Year and a Day Rule) Act 1996

The rule known as the 'year and a day rule' (that is the rule that, for the purposes of offences involving death and suicide, an act or omission is conclusively presumed not to have caused a person's death if more than a year and a day has elapsed before he died) is abolished for all purposes.

Comment

As a result of this legislation, a causal link between D's act and V's death can be established at any time and the case of *Dyson* no longer applies. This reflects the advancement of medical science in the 20th century and the act that it is possible for V to be kept alive notwithstanding his or her injuries for some considerable time (possibly even years). Now D's liability is not negated by this lapse of time.

1.2   Mens rea of murder

1.2.1   Intention to kill or cause grievous bodily harm

Smith (1961): Meaning of grievous bodily harm

Facts

D, in possession of stolen goods, was driving a car when a policeman, V, ordered him to pull over. D sped away with V clinging to the door, resulting in V's fatal collision with another car.

Decision

The House of Lords found D guilty of murder. *Per* Viscount Kilmuir LC:

> [1] The words 'grievous bodily harm' are to be given 'their ordinary and natural meaning'. 'Bodily harm' needs no explanation, and 'grievous' means ... 'really serious' [2] [I]t matters not what the accused in fact contemplated as the probable result or whether he ever contemplated [it] at all ... the sole question is whether the unlawful and voluntary act was of such a kind that grievous bodily harm was the natural and probable result. The only test available for this is what the ordinary responsible man would, in all the circumstances of the case, have contemplated as the natural and probable result.

Comments

See *Woollin* (1998) below where Lord Steyn stated: 'There was widespread and severe criticism of the second part of the decision in *Smith*. In retrospect, it is now clear the criminal law was set on a wrong course. By s 8 of the Criminal Justice Act 1967, Parliament reversed the effect of *Smith*.' It was also stated in *Frankland and Moore* (1987) that part [2] of the decision in *Smith* was wrong.

Hyam v DPP (1975): Intention as foresight of probable consequences

Facts

D sought to frighten an occupant of a house by pouring petrol through the letterbox and then igniting it, resulting in the death of two occupants by asphyxia.

Decision

The House of Lords found D guilty of manslaughter. *Per* Lord Hailsham LC, intention is to be distinguished from desire and foresight of probable consequences: '... a man may desire to blow up an aircraft in flight in order to obtain insurance moneys. But, if any passengers are killed, he is guilty of murder, as their death will be a moral certainty if he carries out his intention.' Therefore, intention is established 'where the defendant knows that there is a serious risk that death or grievous bodily harm will ensue from his acts, and commits those acts deliberately and without lawful excuse ... It does not matter that the act and the intention were aimed at a potential victim other than the one who succumbed.' *Per* Viscount Dilhorne:

> A man may do an act with a number of intentions. If he does it deliberately and intentionally, knowing that when he does it that it is highly probable that grievous bodily harm will result ... [then] whatever other intentions he may have had as well, he at least intended grievous bodily harm.

Cunningham (1981): Intention to cause grievous bodily harm

Facts

D attacked V in a pub, hitting him with a chair, which resulted in V's death.

Decision

The House of Lords found D guilty of murder. Intention to cause grievous bodily harm, but not to cause death, is sufficient to establish the *mens rea* for murder. *Per* Lord Hailsham LC: '... malice aforethought has never been limited to the intention to kill or to endanger life.' *Per* Lord Edmund-Davies (dissenting):

> I find it strange that a person can be convicted of murder if death results from, say, his intentional breaking of another's arm, it no doubt constituting 'serious harm'. But I recognise the force of the contrary view that the outcome of intentionally inflicting serious harm can be so unpredictable that anyone prepared to act so wickedly has little ground for complaint if, where death results, he is convicted and punished as severely as one who intended to kill.

AG's Reference (No 3 of 1994) (1997)

See 1.1.1 above.

1.2.2 Intention includes knowledge or foresight

Moloney (1985): Foresight of natural consequences

Facts
During a late night of drinking, D and V had a contest as to loading and firing a shotgun. At V's taunting of D to fire the gun, D shot V without aiming.

Decision
In finding D not guilty of murder, the House of Lords stated:

> ... foresight of consequences, as an element bearing on the issue of intention in murder, or indeed any other crime of specific intent, belongs, not to the substantive law, but to the law of evidence ... In rare cases in which it is necessary for the judge to direct a jury by reference to foresight of consequences, I do not believe it is necessary for the judge to do more than invite the jury to consider two questions. First, was death or really serious injury in a murder case (or whatever relevant consequence must be proved to have been intended in any other case) a natural consequence of the defendant's voluntary act? Secondly, did the defendant foresee that consequence as being a natural consequence of this act? The jury should then be told that if they answer yes to both questions, it is a proper inference for them to draw that he intended that consequence (*per* Lord Bridge).

Hancock and Shankland (1986): Foresight of highly probable consequences

Facts
In the midst of a miners' strike, in which they were participating, H and S pushed a concrete block and post from a bridge over the road along which M was being driven by V; V was killed in the collision.

Decision
The House of Lords held that H and S were not guilty of murder. *Per* Lord Scarman, the issue of probability regarding death or serious injury is critical to determining intention, yet the House of Lords in *Moloney* omitted any reference in its guidelines to this issue:

> ... therefore, the *Moloney* guidelines as they stand are unsafe and misleading. They require a reference to probability. They also require an explanation that the greater the probability of a consequence the more likely it is that the consequence was foreseen and that, if that consequence was foreseen, the greater the probability is that that consequence was also intended.

Comment
This decision overruled the decision in *Moloney*.

Nedrick (1986): Foresight of virtually certain consequences

Facts
D poured paraffin through the letterbox of a house and set it alight, resulting in the death of a child.

Decision

In finding D guilty of manslaughter, not murder, the Court of Appeal stated:

> [A] Where the charge is murder and in the rare cases where the simple direction [on intent] is not enough, the jury should be directed that they were not entitled to infer the necessary intention unless they feel sure that death or serious bodily harm was a virtual certainty (barring some unforeseen intervention) as a result of the defendant's actions, and that the defendant realised that such was the case. [B] Where a man realises that it is for all practical purposes inevitable that his actions will result in death or serious harm, the inference may be irresistible that he intended that result, however little he may have desired or wished it to happen. The decision is one for the jury, to be reached on consideration of all the evidence (*per* Lord Lane CJ).

Comments

The Court of Appeal's model direction in this case was affirmed by the House of Lords in *Woollin* below.

Woollin (1998): Foresight of a substantial risk not enough for murder

Facts

D lost his temper and threw his son, aged three months, on to a hard surface, resulting in his fractured skull and death.

Decision

The House of Lords held that D was not guilty of murder. *Per* Lord Steyn: a foresight of 'substantial risk' will not constitute murder, because it 'blur[s] the line between intention and recklessness, and hence between murder and manslaughter … Lord Lane's judgment in *Nedrick* (1986) provided valuable assistance to trial judges. The model direction is by now a tried and tested formula. Trial judges ought to continue to use it, subject to [the following] observations on matters of detail; namely, the words "to find" should replace Lord Lane's words "to infer" under [in part A of the above excerpt] and the first sentence [in part B] does not form part of the model direction.'

Matthews and Alleyne (2003): Model direction on intention

Facts

V was assaulted by A and C outside a nightclub. V's bank card was stolen and after the attack A and M tried unsuccessfully to obtain money from a cash point using V's card. V fled and tried to flag a lift from a passing motorist. Instead he was forced into C's car, driven to a bridge and thrown into the river below. V drowned. At the trial for his murder, some of the defendants argued that the death was not intended and was an accident. The judge directed the jury to find intention where the death had been foreseen by the defendants as a virtually certain consequence of their actions.

Decision

The Court of Appeal stated that the law had not yet reached a definition of intent in murder in terms of virtual certainty as the judgment in *Woollin* (above) was not regarded as laying down a substantive rule of law – it merely developed the judgment in *Nedrick* (above). The proper direction was that the jury were 'not entitled to find the necessary intention unless they felt sure that death, or serious bodily harm, was a virtual certainty as a result of the defendant's actions and that the defendant appreciated that this was the case'. There is a difference between appreciation of virtually certain consequences and foresight of merely probable consequences.

Walker and Hayles (1990): The degree of probability required for murder

Facts

W and H threw V from a third floor balcony. V was not killed.

Decision

In finding W and H guilty of attempted murder, the Court of Appeal stated:

> … once one departs from absolute certainty, there is bound to be a question of degree. Reading Lord Scarman's speech in *Hancock* and [reading] *Nedrick*, we are not persuaded that is only when death is a virtual certainty that the jury can infer intention to kill. Providing the dividing line between intention and recklessness is never blurred, and provided it is made clear … that it is a question for the jury to infer from the degree of probability in the particular case whether the defendant intended to kill, we would not regard the use of the words 'very high degree of probability' as a misdirection (*per* Lloyd LJ).

Janjua (1999): Foresight of 'serious' harm

Facts

V was stabbed to death with a five and a half-inch knife, which penetrated his heart. D was charged with murder. He appealed against his conviction on the grounds that, in his direction to the jury regarding the *mens rea* of murder, the trial judge had omitted the word 'really' before the phrase 'serious bodily harm'.

Decision

The Court of Appeal upheld D's conviction. Given the weapon used – in this case a five and a half-inch bladed knife – and the subsequent injuries caused to V, the word 'really' did not need to precede the phrase 'serious bodily harm'. There was no risk that D had been convicted on a lower standard of *mens rea* than that required for a conviction for murder. *Per incuriam*: in other factual situations it may be necessary for the judge to use the word 'really' – but that is a matter for the discretion of the judge. The word is not necessary in all cases.

1.2.3   Constructive malice

Vickers (1957): Constructive malice applied

Facts

During D's burglary of V's shop, D was discovered by V, whereupon D struck V with several blows. V eventually died from shock due to general injuries.

Decision

The Court of Appeal found D guilty of murder because:

> ... he has killed a person with the necessary malice aforethought being implied from the fact that he intended to do grievous bodily harm ... in considering the construction of s 1(1) [of the Homicide Act 1957], it is impossible to say that the doing of grievous bodily harm is the other offence which is referred to in the first line and a half of the sub-section [which abolishes constructive malice]. It must be shown that independently of the fact that the accused is committing another offence, the act which caused the death was done with malice aforethought as implied by law (*per* Lord Goddard CJ).

Comments

Section 1 of the Homicide Act 1957 abolished what was commonly referred to as constructive malice, or the murder felony rule; that is, constructing or imputing malice aforethought in a *legal* sense where it did not exist in reality in circumstances where the defendant caused death during the course of carrying out another felony which involved violence. Under the abolished rule, this would have constituted murder, despite the absence of an intention to kill or cause grievous bodily harm. In the above case, the defendant's *mens rea* was established from his intention to cause grievous bodily harm during the attack and not constructed from his intention in relation to the burglary.

CHAPTER 2

VOLUNTARY MANSLAUGHTER

Introduction

Voluntary manslaughter refers to cases where the *actus reus* and *mens rea* for murder exists and a murder charge has been brought, but the defendant raises a defence under the Homicide Act 1957. Where these defences are successfully pleaded, the court may convict the defendant of manslaughter instead of murder.

The reduction of murder to manslaughter by reason of provocation is governed by s 3 of the Homicide Act 1957. It entails, first, a subjective determination of whether D was in fact provoked to lose self-control ('whether by things done or by things said or by both together') and secondly, an objective determination of 'whether the provocation was enough to make a reasonable man do as [D] did'. The case law in this area has focused on both parts of the test.

First, there is the question of whether the defendant actually lost self-control, and cases where the defendant had time to reflect or plan the killing have not been considered cases of provocation. For example, Ahluwalia's loss of self-control took place over a number of years and her slow-burn anger did not provide the sudden loss of temper and control required.

Secondly, the courts have addressed how far, in applying the objective test as to the gravity of the provocation, the jury may share some of the defendant's characteristics which may be relevant to their reaction to the provocation. To some extent, allowing the jury to share the defendant's characteristics reduces the objectivity of the test, but the courts have been reluctant to allow the jury to share general features of the defendant (for example, drug addiction, impotence of emotional affectations) unless the defendant was actually taunted about those features. Note too that battered woman syndrome, which occurs frequently in these cases, has not been a characteristic relevant to this objective test. The courts have preferred defendants suffering from this syndrome to plead the defence of diminished responsibility, under which it can be considered an abnormality of mind.

Under s 2 of the Homicide Act 1957, the defendant can plead the defence of diminished responsibility where they are judged to have 'an abnormality of mind arising from a condition of arrested or retarded development of mind or any inherent causes, or was induced by disease or injury and that the said abnormality substantially impaired his mental responsibility for his acts in doing or being a party to a killing'. Therefore, again, there are two requirements that the courts have addressed in the case law.

First, there is the question of whether any mental disorder falls within the statutory definition of abnormality of mind. Generally the cases show that the courts are prepared to accept any physical or psychological condition for which there is sufficient medical or other evidence and provided it is a professionally recognised condition (for example, battered woman syndrome). The main exception to this has been alcoholism, which the courts have not recognised, unless the intake of alcohol has been so great as to cause physical brain damage. Secondly, it has to be established that the mental abnormality sufficiently impaired the defendant's responsibility for his actions. In particular, the case of *Dietschmann* (2003) explores the impact of intoxication on this impairment.

2.1 Provocation

2.1.1 Sudden and temporary loss of self-control subjectively determined

Ibrams and Gregory (1981): Desire for revenge not evidence of loss of self-control

Facts
I, G and W had been repeatedly bullied and otherwise provoked by V up to and including a week before I and G attacked V in his sleep, pursuant to their plot with W to avoid further bullying. V died as a result of the attack, which was intended to break V's arms and legs.

Decision
The Court of Appeal found I and G were guilty of murder. *Per* Lawton LJ:

> Nothing happened on the night of the killing which caused [I] to lose his self-control. There having been a plan to kill [V], his evidence that when he saw him, all the past came to his mind does not … provide any evidence of loss of self-control … Indeed, circumstances which induce a desire for revenge are inconsistent with provocation, since the conscious formulation of a desire for revenge means that a person has had time to think, to reflect, and that would negative a sudden and temporary loss of self-control, which is the essence of provocation [*per* Devlin J in *Duffy* (1949)].

Thornton (No 1) (1992): Sudden and temporary loss of self-control

Facts
D was abused by her husband throughout their first year of marriage. One night, her husband was intoxicated and called D a whore; D then obtained a carving knife for protection. The husband threatened to kill D in her sleep and sarcastically taunted D to kill him first. D stabbed him once in the stomach, causing his death. D initially told the police that she wanted to kill him.

Decision
The Court of Appeal found D guilty of murder. To establish provocation there must be a 'sudden and temporary loss of self-control' (*per* Devlin J in *Duffy* (1949)). *Per* Beldam LJ, in cases involving a history of domestic violence '… the question for the jury is whether at the moment the fatal blow was struck, the accused had been deprived for that moment of the self-control which previously he or she had been able to exercise'.

Comments

The conviction of Thornton in this case was later overturned in *Thornton (No 2)* (1995) – set out below. The latter case was the appeal referred to the Court of Appeal by the Home Secretary pursuant to s 17 of the Criminal Appeal Act 1968, based primarily on further medical evidence and its impact on the defence of provocation.

Thornton (No 2) (1995): Battered woman syndrome and provocation

Facts

The facts are set out above in *Thornton (No 1)*. New evidence had arisen from establishing that D had a personality disorder and had suffered from 'battered woman syndrome'.

Decision

The Court of Appeal ordered a retrial having quashed D's conviction for murder. Even if suffering from battered woman syndrome, D could not succeed in relying on provocation unless the jury considered she suffered, or might have suffered, a sudden and temporary loss of self-control at the time of the killing. *Per* Lord Taylor of Gosforth, the relevance of battered woman syndrome is that:

> First, it may form an important background to whatever triggered the *actus reus*. A jury may more readily find there was a sudden loss of control triggered by even a minor incident if the defendant has endured abuse over a period, on the 'last straw' basis. Secondly, depending on the medical evidence, the syndrome may have affected the defendant's personality so as to constitute a significant characteristic relevant ... to the second question the jury has to consider in regard to provocation.

Ahluwalia (1993): 'slow-burn' reaction and provocation

Facts

D, subjected to 10 years of spousal violence and degradation, threw petrol in her husband's bedroom and set it alight, causing his death.

Decision

The Court of Appeal ordered a retrial, having quashed D's conviction for murder. *Per* Lord Taylor CJ:

> [1] Only Parliament, not the courts, could permit a provocation defence in circumstances of a 'slow-burn' reaction [to long term spousal violence] rather than by an immediate loss of self-control. [2] The subjective element in the defence of provocation would not as a matter of law be negatived simply because of the delayed reaction in such cases, provided that there was at the time of the killing a 'sudden and temporary loss of self-control' caused by the alleged provocation. However, the longer the delay and the stronger the evidence of deliberation on the part of the defendant, the more likely it will be that the prosecution will negative provocation. [3] No evidence was adduced at trial that D suffered from a post-traumatic stress disorder or 'battered woman syndrome' so as to affect the characteristics relevant to the reasonableness of D's actions under the second part of the provocation test. (See 2.1.2 below.)

Baillie (1995): Cooling off within a chain of events

Facts

D, who had consumed a large amount of alcohol on the evening in question, was told by his son that the latter had been threatened by V (who supplied the son with soft drugs). D went up into his attic, collected a sawn-off shotgun and a cut-throat razor, drove his car for some two miles, stopped to fill his car with petrol, then went to V's house. On entering V's house, he inflicted wounds on V using the razor. V fled the house and D followed, firing the shotgun twice. V died as a result of wounds from metal shards from a fence which had been hit by the bullets. D pleaded provocation as a defence to the charge of murder, but the trial judge refused to leave the defence with the jury, claiming that there was insufficient evidence.

Decision

The Court of Appeal held that the trial judge was wrong not to leave the defence of provocation with the jury. Whether the evidence is sufficient to raise such a defence is a value judgment for the jury and not the judge. In this case, there was no natural break between the conversation between D and his son and the eventual shooting, notwithstanding that D stopped to fill his car with petrol. Further, D acted in a way 'apparently quite inconsistent with anything he had done before', notwithstanding his intoxicated state. Therefore the jury should have been given the opportunity to assess this evidence and make their own judgment as to whether the defence of provocation could succeed.

2.1.2   *Provocation of such gravity as to make a reasonable man commit homicide*

Bedder (1954): Relevance of sexual impotence as characteristic of defendant

Facts

D attempted sexual intercourse with a prostitute, but failed due to his impotence. She taunted D, punched and slapped him, and kicked him in the groin, whereupon D stabbed her twice, causing her death.

Decision

The House of Lords found D guilty of murder. The jury should consider the effects of the taunts and violence upon D without regard to his sexual impotence. *Per* Lord Simmons LC:

> It would be plainly illogical not to recognise an unusually excitable or pugnacious temperament in the accused as a matter to be taken into account but yet to recognise for that purpose some unusual physical characteristic, be it impotence or another.

Comments

This latter proposition was overruled by the House of Lords in *DPP v Camplin* (below), as modified by the Homicide Act 1957.

Brown (1972): Relationship between the provocation and the retaliation

Facts

D accused his wife of adultery, resulting in a violent struggle between the two. D claimed he blacked out shortly before cutting her throat with a razor, causing her death.

Decision

The Court of Appeal upheld D's conviction for murder. The manner of retaliation to the provocation is relevant to determining the reasonableness of D's actions. *Per* Talbot J: '… a jury should be instructed to consider the relationship of the accused's acts to the provocation when asking themselves the question "Was it enough to make a reasonable man do as he did?"'

DPP v Camplin (1978): Age and sex relevant characteristics of D

Facts

D, aged 15, claimed to have been subjected to anal intercourse by V, without D's consent, after which V 'laughed at' D. D thereupon killed V by splitting his skull with a heavy pan.

Decision

The House of Lords found that D was guilty of manslaughter, not murder. Section 3 of the Homicide Act 1957 retains a dual test, *per* Lord Diplock:

> … the provocation must not only have caused the accused to lose his self-control but also be such as might cause a reasonable man to react to it as the accused did … the reasonable man … is a person having the power of self-control to be expected of an ordinary person of the sex and age of the accused, but in other respects sharing such of the accused's characteristics as they [the jury] think would affect the gravity of the provocation to him.

Newell (1980): Relevance of immutable characteristics to level of self-control

Facts

D, a chronic alcoholic, battered his friend V to death after V made insulting remarks about D's former cohabitee.

Decision

The Court of Appeal upheld D's conviction of murder. In assessing the reasonableness of D's actions, by reference to D's characteristics as per *Camplin* above, the jury may consider immutable characteristics of the accused going to the gravity of the provocation (for example, race), but not characteristics going to the level of self-control such as alcoholism, grief, mental deficiency or weak-mindedness. 'In short, there must be some direct connection between the provocative words or conduct and the characteristic sought to be invoked as warranting some departure from the ordinary man test (*per* North J in *McGregor* (1962)).'

Doughty (1986): Objective test for provocation must be left to jury

Facts
D killed his 17 day old son, raising the defence that the baby's persistent crying and restlessness constituted provocation.

Decision
The Court of Appeal found D guilty of manslaughter, not murder. The trial judge erred in refusing to leave the defence of provocation to the jury. The Homicide Act 1957 requires the trial judge to leave to the jury the issue of the objective test, that is, the second part of the test set out in s 3 of the Act.

Johnson (1989): Prior fault does not vitiate defence of provocation

Facts
D and V were drinking at a nightclub. V's girlfriend taunted D, who proceeded to threaten both her and V himself. When D attempted to leave the club, V poured beer over D and pinned him against the wall, whereupon D was attacked by V's girlfriend. D stabbed V, causing his death.

Decision
The Court of Appeal found D guilty of manslaughter, not murder. The presence of prior fault does not *ipso facto* vitiate provocation. *Per* Watkins LJ:

> ... whether or not there were elements in [D's] conduct which justified the conclusion that he had started the trouble and induced others, including [V], to react in the way they did ... the defence of provocation should have been left to the jury.

Clarke (1991): Jury must consider D's whole conduct in considering provocation

Facts
V told her boyfriend, D, that she was having an abortion. D lost self-control, hitting and strangling V, the act perhaps killing her. D then panicked and electrocuted V with live wires from a lamp.

Decision
The Court of Appeal found D guilty of murder. Provided that the conduct causing death was part of one continuing assault, the jury should look at everything the accused had done in considering whether a reasonable man would have acted in the same way. However, some factors (for example, disposing of the body) may be too remote for consideration.

Egan (1992): Effects of alcohol and drugs irrelevant

Facts
D, said to be mentally unstable, was intoxicated when he forcibly entered the bungalow of a 78 year old widow, severely assaulting and killing her.

Decision
The Court of Appeal found D guilty of murder. Following *Gittens* (1984), a jury should be directed to disregard the effects of alcohol or drugs and determine if the

combined effect of any abnormalities of mind was substantially to impair D's responsibility.

Ahluwalia (1993): Battered woman syndrome

See 2.1.1 above.

Morhall (1995): Solvent abuse addiction a relevant characteristic if subject of provocation

Facts

D was addicted to glue sniffing and had killed V after he had nagged D over a protracted period about his solvent abuse habit.

Decision

In finding D guilty of manslaughter, not murder, the House of Lords stated that the reasonable person is:

> ... a hypothetical person having the power of self-control to be expected of an ordinary person of the age and sex of the defendant, but, in other respects, having such of the defendant's characteristics as they think would effect the gravity of the provocation to him ... [A jury] must take into account the entire actual situation (and, in particular, the fact that the provocation was directed at a habitual glue sniffer taunted with his habit) when considering the question whether the provocation was enough to cause a man possessed of an ordinary man's power of self-control to act as the defendant did (*per* Lord Goff).

Humphreys (1995): Relevance of attention seeking personality

Facts

D was living in a tempestuous relationship with V. V was very possessive and jealous of D and regularly assaulted her. One evening D attempted to cut her own wrists. When V returned to the house he taunted her about her failed attempts. D stabbed and killed V. D was charged with murder but pleaded the defence of provocation on the grounds that her immature, explosive and attention seeking characteristics caused her to lose her self-control. D was convicted of murder and appealed.

Decision

The Court of Appeal held that the jury should have been allowed to consider the defendant's particular characteristics. Attention seeking behaviour was a permanent characteristic and was not inconsistent with the concept of the reasonable man.

Dryden (1995): Obsessive and eccentric personality as a relevant characteristic

Facts

D built a bungalow without planning permission. The local authority formed the view that D was unlikely to get planning permission for the building and therefore issued a demolition order. V, a local planning officer, arrived at the property as the demolition was due to begin in order to remove D from the premises. D emerged from the bungalow and shot and killed V. D pleaded provocation in defence to his murder charge. He claimed his eccentric and obsessive personality caused him to lose his self-control. D was convicted of murder.

Decision

The Court of Appeal quashed D's conviction for murder. The jury were entitled to consider any characteristics which distinguished D from the ordinary person in the community. Therefore, D's eccentric and obsessive personality should have been considered by the jury in applying the reasonable man test.

Luc Thiet-Thuan (1996): Mental infirmity only relevant if subject of provocation

Facts

D and others robbed V, an ex-girlfriend; then, during an altercation, D stabbed and killed V. Evidence was adduced that D, following a fall in which he was rendered unconscious, was prone to lack of control when provoked.

Decision

The Privy Council found D guilty of murder. *Per* Lord Goff:

> ... there is no basis upon which mental infirmity on the part of the defendant, which has the effect of reducing his powers of self-control below that to be expected of an ordinary person, can, as such, be attributed to the ordinary person for the purposes of the objective test in provocation. [Nevertheless] ... mental infirmity of the defendant, if itself the subject of taunts by the deceased, may be taken into account as going to the gravity of the provocation as applied to the defendant.

Per Lord Steyn (dissenting): '... brain damage, and its impact on [D's] response to provocation, depending on what the jury made of it, was relevant to the objective requirement of provocation.'

Horrex (1999): Affectionate feelings not a relevant 'characteristic'

Facts

D, V and G were all vagrants living in Oxford. D had a strong emotional attachment to G, and described her as a 'mother figure'. D was also having a sexual relationship with V. After V had attacked G, D became angry and had a fight with V. V died and D was charged with murder. At trial, the defence of provocation was left to the jury. D was convicted and appealed, claiming that D's feelings for G should have been considered by the jury in applying the objective *Camplin* test for provocation.

Decision

The Court of Appeal held that the word 'characteristic' should not be applied to the affectionate feelings. Such emotions which commonly arise in close relationships could not themselves amount to a characteristic for the purpose of the test under s 3 of the Homicide Act 1957, as opposed to medical or other evidence, which showed that D was distinguished from other ordinary members of the community.

Smith (2001): Depressive condition as a relevant characteristic

Facts

D and an intoxicated V had an argument. D picked up a knife and stabbed V, but had no recollection of doing this. D had a depressive condition, but it did not constitute an abnormality of mind for the defence of diminished responsibility.

Decision

The House of Lords stated that the trial judge was wrong to direct the jury to ignore D's depressive condition in applying the objective test. Whilst generally the same standards of self-control apply to everyone in society when applying such a test, 'in an appropriate case the judge should make clear that the standard may need to be adjusted to accommodate the defendant's reduced capacity for self-control which may have any number of different explanations' (*per* Lord Slynn):

> While I fully recognise the importance of not allowing the effects of a quarrelsome or choleric temperament to serve as a factor which may reduce the crime of murder to one of manslaughter, nevertheless I consider that justice cannot be done without regard to the particular frailties of particular individuals where their capacity to restrain themselves in the face of provocation is lessened by some affliction which falls short of a mental abnormality (*per* Lord Clyde).

Although delivering a dissenting judgement, Lord Millett gave further guidance on how the reasonable man test should be applied:

> The expression the 'reasonable man'... is not intended to invoke the concept of reasonable conduct: it can never be reasonable to react to provocation by killing the person responsible for it. Nor by pleading provocation does the accused claim to have acted reasonably. His case is that he acted unreasonably, but only because he was provoked. But while this may not be reasonable it may be understandable, for even normally reasonable people may lose their self-control and react unreasonably if sufficiently provoked.

Hence Lord Millett is stating that the defence of provocation is a justificatory defence. That is, the law is not stating that it is right to kill another who provokes D, but that it is understandable in certain circumstances given D's particular characteristics.

Comment

Lord Hoffmann was keen to emphasise that: '[the judge] should not be obliged to let the jury imagine that the law now regards anything whatever which caused loss of self-control (whether an external event or a personal characteristic of the accused) as necessarily being an acceptable reason for loss of self-control.' As an indication of where to draw the line he further stated that 'possessiveness and jealousy should not today be an acceptable reason'. However, see *Weller* (2004) below.

Martin (2002)

See 8.2.1 below.

Weller (2004): Possessiveness and jealousy as relevant characteristics

Facts

D and V were lovers. V decided to end the relationship because of V's possessiveness and jealousy. An argument ensued during which D strangled V to death. D pleaded provocation but was convicted of murder.

Decision

The Court of Appeal stated that in deciding whether the reasonable man would have reacted to the provocation in the way that D did, the jury should have been directed to consider all of D's characteristics relevant to the issue of loss of self-control, including in this case D's possessiveness and jealousy.

2.1.3   Proportionality

Rampharry (1999): Retaliation must be proportionate to the provocation

Facts
D accused his ex-wife of promiscuity, and alleged that she had thrust a knife in his face. D alleged a struggle, then 'pounded' her with the knife. She died of stabbing wounds to the chest.

Decision
The Privy Council found D guilty of murder. Regardless of whether provocation actually occurred, D's response cannot be disproportionate to the provocation. Whether 'the retaliation of the accused must be proportionate to the provocative acts' was considered in the context of 'the reaction to be expected of the ordinary person' (*per* Sir Leggatt).

2.1.4   Duty to leave the defence of provocation before the jury

Dhillon (1997): Prima facie evidence of provocation

Facts
D and V were members of rival factions. One evening there was an altercation between members of the rival factions and a fight broke out. D drove a van at V and struck him, causing V's death. D claimed that he had been threatened my members of the rival group, was intending to drive away in the van, and therefore V's death was an accident. D also raised the defence of provocation at his trial. D was convicted of murder and appealed.

Decision
The Court of Appeal held that the trial judge was wrong not to leave the defence of provocation to the jury. Whilst D's plea of provocation did not sit comfortably next to his plea that the killing was an 'accident', there was evidence in this case that D was being threatened at the time he struck V, D did appear to lose his temper and that D had not gone 'looking for trouble'. This provided sufficient *prima facie* evidence of the defence, which imposed a duty on the judge to leave the issue to the jury. Since his murder conviction was unsafe, D's conviction was reduced to manslaughter.

2.2   Diminished responsibility

2.2.1   Abnormality of the mind impairing mental responsibility

Byrne (1960): Meaning of 'abnormality of mind'

Facts
D strangled to death and then mutilated a young woman, confessing to both in full. D raised the defence of diminished responsibility.

Decision

The Court of Appeal held that D was not guilty of murder by reason of diminished responsibility:

(1)   To satisfy the requirements of this defence under s 2 of the Homicide Act 1957, D must demonstrate that he suffered from an 'abnormality of mind' arising from a condition of arrested or retarded development of mind or any inherent causes, or was induced by disease or injury, and that the said abnormality substantially impaired his mental responsibility for his acts in doing or being a party to a killing.

(2)   An abnormality of mind is to be defined widely, per Lord Parker CJ: '… a state of mind so different from that of ordinary human beings that the reasonable man would term it "abnormal" and covering all cognitive aspects, from perception to rationality and "will power".'

Comments

Although the charge of manslaughter was substituted for murder, D was still sentenced by Lord Parker CJ to imprisonment for life.

Walton (1978): Non-medical evidence may be relevant to establish abnormality of mind

Facts

D was driving with his girlfriend, who thought he was 'acting funny' when he stopped the car. After she flagged down a car for assistance, D shot and killed a passenger in that car.

Decision

The Privy Council found D guilty of murder. *Per* Lord Keith:

> … upon an issue of diminished responsibility, the jury are … bound to consider not only the medical evidence, but the evidence upon the whole facts and the circumstances of the case. These include the nature of the killing, the conduct of the accused before, at the time of and after it and any history of mental abnormality.

Tandy (1989): Alcoholism not abnormality of mind unless intoxication caused brain damage

Facts

D, an alcoholic, had drunk nearly a bottle of vodka when she strangled her daughter.

Decision

The Court of Appeal found D guilty of murder. Alcoholism or drug addiction is relevant to determining an abnormality of mind only as a cause of diminished responsibility, not an effect. *Per* Watkins LJ:

> If the alcoholism has reached the level at which her brain had been injured by the repeated insult from intoxicants so that there was gross impairment of her judgment and emotional responses, then the defence of diminished responsibility was available to her … if her drinking was involuntary, then her abnormality of mind at the time of the act of strangulation was induced by her condition of alcoholism.

Ahluwalia (1993): Battered woman syndrome as an abnormality of mind

See 2.1.1 above.

Hobson (1997): Battered woman syndrome is an abnormality of mind

Facts
D had killed her alcoholic partner after a long and abusive relationship, and was convicted of murder. At trial she pleaded self-defence, and the defence of provocation was also left to the jury. She appealed against her conviction on the grounds that she was suffering from 'battered woman syndrome' at the time of the offence, and this gave rise to the defence of diminished responsibility. She had not pleaded this defence at trial, as battered woman syndrome was not classified at that time as a disease recognised by psychiatrists in Britain.

Decision
The Court of Appeal held that since battered woman syndrome is now part of the British classification of mental diseases and, given that there was supporting psychiatric evidence in this case, the defence should have been left to the jury. Accordingly, the conviction was unsafe and a retrial was ordered.

Sanderson (1994): Abnormality of mind includes psychosis caused by upbringing

Facts
D had a violent argument with his girlfriend, whom he killed by hitting her 100 times with a wooden object. Medical evidence established that D suffered from a paranoid psychosis arising from inherent causes, namely, his upbringing.

Decision
The Court of Appeal found D guilty of manslaughter by diminished responsibility. A permissible cause of an abnormality of the mind includes 'any inherent cause', which covers functional mental illness as well as organic or physical injury or disease of the body, including the brain.

Luc Thiet-Thuan (1996): Brain damage
See 2.1.2 above.

Antoine (1999): Unfitness to plead

Facts
D was charged with murder and found unfit to plead by reason of disability. A jury was especially formed to decide whether D 'had done the act charged against him as an offence' under s 4A Criminal Procedure (Insanity) Act 1964. (This section requires that there be a *prima facie* finding that D carried out the *actus reus* of the offence; if there is then they can find him unfit to plead. If not they should acquit.) D tried to plead diminished responsibility as a defence, thereby establishing that the *actus reus* of murder had not been committed. The judge refused the defence to be left to the jury and D appealed.

Decision
The House of Lords held that a defendant cannot plead diminished responsibility where a court has already made a finding of unfitness to plead through insanity. In

these circumstances, the court still has to consider whether an offence of murder has been committed, although only proof of the *actus reus* will be required. The defence of diminished responsibility can only be relevant to the determination of this question if it establishes that the defendant acted involuntarily, for example, where a person strikes another during an uncontrollable fit brought on by a medical condition. Where the defence of diminished responsibility merely establishes that D did not have the requisite *mens rea* for the offence of murder, then it is inadmissible in the determination of the question of fitness to plead.

Comment

See also *Grant (Heather)* (2002), where it was held that the defence of provocation could never be relevant to the determination of *actus reus* for the purposes of a finding of unfitness to plead. The defence of provocation is only concerned with D's state of mind at the time of the killing and presupposes that D carried out the killing with intention to kill or cause grievous bodily harm.

Dietschmann (2003): Abnormality of mind and intoxication

Facts

D, under the influence of alcohol, killed V whom he believed had insulted D's aunt. At his trial, D introduced evidence that at the time of the offence he was suffering from depressive grief as a result of his aunt's death. The judge directed the jury that in order to plead the defence of diminished responsibility D had to show that if he had not been intoxicated he would still have killed V, and that he would still have been operating under an abnormality of mind.

Decision

The House of Lords held that D was entitled to use diminished responsibility as a defence if he could establish that, despite the effects of alcohol on him, his abnormality of mind had substantially impaired his mental responsibility for his actions. Section 2 of the Homicide Act 1957 did not require the abnormality of mind to be the sole cause of D's actions. Even if D would not have killed V without consuming alcohol, the causative effect of the alcohol did not necessarily affect his abnormality of mind, substantially impairing his mental responsibility.

CHAPTER 3

INVOLUNTARY MANSLAUGHTER

Introduction

Charges of involuntary manslaughter arise where the defendant causes the victim's death but without the intention to kill or cause serious bodily harm required for the *mens rea* of murder. Hence the use of the word 'involuntary' to distinguish from cases of voluntary manslaughter, where such intention does exist but other defences partially negate liability. There are essentially three types of involuntary manslaughter and the cases below set out how these three offences have been developed by the common law.

First, where a defendant commits an unlawful act which results in V's death, he may be convicted of manslaughter. In this case there need be no *mens rea* on the part of the defendant relating to the death. The offence is proved where the *actus reus* requirements are present and death is caused and there is a high degree of negligence. Hence the cases have principally focused on the nature of the unlawful act and the causation issue. The act must be unlawful in the sense that it breaches the criminal law (a civil wrong will not suffice) and it must be dangerous, assessed objectively by the jury. On the causation issue there is a requirement that the act be 'directed' at the victim. This has been construed by the courts rather generously as meaning that there was no intervening act which may have caused the death. Hence a person who supplies a prohibited drug to another who subsequently dies as a result of taking the drug may be found guilty of this offence. This is because the supply of the drug is unlawful, it may be considered to be dangerous as the drug is prohibited and there was no break in the chain of events between the supply of the drug, V taking it and then dying (see *Kennedy* below).

Secondly, manslaughter may be committed where the defendant causes the death of the victim by committing acts (lawful or otherwise) which are grossly negligent. Negligence bears the same meaning as it does in the law of torts, but for a criminal charge the negligence must be 'gross' (see *Adomako* (1994) below). This means that the defendant must breach a duty owed to the victim, and act with a very high degree of negligence or disregard for an obvious risk of death to the victim. Manslaughter by gross negligence was established as an offence in *Andrews v DPP*, although briefly the courts used the objective test of recklessness as the *mens rea* for manslaughter after *Lawrence* (1981). In *Adomako* (1994), the House of Lords rejected the objective test of recklessness in this context and re-confirmed that gross negligence was the appropriate *mens rea* for this offence.

Thirdly, where the victim's death is caused by the defendant failing to act (such as in a case of neglect) the defendant may be charged with involuntary manslaughter. In these cases the requirements of the offence are the same as the second category above; namely the defendant must breach a duty of care owed to the victim and must do so with a high degree of negligence. The difference between the two categories is in the way that the death is caused – by an act in the former category and by a failure to act in the latter.

3.1 Unlawful act manslaughter

3.1.1 Predicate offence causing death must be an unlawful act

Franklin (1883): A civil wrong is not an unlawful act for a manslaughter charge

Facts

D took a box from another man's stall on a pier and threw it into the sea. The box struck and killed V who was swimming.

Decision

D was not guilty of manslaughter. A civil wrong is immaterial to a charge of manslaughter (rejecting *Fenton* (1830)). *Per* Field J: ' ... the mere fact of a civil wrong committed by one person against another ought not to be used as an incident which is a necessary step in a criminal case.'

Andrews v DPP (1937): Reckless lawful act not sufficient

Facts

D had been dispatched by his employer to assist a disabled vehicle. D killed a pedestrian whilst attempting to pass another car by driving well over on the offside of the road.

Decision

The House of Lords found D guilty of manslaughter by gross negligence, not by an unlawful act. *Per* Lord Atkin:

> [1] There is an obvious difference in the law of manslaughter between doing an unlawful act and doing a lawful act with a degree of carelessness which the legislature makes criminal. If it were otherwise, a man who killed another while driving without due care and attention would *ex necessitate* commit manslaughter. [2] ... a very high degree of negligence is required to be proved before the felony is established.

Lamb (1967): Unlawful act must be criminally wrong

Facts

D, in jest, pointed a revolver at his best friend V and pulled the trigger, believing that it would not fire because no bullet was opposite the barrel. As a revolver, the gun did fire, killing V.

Decision

The Court of Appeal found D not guilty of unlawful act manslaughter:
(1) ' ... it is long settled that it is not in point to consider whether an act is unlawful merely from the angle of civil liberties' (*per* Sachs LJ).
(2) For the act to be unlawful, it must constitute at least a technical assault, which was not established by the evidence in this case.
(3) Regarding criminal negligence, D might properly be convicted if his belief that there was no danger in pulling the trigger was formed in a criminally negligent way.

Newbury and Jones v DPP (1977): Objective test for dangerousness of unlawful act

Facts

N and J pushed a paving stone off a railway bridge on to the train below, causing the death of a railwayman.

Decision

The House of Lords found N and J guilty of unlawful act manslaughter. *Per* Lord Salmon, the test for liability is '... an objective test. In judging whether the act was dangerous, the test is not 'did the accused recognise that it was dangerous' but 'would all sober and reasonable people recognise its danger'.

Jennings (1990): Carrying a knife for protection not an unlawful act

Facts

D was restrained by his brother V from attacking E with a sheath knife, which ended up entering V's body and killing him.

Decision

The Court of Appeal found D not guilty of unlawful act manslaughter. It was not established at trial that carrying a sheath knife for protection was an unlawful act – a necessary prerequisite for this offence.

Scarlett (1993): Use of reasonable force not an unlawful act

Facts

D, a publican, 'bundled' a drunken customer towards the exit of his pub, causing him to fall backwards down some steps to his death.

Decision

The Court of Appeal found D not guilty of unlawful act manslaughter:

(1) The question whether the appellant's action amounted to an assault and was unlawful and the question whether it was dangerous should have been considered separately by the jury.

(2) *Per* Beldam LJ, the jury ought not convict D 'unless they are satisfied that the degree of force used was plainly more than was called for by the circumstances as he believed them to be, and, provided he believed the circumstances called for the degree of force used, he is not convicted, even if his belief is unreasonable'.

(3) *Per curiam* the present law relating to unlawful act manslaughter is in urgent need of reform.

Dias (2002): Injecting oneself with heroin not an unlawful act

Facts

D and V jointly bought some heroin. D prepared it in a syringe and handed it to V who injected himself with it. V died as a result and D was convicted of manslaughter. D appealed claiming that he had not committed an unlawful act.

Decision

The Court of Appeal held that it was not an offence under the Offences Against the Person Act 1861, the Misuse of Drugs Act 1971 or in common law to inject oneself with heroin. Therefore, it could not be said that D's encouragement or assistance to V to inject himself was an unlawful act. Although it is unlawful to supply heroin, the judge had not directed the jury to consider whether the supply of the drug by D had caused V's death.

Comment
Kennedy (1998) below was distinguished on its facts. In this case, the conviction was quashed, as the jury had not been asked to consider supply as an unlawful act, whereas in *Kennedy* they had.

Rogers (2003): Assistance of another in self-injection of heroin is an unlawful act
Facts
V bought some heroin for D and V to share. V injected D with some of the drug. D then formed a tourniquet on V's arm while V injected himself with the rest of the drug. V died as a result and D was convicted of manslaughter. D appealed on the grounds that V's self-injection of heroin was not an unlawful act and therefore assisting him in that act was not unlawful either.

Decision
The Court of Appeal held that D could not be liable as a secondary party to V's self-injection as that was not in itself an offence. However, by applying and holding the tourniquet in order to raise a vein into which V could inject the heroin, D could be said to be a principal actor in the offence of administering a poison contrary to s 23 of the Offences Against the Person Act 1861. Therefore D had committed an unlawful act and was rightly convicted of manslaughter.

3.1.2   The unlawful act must cause the death of another

Cato (1976): Possession of heroin an unlawful act causing death
Facts
D injected V with heroin several times throughout the evening, at V's request. The intoxication caused V's respiratory failure.

Decision
The Court of Appeal found D guilty of unlawful act manslaughter:
(1)   Although administering heroin is not an offence known to law, the unlawful act causing death was either possession of heroin or administering a noxious substance.
(2)   *Per* Lord Widgery CJ: 'As a matter of law, it was sufficient if [the heroin injection] was a cause, provided that it was a cause outside the *de minimus* range, and effectively bearing upon the acceleration of the moment of the victim's death.'

Dalby (1982): Unlawful act must be 'directed at V'
Facts
D supplied Diconal tablets, a controlled drug, to V, who then injected himself intravenously with the drug and later died.

Decision
The Court of Appeal found D not guilty of unlawful act manslaughter. *Per* Walter LJ: '… the act of supplying a scheduled drug was not an act which caused direct harm.' In

order to establish criminal liability 'where the charge of manslaughter is based on an unlawful and dangerous act, it must be directed at the victim and likely to cause immediate injury, however slight'.

Comment

For contrary guidance on the 'directed at V' requirement, see *Goodfellow* (1986) below.

Mitchell (1983): D's unlawful act must cause death

Facts

D hit a man who fell against V, an elderly woman, causing her to fall over. V sustained injuries and later died. D was convicted of manslaughter.

Decision

The Court of Appeal held that this case could be distinguished from *Dalby* (see above) because although there was no direct contact between D and V, V died as a direct result of injuries sustained through D's actions. The jury were therefore right to conclude that D's acts caused V's death.

Goodfellow (1986): Causation established where there was no intervening cause

Facts

D wished to move from his council house but could not, so he set fire to it as part of a scam. His wife, son and another woman died in the fire.

Decision

The Court of Appeal found D guilty of manslaughter by either unlawful act or recklessness. *Per* Lord Lane CJ:

(1)   'What [Walter LJ in *Dalby*] was, we believe, intending to say was that there must be no fresh intervening cause between the act and the death.'

(2)   D would not be liable for reckless manslaughter if D either was inadvertent as to the risk of injury to others entailed in setting fire to the house, in circumstances where 'it would have been obvious that there was some risk', or was aware of the risk but adverted to it nonetheless '… in the circumstances of this case, if there was risk of injury at all to the people upstairs, then it must follow that there was a risk of death'.

Comment

Does holding (1) in this case render the 'directed at V' requirement of *Dalby* meaningless, or at least redundant? This question is discussed further in *Pagett* (1983) below in section 13.2.1.

AG's Reference (No 3 of 1994) (1997): Foetus part of mother for causation purposes

See 1.1.1 above.

Kennedy (1998): Causation established where D is responsible for death jointly with intervening cause

Facts

D supplied heroin to V, who immediately injected himself, dying as a result.

Decision

The Court of Appeal found D guilty of manslaughter. *Per* Waller LJ:

> Whether one talks of *novus actus interveniens* or simply in terms of causation ... the critical question ... where... there is an act causative of death performed by ... the deceased himself, is whether [D] can be said to be jointly responsible for the carrying out of that act.

3.1.3　The unlawful act must be objectively dangerous

Church (1965): Objective test of dangerousness of unlawful act

Facts

D claimed to have taken V to a van for sexual purposes. In the van V mocked D and slapped him, leading to a fight in which D knocked V unconscious. Unable to revive her, D panicked and dragged V out of the van into a river. V was drowned.

Decision

The Court of Appeal found D guilty of manslaughter. D's conduct amounted to a series of acts which culminated in V's death and thus constituted manslaughter. *Per* Edmund-Davies J:

> ... an unlawful act causing the death of another cannot, simply because it is an unlawful act, render a manslaughter verdict inevitable. For such a verdict inexorably to follow, the unlawful act must be such as all sober and reasonable people would inevitably recognise must subject the other person to, at least, the risk of some harm resulting therefrom, albeit not serious harm.

Newbury and Jones v DPP (1977): Objective test of dangerousness of unlawful act

See 3.1.1 above.

Dawson (1985): Jury view circumstances with same knowledge as D

Facts

D and E robbed V's petrol station wearing masks and armed with a pickaxe handle and replica firearm. When V pushed the alarm, they fled. Soon after V, who had a severe heart condition, died from a heart attack.

Decision

The Court of Appeal found D not guilty of unlawful act manslaughter. *Per* Watkins LJ, since the test in this case '... can only be undertaken upon the basis of the knowledge gained by a sober and reasonable man, as though he were present at the scene of and watched the unlawful act being performed', the jury ought not to have taken into account V's heart condition and, therefore, the increased chance that D's actions would induce a heart attack.

Ball (1989): Reasonable man not endowed with D's mistaken belief

Facts

D loaded a gun with two cartridges taken from his pocket, containing both live and blank cartridges. D claimed to intend only to frighten V by using a blank cartridge, but the gun fired and killed V.

Decision

The Court of Appeal found D guilty of unlawful act manslaughter. The reasonable man cannot be endowed with D's mistaken belief. *Per* Stuart-Smith LJ:

> [Once it is] established ... that the act was both unlawful and that he intended to commit the assaults, the question whether the act is a dangerous one is to be judged not by the appellant's appreciation, but by that of the sober and reasonable man, and it is impossible to impute into this appreciation the mistaken belief of [D] that what he was doing was not dangerous, because he thought he had a blank cartridge in the chamber. At that stage [D's] intention, foresight or knowledge is irrelevant.

Watson (1989): Reasonable man's view of the circumstances of the case

Facts

D and E threw a brick through the window of V's house and entered it, confronting V who was 87 years old and suffering from a severe heart condition. After verbally abusing V, they left and V died 90 minutes later of a heart attack.

Decision

The Court of Appeal found D not guilty of manslaughter (on other grounds). The reasonable person in this case would be appraised of the 'whole of the burglarious intention' (*per* Lord Lane CJ), including the observation that V was very elderly and frail.

3.2 Manslaughter by gross negligence

3.2.1 Manslaughter by gross negligence subsumes reckless manslaughter

Bateman (1925): For criminal liability there must be more than mere negligence

Facts

D attended the confinement of a woman who died while giving birth.

Decision

The Court of Appeal found D not guilty of manslaughter. *Per* Lord Hewart CJ:

> ... in order to establish criminal liability, the facts must be such that, in the opinion of the jury, the negligence of the accused went beyond a mere matter of compensation between subjects and showed such disregard for the life and safety of others as to amount to a crime against the state and conduct deserving punishment.

Andrews v DPP (1937): A very high degree of negligence required

See 3.1.1 above.

Lawrence (1981): Manslaughter by recklessness

Facts

D was driving a motorcycle along an urban street and collided with a pedestrian, causing her death.

Decision
The House of Lords found D not guilty of manslaughter. *Per* Lord Diplock, manslaughter by recklessness is established first where D is '... driving the vehicle in such a manner as to create an obvious and serious risk of causing physical injury to some other person who might happen to be using the road or of doing substantial damage to property'; furthermore, where D 'did so without having given any thought to the possibility of there being any such risk, or, having recognised that there was some risk involved, had nonetheless gone on to take it'.

Comment
The House of Lords in *Seymour* (1983) and *Kong Chuek Kwan* (1985) established this test as governing manslaughter involving gross negligence. However, see *Adomako* (1994) below.

Goodfellow (1986): Recklessness through inadvertence to risk or advertently running an obvious risk
See 3.1.2 above.

Adomako (1994): Manslaughter by gross negligence. Reckless manslaughter abolished

Facts
D, an anaesthetist, failed to observe during an eye operation that the tube inserted in V's mouth had become detached from the ventilator, causing V to suffer a cardiac arrest and eventually die.

Decision
The House of Lords found D guilty of manslaughter by gross negligence, which is established where D breached a duty of care towards V that caused V's death, and that amounted to gross negligence. Gross negligence depends '... on the seriousness of the breach of duty committed by the defendant, in all the circumstances in which he was placed when it occurred and whether, having regard to the risk of death involved, the conduct of the defendant was so bad in all the circumstances as to amount, in the jury's judgment, to a criminal act or omission' (*per* Lord McKay LC).

Comment
The House of Lords in this case overruled its previous decision in *Seymour* (1983), thereby reducing the applicability of recklessness as defined in *Lawrence* (1981) to the offence of criminal damage (*Caldwell* (1982)). See Chapter 19 below.

R v DPP ex p Jones (1996): How gross is 'gross'?

Facts
D, a landlord, failed to implement fire safety precautions required by the local authority. A fire took place in the building, killing a tenant.

Decision
The Court of Appeal found D not guilty of manslaughter. *Per* Auld LJ, judges should not apply '... Lord Mackay's reasoning in *Adomako* as if it were a statutory formulation to be incanted to demonstrate its application ... the necessarily imprecise

Adomako test [is] ... whether there was a realistic prospect of proving [that the defendant's] breach of duty was so serious or "gross" or so bad in all the circumstances as to amount ... to a criminal act'.

3.3 Manslaughter by omission

3.3.1 Distinction between unlawful commission and omission

Senior (1899): Meaning of 'wilful'

Facts

D belonged to a religious sect and refused to seek medical assistance for his ill child, who then died.

Decision

The Court of Appeal found D guilty of unlawful act manslaughter. Wilful neglect of the child was the unlawful act causing death. *Per* Lord Russell CJ: '"Wilfully" is defined as "deliberately and intentionally, not by accident or inadvertence ..." and "neglect" as "the want of reasonable care – that is, the omission of such steps as a reasonable parent would take, such as are usually taken in the ordinary experience of mankind".'

Lowe (1973): Manslaughter charge not inevitable in case of omission

Facts

D failed to call a doctor when his nine week old child became ill, but claimed to have told his wife to do so. She did not do so, and the child died 10 days later.

Decision

The Court of Appeal found D not guilty of unlawful act manslaughter. *Per* Phillimore LJ:

> ... there is a clear distinction between an act of omission and an act of commission likely to cause harm ... if I strike a child in a manner likely to cause harm, it is right that, if the child dies, I may be charged with manslaughter. If, however, I omit to do something with the result that it suffers injury to health which results in death ... a charge of manslaughter should not be an inevitable consequence, even if the omission is deliberate.

Stone and Dobinson (1977): Manslaughter by negligent omission

Facts

S and D allowed an ill and otherwise unstable relative, whom they permitted to live in their house, to die without medical attention.

Decision

The Court of Appeal found S and D guilty of manslaughter by gross negligence. *Per* Lane LJ:

> The duty which the defendant has undertaken is a duty of caring for the health and welfare of the infirm person. What the prosecution have to provide is a breach of duty in such circumstances that the jury feel convinced that the defendant's conduct can properly be described as reckless, that is to say, a reckless disregard of danger to the health and welfare of the infirm person. Mere inadvertence is not enough. The

defendant must be proved to have been indifferent to an obvious risk of injury to health, or actually to have foreseen the risk, but to have determined nevertheless to run it.

Khan (1998): Duty of care must be established in case of manslaughter by omission

Facts
D sold heroin to a 15 year old prostitute, giving her a dose which was twice the amount which would be taken by an experienced heroin user. She went into a coma and D fled the scene, after which the girl died.

Decision
The Court of Appeal found D not guilty of manslaughter (due to a faulty direction to the jury at trial). Manslaughter by omission or willful neglect is not a freestanding offence. The trial judge must rule precisely how the defendant had a duty of care to the deceased and give the jury full directions on the topic.

Singh (Gurphal) (1999): Proximity
See 18.2 below.

Wacker (2003): Assumption of responsibility gives rise to a duty of care

Facts
D was a Dutch lorry driver who arrived in England via a cross channel ferry. 58 Chinese illegal immigrants had stowed themselves in his lorry and suffocated. D was charged with their manslaughter. D claimed that he did not owe the Vs a duty of care because they were engaging in a criminal enterprise and the law of negligence did not recognise a duty of care between participants of such an enterprise.

Decision
The Court of Appeal held that, as a matter of public policy there is no reason why criminal law would refuse to hold D criminally liable for the Vs' death just because Vs were engaged in a joint unlawful enterprise. D had assumed a responsibility for the immigrants and a duty of care arose at the time that D shut off the air vents in the lorry. That duty of care continued until such time as the air vents were opened again since during that time D knew that his failure to act would cause the Vs to suffocate.

CHAPTER 4

OFFENCES AGAINST THE PERSON AND CONSENT

Introduction

Offences against the person involve assaults and the causing of injuries which do not cause death. These offences range from very simple assaults (for example, through a threat or gesture) to the infliction of very serious injuries to the victim. These offences are all currently governed by the Offences Against the Person Act (OAPA) 1861 and, not surprisingly, the courts have had to introduce modern meanings to some of the antiquated terms used in that Act. Indeed, for some time there has been academic and judicial pressure to re-codify these offences using more modern terms and to cover a wider range of activities amounting to an assault not adequately covered by the old legislation. The Law Commission has drafted suggested new offences in their Draft Criminal Code.

The most minor forms of assault – assault and battery – are common law offences and the cases have developed the law in this area to establish the lower limits of behaviour which amount to an offence. Assault at common law amounts to causing the victim to apprehend immediate force. This is a result crime in the sense that whether a crime is made out depends on the victim's reaction to the defendant's behaviour. It is for this reason that an assault can be committed without the defendant actually touching the victim, and merely by issuing a verbal threat or making a gesture which frightens the victim into believing they may anticipate the immediate use of force. Battery is a separate offence at common law (although it is common for defendants to be charged with assault and battery). Battery involves the actual infliction of unlawful force, although for this minor offence the force may not be serious. Unwanted touching may suffice (*Faulkener v Talbot* (1981); *Wilson v Pringle* (1986)). Technically, therefore, you may commit a battery every time you brush against another person on a crowded bus, for example, although you would not necessarily be charged for this since people are generally deemed to consent to a certain degree of physical contact in such circumstances.

The statutory offences range in seriousness from assault occasioning actual bodily harm (ABH) at the lower end (s 47), malicious wounding or inflicting grievous bodily harm (GBH) in the middle (s 20), to wounding or causing grievous bodily harm with intent (s 18) as the most serious offence. The difference between actual bodily harm and serious bodily harm is a question of degree. All that the cases tell us is that serious bodily harm means 'really serious bodily harm' (*Smith* (1961)) and we should therefore assume that actual bodily harm amounts to injuries falling short of that benchmark. The cases have been more concerned with defining the words 'inflict' and 'occasion'. The courts have, though, in recent years, ruled that both ABH and GBH may include psychiatric injuries caused to the victim (*Ireland; Burstow* (1997); *Morris* (1998)). These rulings were made in those cases to deal with the issue of 'stalking'. Silently making unwanted telephone calls, following the victim or relentlessly making unwanted communication with the victim with the result that the victim suffers some sort of psychiatric harm such as depression, are activities that do not sit comfortably within the OAPA 1861, which primarily deals with physical assaults. However, the practice of stalking has been highlighted in recent years as a growing menace with serious consequences for the victim, and so, not surprisingly, the courts initially argued that such behaviour amounts to an assault or an infliction and that the harm caused amounts to either ABH or GBH. Since 1997, with the enactment of the Protection From Harassment Act, the courts no longer have to contort the OAPA 1861 in this way, since the 1996 Act specifies the offence of harassment to cover these situations.

The *mens rea* of all of the offences against the person, whether in common law or under the OAPA 1861, involves either intention to cause the relevant level of harm to the victim or recklessness as to whether that harm is caused, recklessness bearing its subjective meaning (see Chapter 19).

The other issue discussed in this chapter is that of consent. Since all assault offences involve 'hostile' or unwanted physical contact with the defendant, where the victim consents, clearly the defendant would have a defence. In some cases however, the courts have ruled that the victim's actual consent is irrelevant because there are public interest reasons for overruling that consent and declaring the behaviour of the defendant unlawful. The landmark (and most controversial) case on this issue is *Brown* (1993), where a group of people practising private and consensual acts of sado-masochism were successfully prosecuted for assault. The European Court of Human Rights (ECtHR) agreed with the House of Lords in this case that there were strong public interest reasons for interfering with the defendant's right to privacy and declaring their practices unlawful in order to protect the moral and physical health of the public at large. Other activities (arguably as harmful) have attracted a different reaction from the courts, and injuries incurred on a sports field (*Billingshurst* (1978)), through 'horse play' (*Aitken* (1992)) or through schoolboys' 'rough and tumble' behaviour (*Jones* (1986)) have been deemed to be consented to.

The issue of consent will be discussed further in Chapter 5 where it relates to sexual offences.

4.1   Assault

4.1.1   *Actus reus – apprehension of immediate force*

Meade and Belt (1823): Words do not constitute an assault

Facts
D and others gathered at V's house were 'singing songs of menace and using violent language'.

Decision
D was not guilty of assault: '... no words of singing are equivalent to an assault' (*per* Holroyd J).

Light (1857): Words and actions constitute an assault

Facts
D raised a sword over his wife's head, saying: 'Were it not for the bloody policeman outside, I would split your head open.'

Decision
The Crown Court found D guilty of assault.

Wilson (1955): Assault by threats

Facts
D uttered threats towards, and then kicked, a gamekeeper.

Decision
The Court of Appeal found D guilty of assault and battery. *Per* Lord Goddard: '[D] called out "get out the knives" which itself would be an assault, in addition to kicking the gamekeeper.'

Fagan v Metropolitan Police Commissioner (1969): No assault by omission but by a continuing act

Facts
D was told by a policeman, V, to park his car. D drove onto V's foot, then realised he had done so and refused to reverse off.

Decision
The Queen's Bench Divisional Court found D guilty of assaulting a police officer in the execution of duty. An assault is any act which intentionally, or possibly recklessly, causes another person to apprehend immediate and unlawful personal violence. *Per* James J:

> [1] A mere omission to act cannot amount to an assault. [2] For an assault to be committed, both the elements of *actus reus* and *mens rea* must be present at the same time. [3] It is not necessary that *mens rea* should be present at the inception of the *actus reus*; it can be superimposed upon an existing act. [4] On the other hand, the subsequent inception of *mens rea* cannot convert an act which has been complete without *mens rea* into an assault.

Smith v Superintendent of Woking Police Station (1983): Apprehension of violence

Facts
D frightened V by looking through her bedroom window late at night.

Decision
D was guilty of assault as V apprehended unlawful personal violence.

Collins v Wilcock (1984): Implied consent to physical contact

Facts
D refused to speak to P, a police officer, who eventually took hold of D's arm to restrain her. D, in turn, scratched P's arm.

Decision

The Court of Appeal found D not guilty of assaulting a police officer in the execution of duty. *Per* Goff LJ:

> [1] An assault is an act which causes another person to apprehend the infliction of immediate, unlawful force on his person ... any touching of another person, however slight, may amount to a battery. [2] ... consent is a defence to battery, and most of the physical contacts of ordinary life are not actionable because they are impliedly consented to by all who move in society and so expose themselves to the risk of bodily contact. [3] Notwithstanding [2], it is more common nowadays to treat [everyday jostling] as falling within a general exception embracing all physical contact which is generally acceptable in the ordinary conduct of daily life.

Little (1992): Assault and battery separate offences

Facts

The prosecution alleged that 'L ... did unlawfully assault and batter J'.

Decision

The Court of Appeal quashed L's conviction on the grounds of duplicity. The offence of assault is separate from battery *de jure* and both are statutory offences under s 39 of the Criminal Justice Act 1988.

Ireland; Burstow (1997): Assault by words or gestures

Facts

For facts see 4.3.1 below.

Decision

In the House of Lords, Lord Steyn held:

> The proposition that a gesture may amount to an assault, but that words can never suffice is unrealistic and indefensible. A thing said is also a thing done. There is no reason why something said should be incapable of causing an apprehension of immediate personal violence.

Per Lord Hope:

> ... it is not true to say that mere words or gestures can never constitute an assault ... The words or gestures must be seen in their whole context ... In my opinion, silent telephone calls of this nature are just as capable as words or gestures, said or made in the presence of the victim, of causing an apprehension of immediate and unlawful violence.

Constanza (1997): Stalking and assault

Facts

For a period of nearly two years D 'stalked' V by following her home, making silent telephone calls, sending over 800 letters, driving past her home repeatedly and writing offensive words on her front door. V was diagnosed as suffering from clinical depression and anxiety as a result of D's behaviour. V claimed that she thought D might attack her at any time. D was convicted of assault occasioning actual bodily harm, but appealed on the ground that his behaviour did not constitute an assault, as V did not apprehend 'immediate' force.

Decision

The Court of Appeal held that the prosecution merely had to prove that D caused a fear of violence at some time, either immediately or in the near future. The fact that D lived near V (which made V think that something might happen at any time) was sufficient evidence for the jury to find that she feared immediate violence.

Comments

'Stalking' in these cases resulted in convictions for assault occasioning actual bodily harm under s 47 of the Offences Against the Person Act 1861. However, a new offence of harassment was created in the Protection From Harassment Act 1997. Section 4 defines harassment as causing 'another to fear, on at least two occasions, that violence will be used against him'. Had *Ireland; Burstow* and *Constanza* been charged with this new offence, there would have been no need to prove an assault.

4.1.2   Mens rea of intention to cause apprehension of violence or recklessness thereto

Fagan v Metropolitan Police Commissioner (1969): Mens rea and continuing act

See 4.1.1 above.

Venna (1975): Mens rea of assault and battery

Facts

D struggled with police officers attempting to arrest him. D fell to the ground and lashed out wildly with his legs, striking the hand of an officer.

Decision

The Court of Appeal found D guilty of assault occasioning actual bodily harm. *Per* James LJ: '... the element of *mens rea* in the offence of battery is satisfied by proof that the defendant intentionally or recklessly applied force to the person of another.'

4.2   Battery

4.2.1   Inflicting unlawful personal violence with intention or recklessness

Martin (1881): Intention of natural consequences

Facts

D placed an iron bar across an exit, turned out the lights on a staircase and yelled 'Fire!'. As a result, several people were injured.

Decision

The Court of Appeal found D guilty of assault causing grievous bodily harm. *Per* Lord Coleridge CJ: 'The prisoner must be taken to have intended the natural consequences of that which he did.'

Faulkner v Talbot (1981): Intentional touching

Facts
V, a 14 year old boy, was forced to have sexual intercourse with D.

Decision
The Court of Appeal, in finding D guilty of indecent assault, held:

> [1] An assault is any intentional touching of another person without the consent
> of that person and without lawful excuse. It need not necessarily be hostile or rude
> or aggressive. [2] It was intentional touching; it was touching without lawful
> excuse, and in view of s 15(2) [of the Sexual Offences Act 1956] it was touching to
> which the boy could not in law consent and therefore did not consent (*per* Lord
> Lane CJ).

Wilson v Pringle (1986): Hostile touching

Decision
The Court of Appeal held:

> ... in a battery, there must be an intentional touching or contact in one form or
> another of the plaintiff by the defendant. That touching must be hostile ... hostility
> cannot be equated with ill will or malevolence. It cannot be governed by the obvious
> intention shown in acts like punching, stabbing or shooting. But by the element of
> hostility, in the sense in which it is now to be considered, must be a question of fact
> for [the jury] (*per* Croom-Johnson LJ).

K (1990): Indirect occasioning of harm

Facts
D had placed acid in a hot air dryer to conceal it from his teachers. When V next used
the dryer, he suffered burns on his face.

Decision
The Court of Appeal found D guilty of assault occasioning bodily harm. D had 'just as
truly assaulted the next user of the machine [V] as if [D] had himself switched the
machine on (*per* Parker LJ)'.

Lynsey (1995): Indirect physical force

Facts
D spat in the face of a police officer who was arresting him. The spittle hit the police
officer on the bridge of his nose and went in his eyes. D was charged with battery.

Decision
The Court of Appeal held that, despite the fact that D did not touch V, physical force
was used and this constituted a battery.

Comment
Harm to V need not have been proven if the charge was simply battery. Touching is
not necessary, but the force must be physical.

Brown (1993): Absence of consent

Facts

Five men engaged in various homosexual sado-masochistic practices in private, including genital torture and involving the infliction of various injuries, none requiring medical treatment.

Decision

The House of Lords found all five defendants guilty of assault occasioning actual bodily harm and three were also guilty of unlawful wounding:

(1) Absence of consent is not an element of assault occasioning actual bodily harm or unlawful wounding.

(2) Consent is a defence to the infliction of bodily harm in the course of some lawful activity, but ought not to be extended to sado-masochistic encounters.

Lord Mustill, dissenting, held that 'these consensual private acts are [not] offences against the existing law of violence' and Lord Slynn, also dissenting, found no compelling reasons for creating criminal liability in this case.

A v UK (1998): Unlawful chastisement of a child

Facts

D used a garden cane to chastise his stepchild. He was convicted for assault occasioning actual bodily harm and appealed on the grounds that he had not committed a battery, because the conduct constituted reasonable chastisement and was, therefore, not unlawful.

Decision

The ECtHR held that D's conduct breached Art 3 of the European Convention on Human Rights (which provides that no one shall be subjected to torture or inhuman or degrading treatment or punishment).

Comment

The ECtHR did not hold that reasonable chastisement could never render personal force lawful. However, D's conduct in this case fell beyond the limit of reasonable chastisement and therefore amounted to unlawful force. This will be a question of degree in any case.

4.3 Assault occasioning actual bodily harm (s 47 of the OAPA 1861)

4.3.1 Actus reus of assault or battery causing actual bodily harm

Miller (1954): Non-physical injury

Facts

D had non-consensual sexual intercourse with his wife, after which she was 'in a hysterical and nervous condition'.

Decision

The Queen's Bench Divisional Court found D guilty of assault occasioning actual bodily harm. *Per* Lynskey J: '… if a person is caused hurt or injury resulting, not in any physical injury, but in an injury to his mind for the time being, that is within the definition of "actual bodily harm".'

Chan-Fook (1994): Psychiatric and emotional injuries

Facts

D subjected V to aggressive questioning about the theft of a ring, and then dragged V to an upstairs room and locked him in. Fearing D's return, V escaped through a window, causing him injury.

Decision

The Court of Appeal found D not guilty of assault occasioning actual bodily harm:

(1) 'Actual bodily harm' is capable of including psychiatric injury, but does not include emotions, such as fear or panic, nor states of mind that are not themselves evidence of some identifiable clinical condition. Apart from expert evidence to this effect, no mention should be made to the jury regarding psychiatric injury. *Per* Hobhouse LJ: 'The body of the victim includes all parts of the body, including his organs, his nervous system and his brain. Bodily injury therefore may include injury to any of those parts of the body responsible for his mental health and other faculties.'

(2) *Per curiam*: the phrase 'state of mind' is unscientific, confusing and should be avoided when considering whether psychiatric injury has been caused.

Ireland; Burstow (1997): Psychiatric injury; confirmation of Chan-Fook

Facts

D1 made repeated silent telephone calls to three victims. In some calls he resorted to heavy breathing. V suffered psychiatric illness as a result in all three cases. D1 was convicted under s 47 of the Offences Against the Person Act 1861. D2 stalked V for eight months, resulting in V's severe depression. D2 was convicted under s 20 of the Offences Against the Person Act 1861. Both appealed on the ground that 'bodily harm' under both s 47 and s 20 could not include psychiatric illness.

Decision

In the House of Lords, Lord Steyn held:

> In my view, the ruling in [*Chan-Fook*] was based on principled and cogent reasoning and it marked a sound and essential clarification of the law. I would hold that 'bodily harm' in ss 18, 20 and 47 must be interpreted so as to include recognisable psychiatric illness.

Morris (1998): Psychiatric evidence of non-physical injuries

Facts

D had stalked V, causing her to suffer pains in her joints and abdomen, sleeplessness, tension and fear of being alone. At D's trial for assault occasioning actual bodily harm, the judge refused an adjournment for the prosecution to adduce psychiatric evidence of V's symptoms, because he thought her non-physical injuries could not amount to actual bodily harm.

Decision

The Court of Appeal held that in such a case as this, where V claimed to have suffered non-physical injuries as a result of a non-physical assault, psychiatric evidence as to whether the injuries may have been caused by D's conduct must be adduced before the case goes before the jury. The evidence must be sought notwithstanding that the injuries were not directly inflicted as they might have been in the case of physical injuries.

4.3.2   Mens rea of intention or recklessness to cause apprehended or actual force

Roberts (1971): Reasonably foreseeable harm

Facts

While driving, D sought to make advances towards V, who then jumped out of the car, sustaining injuries.

Decision

The Court of Appeal found D guilty of assault occasioning actual bodily harm. V's reaction does not negate causation, provided it was reasonably foreseeable, that is, provided it was not '… so "daft" … or so unexpected … that no reasonable man could be expected so foresee it', thereby constituting a *novus actus interveniens*' (*per* Stephenson LJ).

Savage; Parmenter (1992): Mens rea of common assault will suffice

Facts

When S intentionally threw beer at V, the glass left her hand and struck V causing a cut. P roughly handled his child, causing the breaking of arms and legs.

Decision

The House of Lords found S not guilty of assault occasioning actual bodily harm; P was guilty of the same. The offence requires an *actus reus* of assault occasioning actual bodily harm and the *mens rea* for a common assault. *Per* Lord Ackner: 'The prosecution are not obliged to prove that the defendant intended to cause some actual bodily harm or was reckless as to whether such harm would be caused.'

Chan-Fook (1994): Psychological harm reasonably foreseeable

See 4.3.1 above.

4.4   Malicious wounding or inflicting grievous bodily harm (s 20 of the OAPA 1861)

4.4.1   Actus reus of unlawfully and maliciously wounding another or inflicting grievous bodily harm

JJC v Eisenhower (1983): Meaning of wound

Facts

V was shot with an air gun pellet near the eye, resulting in a bruise below the eyebrow and fluid filling the front of his eye.

Decision

The Court of Appeal found D not guilty of maliciously wounding. A wound is a break in the continuity of the whole skin; an internal rupturing of the blood vessels is not a wound.

Wilson (1984): Infliction need not involve assault

Facts

After D, a motorist, nearly ran down V, D got out of his car and punched V in the face.

Decision

The House of Lords found D guilty of assault occasioning actual bodily harm. An infliction of grievous bodily harm, *contra* to s 20 may be committed without establishing first an assault. *Per* Lord Roskill, citing *Salisbury* (1976):

> ... grievous bodily harm may be inflicted ... either where the accused has directly and violently 'inflicted' it by assaulting the victim, or where the accused has 'inflicted' it by doing something, intentionally, which, though it is not itself a direct application of force to the body of the victim, does directly result in force being applied violently to the body of the victim, so that he suffers grievous bodily harm.

Gelder (1994): Psychiatric injury as GBH

Facts

D made persistent indecent telephone calls to V, causing psychiatric injury.

Decision

The Court of Appeal found D not guilty of assault causing grievous bodily harm with intent, *contra* to s 18 of the Offences Against the Person Act 1861. The jury had been misdirected as to whether D intended the resulting injury.

Comment

Unfortunately the Court of Appeal did not comment on whether such psychiatric injury could constitute grievous bodily harm. But see *Ireland; Burstow* (1997) above, where the House of Lords clarified this point.

4.4.2   Mens rea of intentionally or recklessly causing some physical harm

Mowatt (1967): Foresight of even minor harm

Facts

V seized D by the lapels and demanded to know where D's companion had taken off to with V's money. D struck V several times, rendering V unconscious.

Decision

The Court of Appeal found D guilty of malicious wounding. Intention or recklessness as to the resulting wounding or grievous bodily harm need not be proved. *Per* Diplock LJ:

> [1] It is enough that [D foresaw] ... that some physical harm to some person, albeit of a minor character, might result. [2] *Per curiam*, the intent expressly required by s 18 of the Offences Against the Person Act 1861 is more specific than the element of

foresight of consequences implicit in the word 'maliciously' in that enactment and, in directing a jury on this offence, the word 'maliciously' is best ignored; in the offence of unlawful wounding (s 20 of the Offences Against the Person Act 1861) the word 'maliciously' imports, on the part of the person who unlawfully inflicts the wound or other grievous bodily harm, an awareness that his act may have the consequences of causing physical harm to some other person.

Comment

Holding [1] above was confirmed by the House of Lords in *Savage; Parmenter* (1992).

4.5 Wounding or causing grievous bodily harm with intent (s 18 of the OAPA 1861)

4.5.1 Actus reus of wounding or causing grievous bodily harm

Mandair (1994): 'Causing' bodily harm is wider than 'inflicting'

Facts

D came home in a bad temper and, in frustration, threw a container containing an acidic cleanser at his wife, badly injuring her face.

Decision

The House of Lords found D not guilty of causing grievous bodily harm with intent, but D was guilty of a s 20 offence. *Per* Lord Mackay: '"Causing" grievous bodily harm is wider or at least not narrower than the word "inflict".' Thus 'causing' grievous bodily harm under s 18 was wide enough to include 'inflicting' grievous bodily harm under s 20; it was open to the jury to convict a defendant charged under s 18 of the alternative offence of inflicting grievous bodily harm, contrary to s 20.

Ireland; Burstow (1997): Psychological harm

See 4.3.1 above.

4.5.2 Mens rea of intention as to consequences

Mowatt (1967): Foresight of even minor harm

See 4.4.2 above.

Purcell (1986): Model direction on intention

Facts

D attacked V with a hammer and strangled her, causing injury.

Decision

The Court of Appeal found D guilty of causing wounding with intent. *Per* Lord Lane CJ, at a trial of a person charged with causing grievous bodily harm, the following direction should be given to the jury on the issue of intent: 'You must feel sure that the defendant intended to cause serious bodily harm to the victim. You can only decide what his intention was by considering all the relevant circumstances and, in particular, what he did and what he said about it' (citing Lord Bridge in *Moloney* 1.2.2 above).

Morrison (1989): Foresight of actual consequences

Facts

D was seized by a police officer who stated she was arresting D, who then dived through a window pane, dragging her through the glass and resulting in serious cuts to her face.

Decision

The Court of Appeal found D not guilty of a s 18 offence.

4.6   Attempted murder

4.6.1   Mens rea of intending to kill

Fallon (1994): Intent to kill necessary

Facts

In the course of being arrested, D spun around and shot a police officer.

Decision

The Court of Appeal held that the *mens rea* for attempted murder does not include intention to cause grievous bodily harm. Only an intent to kill will suffice.

4.7   Consent

4.7.1   Consent and the public interest

Coney (1882): Consent no defence to assualt

Decision

In the Queen's Bench Divisional Court, Stephen J held:

> The principle as to consent seems to me to be this: when one person is indicted for inflicting personal injury upon another, the consent of the person who sustains the injury is no defence to the person who inflicts the injury, if the injury is of such a nature, or is inflicted under such circumstances, that its infliction is injurious to the public as well as to the person injured.

AG's Reference (No 6 of 1980) (1981): Consent invalid if not in the public interest

Facts

Two youths settled an argument by fighting in the street.

Decision

The Court of Appeal held that the youths may be liable for assault. *Per* Lord Lane CJ:

(1)   One cannot consent to injuries sustained in a fight because 'it was not in the public interest that people should try to cause or should cause each other actual bodily harm for no good reason'.

(2)   The holding in [1] does not affect 'the accepted legality of properly conducted games and sports, lawful chastisement or correction, reasonable surgical interference, dangerous

exhibitions etc. These apparent exceptions can be justified as involving the exercise of a legal right ... or as needed in the public interest in other cases'.

Billinghurst (1978): Consent in sport

Facts

During an off the ball incident at a rugby match, D punched V in the face, fracturing his jaw. D was charged under s 20 of the OAPA 1861. At the trial, evidence was adduced that players were regularly punched in the course of a game. D argued in his defence that V consented to the risk of some injury during a match.

Decision

The Crown Court convicted D, holding that rugby was a game of physical contact which necessarily involved the use of force. Players are deemed to consent to force 'of a kind which could reasonably be expected to happen during a game'. This does not give a player a licence to use unlimited force, and some incidents will inevitably cross the line of that to which a player is deemed to consent. Force used outside the course of play may be distinguished from that used during the course of play.

Jones (1986): Consent to assault

Facts

D and other schoolboys tossed two boys into the air, resulting in a ruptured spleen for one and a broken arm for the other.

Decision

The Court of Appeal found D not guilty of assault causing grievous bodily harm, as D ought to have been able to raise the defence of consent at trial.

Boyea (1992): Consent no defence to serious assault

Facts

D pinned down V on her bed and forced his fingers into her vagina.

Decision

The Court of Appeal found D guilty of indecent assault. *Per* Glidewell LJ: '... an assault intended or which is likely to cause bodily harm, accompanied by indecency, is an offence irrespective of consent, provided that the injury is not "transient or trifling".'

Aitken (1992): Consent of victim

Facts

The defendants were RAF officers. At a party in the officers' mess, some horseplay ensued. They set fire to V, who was very drunk. V suffered severe burns. The Ds were charged under s 20 of the OAPA 1861, but claimed that their actions were normal horseplay and that V consented.

Decision

The Court of Appeal found D not guilty of an offence of assault if he believed that V consented to the activity. As V had taken part in other horseplay activities during the evening, it was possible that his continued presence was an acceptance by him that he consented to such an activity. D had genuinely believed that V consented and therefore his conviction was quashed.

Slingsby (1995): Consensual activities resulting in injury

Facts
During consensual sexual activity, D inserted his hand into V's vagina and rectum. The ring on D's finger caused multiple cuts to V. V was unaware of the seriousness of the injuries and later died from septicaemia. D was charged with unlawful act manslaughter (the unlawful act in this case being battery). D claimed that V had consented to the battery and it was therefore not unlawful.

Decision
The Queen's Bench Divisional Court held: 'It would ... be contrary to principle to treat as criminal, activity which would not otherwise amount to an assault, merely because in the course of the activity an injury occurred (*per* Judge J).'

Brown (1993): Consent to sado-masochism
See 4.2.1 above.

Brown v UK (1997): Consent to sado-masochism and the right to privacy

Facts
D appealed against his conviction for assault occasioning actual bodily harm on the grounds that the judgment breached Art 8 of the European Convention on Human Rights. D claimed that the sexual acts to which the charge applied had all taken place in private and were fully consensual.

Decision
The ECtHR held that the interference with D's private life was justified as it was in pursuance of a legitimate aim, namely the protection of the physical and moral health of the public.

Wilson (1996): Consent and private sexual activities

Facts
D branded his initials on his wife's buttocks with a hot knife. He was convicted of assault occasioning actual bodily harm. He appealed on the grounds that she consented.

Decision
The Court of Appeal held:

> Mrs Wilson not only consented to that which the appellant did, she instigated it. There was no aggressive intent on the part of the appellant ... We are firmly of the opinion that it is not in the public interest that activities such as the appellant's in this appeal should amount to criminal behaviour. Consensual activity between husband and wife, in the privacy of the matrimonial home, is not, in our judgment, a proper matter for criminal investigation, let alone criminal prosecution (*per* Russell LJ).

Richardson (1999): Fraud as to qualifications does not invalidate consent

Facts

D was a registered dental practitioner who was suspended from practice by the General Dental Council. Whilst suspended, she continued to carry out dentistry on patients, one of whom complained to the police. D was convicted of assault occasioning actual bodily harm. She appealed on the ground that the patients consented to the treatment, notwithstanding that they did not know that D had been suspended.

Decision

The Court of Appeal held that consent is only invalidated where there is fraud as to the identity of the perpetrator or fraud as to the nature of the act consented to. In this case D had misled patients as to her qualifications and not as to her identity. Therefore, the consent of the patients was valid and provided a defence.

Tabassum (2000): Fraud as to nature of acts invalidates consent

Facts

D deceived a number of women into consenting to him touching their breasts by claiming that he was medically qualified and was conducting a survey into breast cancer. There was no sexual motive. At his trial for indecent assault, the trial judge concluded that D's deceit as to his medical qualification invalidated the women's consent. D appealed.

Decision

The Court of Appeal held that the victims in this case did not genuinely consent to D's actions because they only consented to acts of a medical nature. As D was not a medical practitioner, and the fundamental quality of the acts was not medical, the women's consent was not genuine.

Comment

The Court of Appeal appears to have reconciled the apparently conflicting decisions of *Richardson* and *Tabassum* above. In the former, V genuinely consented to the nature of the acts, and deceit as to the identity of the perpetrator did not invalidate consent. In the latter, V consented to the nature of the act but was deceived as to its 'fundamental quality', which did invalidate consent.

CHAPTER 5

RAPE AND INDECENT ASSAULT

Introduction

The two sexual offences covered in this chapter are rape and indecent assault. Rape is governed by the Sexual Offences Act 1956, but this legislation has been amended over the years in the light of modern attitudes towards sexual activity. The *actus reus* of the offence is now defined as 'Sexual intercourse with a man or a woman without their consent' (s 142 of the Criminal Justice and Public Order Act 1994). The word 'unlawful' was dropped from the original definition because by the 1990s the only relevant application of this word was to exclude sexual intercourse between a husband and wife. The landmark case of *R v R* in 1991 rendered the word meaningless by expressly stating that a man was capable in law of raping his wife. The offence also now extends to both male and female victims to take into account the growing problem of male rape and to accord it the same legal status as rape of a woman.

Further cases on the *actus reus* element of the offence of rape have defined the precise meaning of the words 'sexual intercourse' which includes only penetrative sex. Any sexual contact falling short of penetration (of the anus or vagina) to which consent is not obtained must be charged as indecent assault.

The issue of consent has been the subject of a great deal of the case law in this area. The courts have been careful to point out the difference between submission to sexual intercourse (which amounts to consent) and lack of consent, although this has been difficult since this often involves an interpretation of the victim's behaviour (*Olugboja* (1981); *McAllister* (1997)). The courts have also had to address cases where the victim consents, but for various reasons their consent may be invalid. Consent obtained through fraud may be invalid where it involves a deception as to the identity of the perpetrator (*Elbekkay* (1995)) or as to the nature of the act (*Flattery* (1877); *Williams* (1923); *Tabassum* (2000)).

The *mens rea* of rape concerns the defendant's attitude towards consent and is established where he either knew the victim did not consent or was reckless as to whether she consented or not (recklessness bearing its subjective meaning (*Pigg* (1982)). The case of *Morgan* (1976) deals with the situation where the defendant did address his mind to whether the victim consented or not, but mistakenly believes that she does. In this case, the jury must consider the defendant's honest belief (a subjective test), and the belief does not have to be reasonable (see *B v DPP*) (although the more unreasonable the belief, the more the jury may consider that it was not honestly held).

The offence of indecent assault involves the defendant committing an assault (as defined in Chapter 4) which is considered to be indecent, since in some situations this may be ambiguous or unclear, such as where a defendant touches a woman's foot to satisfy his shoe fetish. The courts have devised a complex test to be applied by the jury in deciding whether an assault is indecent, which combines subjective and objective elements (*Court* (1989)). First, they must consider whether the assault is indecent according to the standards of the ordinary reasonable person (objective). If it clearly is, then indecency is proved. If it is not clear that the ordinary reasonable person would consider the assault indecent, then the jury should examine the defendant's state of mind and any secret sexual motive he may have had for the assault. If he was acting in a way which he would have considered inherently sexual or indecent, then indecency is proved. If neither the ordinary reasonable person, nor the defendant imputed any indecent quality to the act then it is unlikely to be indecent for the purposes of this criminal offence.

5.1   *Actus reus* of rape

5.1.1   Unlawful

R v R (1991): Marital rape

Facts
D was convicted of attempting to rape his wife. He appealed on the ground that a husband could not be liable for raping his wife in common law.

Decision
The House of Lords held that, although there was clear precedent in common law that a husband cannot be guilty of raping his wife, since sexual intercourse between husband and wife was not unlawful, '… the common law is … capable of evolving in the light of changing social, economic and cultural developments' (*per* Lord Keith). In today's society, marriage is a partnership of equals and the common law proposition that, by marriage, the wife gives her irrevocable consent to sexual intercourse with her husband is 'quite unacceptable'. The word 'unlawful' in s 1(1) of the Sexual Offences Act 1956 can no longer rationally mean outside the bonds of marriage. The use of the word 'unlawful' adds nothing to the definition of rape and therefore there is nothing which prevents a husband being liable for raping his wife.

Comment
This judgment was effectively codified in s 142 of the Criminal Justice and Public Order Act 1994, which drops the word 'unlawful' from the definition of rape and refers merely to sexual intercourse without consent.

5.1.2   With a man or a woman

Matthews (John) (1997): Rape of a transsexual

Facts
V was a male-female transsexual. D visited V in her flat and removed her clothing, touched her genital area and forced his penis into her artificial vagina. D was charged with rape, but claimed that penile penetration of an artificial vagina could not constitute rape.

Decision
The Crown Court held that where the Criminal Justice and Public Order Act 1994 had extended the definition of rape to include anal rape of a man, it also included 'vaginal' rape of a man. D was therefore convicted of rape.

Comment

The definition of rape was amended by s 142 of the Criminal Justice and Public Order Act 1994, so as to include the rape of a man or a woman.

5.1.3 Sexual intercourse

Hughes (1841): Penetration

Decision

The slightest penetration of the vagina by the penis is sufficient proof of sexual intercourse. The hymen need not be ruptured.

Kaitamaki (1985): Withdrawal of consent

Facts

The defendant had sexual intercourse with V, believing at the time of penetration that she consented. When he realised during the intercourse that she did not consent, or was no longer consenting, he did not withdraw and continued having intercourse with her.

Decision

The Court of Appeal ruled that sexual intercourse is a continuing act which only ends with withdrawal. Although the initial act of penetration could not be deemed to be rape, if D at least believed the victim consented, the refusal to withdraw and the continuation of intercourse after consent had been withdrawn could be deemed rape.

Cooper and Schaub (1994): Withdrawal of consent

Facts

The Ds had met V at a pub and had offered her a lift home at the end of the evening. She got into their car and fell asleep. When she awoke D2 had sexual intercourse with her whilst D1 put his penis in her mouth. The Ds then changed places. V did not consent to any of the sexual activity, but the Ds claimed that she had. At the trial for rape, the jury were told that if they found that V initially consented and then withdrew her consent, then this constituted rape. Both Ds were convicted and appealed.

Decision

The Court of Appeal confirmed that penetration is a continuing act. Where a man continues to penetrate a woman after she has withdrawn consent, he commits rape. The judge had therefore not misdirected the jury.

5.1.4 Lack of consent

Olugboja (1981): 'Reluctant acquiescence'

Facts

D offered V and J a lift home. He drove them to his home. He raped J in his car and then dragged V into a bedroom and told her he was going to have sexual intercourse with her. V removed her clothing when told to and D had sexual intercourse with her. The judge directed the jury to consider whether a rape had taken place, even though V submitted to the intercourse and did not struggle or scream and despite the fact that D had made no threats of violence. D was convicted of rape and appealed.

Decision

The Court of Appeal held that the definition of rape was unlawful intercourse without the woman's consent and therefore the offence was not limited to cases where consent was induced through threats of force. 'Consent' is a wide ranging word 'ranging from actual desire ... to reluctant acquiescence' (*per* Dunn LJ). Whether consent was present or not is a matter for the jury to consider, applying their common sense and knowledge of human nature.

Larter and Castleton (1995): Difference between consent and submission

Facts

Both defendants were convicted of raping a 14 year old girl. The girl was alleged to have been asleep at the time of the rape and claimed that she knew nothing of what happened. The defendants claimed that the judge should have directed the jury that the prosecution had to prove that V either physically resisted or was not in a position to decide whether she consented or not.

Decision

The Court of Appeal held that the essential element in the definition of rape is now the absence of consent. The jury should be directed that absence of consent is to be given its ordinary meaning; there is a difference between consent and submission. Every consent involves a submission, but a mere submission does not necessarily involve consent.

McAllister (1997): 'Reluctant acquiescence'

Facts

D was convicted of indecent assault on his estranged wife. D claimed she had consented to the sexual acts which took place. At the trial, the jury had asked the judge to define the difference between consent and submission, but the judge failed to tell them that 'reluctant acquiescence' amounted to consent (*per Olugboja* above).

Decision

The Court of Appeal held that the jury should have used their common sense and experience to decide whether there was consent or not in this case. The judge directed them fully and did not need to spell out the possibility that 'reluctant acquiescence' may constitute consent.

Clarence (1888): Fraud as to a sexually transmitted disease

Facts

D had sexual intercourse with a woman, knowing that he had venereal disease. V contracted the disease. V claimed that, by not telling her he had the disease, he had obtained her consent through fraud and consent was therefore vitiated.

Decision

The Crown Court held that D's deceit did not vitiate V's consent, since it was not fraud as to the nature of the act of sexual intercourse.

Flattery (1877): Fraud as to the nature of sexual intercourse

Facts

D induced V to have sexual intercourse with him by telling her that he was performing a surgical operation.

Decision

The Crown Court convicted D as his fraud related to the nature of the act of sexual intercourse and therefore V's consent was vitiated by the deception.

Williams (1923): Fraud as to the nature of sexual intercourse

Facts

D, who was a singing teacher, induced one of his pupils to have sexual intercourse with him by telling her that he was practising a breathing exercise.

Decision

The Court of Appeal convicted D of rape since his fraud related to the nature of the act of intercourse and therefore V's consent was vitiated. *Per* Lord Hewart CJ: 'Where [V] is persuaded that what is being done to her is not sexual intercourse but is some medical or surgical operation ... then it is rape, although the actual thing that was done was done with her consent, because she never consented to the act of sexual intercourse.'

Linekar (1995): Fraud as to payment for sexual intercourse

Facts

D agreed to pay £25 to have sexual intercourse with a prostitute. After sexual intercourse took place, D made off without paying. V alleged that she had been raped, claiming that she would not have consented to the intercourse unless she had been paid in advance and D had worn a condom. The jury were directed that such fraud on the part of D vitiated V's consent.

Decision

The Court of Appeal held that the only types of frauds which could vitiate consent were those as to the nature of the act itself or as to the identity of the perpetrator. In this case, fraud as to payment for the intercourse did not vitiate V's consent.

Elbekkay (1995): Fraud as to the identity of the perpetrator

Facts

V lived with her boyfriend and D was staying with them. V and D were drunk. V claimed that during the night she was awakened by D getting into her bed and touching her. She thought it was her boyfriend and D and V had sexual intercourse. When V realised D was not her boyfriend, she punched him. D was charged with rape but claimed that V consented, even when she knew who he was.

Decision

The Court of Appeal held that where the consent of a woman is obtained by impersonating her boyfriend, that consent in invalid. This rule no longer merely applies to defendants who impersonate a woman's husband.

Tabassum (2000): Fraud as to sexual nature of acts

See 4.7.1 above.

5.1.5   Defendant knows the woman does not consent

Morgan (1976): Honest belief in consent

Facts

D invited some acquaintances back to his house to have sexual intercourse with his wife. He told them that, although she may protest and struggle, she would be consenting as she preferred it that way. D and his acquaintances all had sexual intercourse with V without her consent. The judge directed the jury that, even though the men believed V was consenting, they should be convicted if their belief was not reasonable.

Decision

The House of Lords held that if D honestly believes that V was consenting, he lacks the *mens rea* for rape. The belief does not have to be reasonable. 'It seems to me to follow as a matter of inexorable logic that there is no room either for a "defence" of honest belief or mistake, or of a defence of honest and reasonable belief or mistake' (*per* Lord Hailsham). If D honestly believes that V was consenting, the prosecution have failed to prove the required *mens rea* of rape and therefore a conviction cannot follow. The presence or absence of reasonable grounds for such a belief is irrelevant, unless the jury consider that the belief is so unreasonable that it is not honestly held by D.

See also 9.2.1 below.

Taylor (1985): Drunken mistaken belief in consent

Facts

D was charged with rape. The issue before the court was whether V consented to the sexual intercourse. D admitted that he had been drinking, but maintained that he genuinely believed V was consenting.

Decision

The Court of Appeal held that it was not necessary to give a detailed direction on mistaken belief in V's consent in most cases. Unless there is an acute dispute in the evidence, in most cases the jury should take the view that if V's account of the events is honest, then there is no room for mistaken belief in her consent on the part of the defendant.

5.1.6   *Recklessness as to V's consent*

Bashir (1982): 'Knowing' and 'recklessness' should be indicted under separate counts

Facts

D had sexual intercourse with V. V had undressed herself and assisted D with penetration. D dropped her home afterwards and V kissed him on the cheek. V claimed that she had not resisted as she was terrified of what would happen if she did. D was charged with rape, initially on the grounds that he had sexual intercourse with a woman knowing that she did not consent. During the trial the judge introduced a second count, namely that D had sexual intercourse with V being reckless as to whether she consented or not. D was convicted on the second count and appealed.

Decision

The Court of Appeal held that the trial judge was right to introduce a second count on the indictment, as separate counts are necessary for 'knowing' the woman did not consent and 'being reckless' as to whether she consented.

Flitter (2001): 'Knowing' and 'reckless' should be indicted under the same count

Facts

D was convicted of rape and appealed. He claimed that the trial judge had misdirected the jury in asking them to consider not only whether D knew that V did not consent to the sexual intercourse, but also whether D was reckless as to whether she consented or not, as part of the same charge.

Decision

The Court of Appeal ruled that the judge was right to direct the jury in the way he did, as 'knowing' and 'reckless' should not be indicted as separate counts for the offence of rape. *Bashir* (above) was not followed.

5.1.7   Strict liability

B v DPP (2002): Sexual offences not strict liability unless Parliament expressly so provides

Facts

V (a girl aged 13) sat next to D (aged 15) on a bus. D asked her several times to perform oral sex on him but she refused. D was charged with inciting a girl under the age of 14 to commit an act of gross indecency (contrary to s 1(1) of the Indecency with Children Act 1960). D claimed he had honestly believed V was aged over 14. The trial judge ruled that this was not a defence to this charge, so D changed his plea to guilty. D appealed against his conviction.

Decision

The House of Lords held that the *mens rea* is an essential ingredient in any offence unless Parliament expressly or impliedly provided that it is a strict liability crime. In s 1(1) of the 1960 Act, Parliament had not so provided in relation to that offence. Therefore, if D had an honest belief (whether reasonable or not) that V was aged over 14, then the offence is not proved.

5.2 Indecent assault

5.2.1 Actus reus

Court (1989): Objective test for indecency

Facts

The defendant worked in a shop. He asked a 12 year old girl who visited the shop whether she would let him spank her. She said 'No' but D seized her and spanked her repeatedly on her backside. When arrested by the police, D admitted to spanking her and, when asked why he had done so, he replied 'I don't know, buttock fetish'.

Decision

The House of Lords ruled that not all indecent assaults will be clearly sexual; they may merely have sexual undertones. Therefore a jury must consider first, whether right-minded persons would regard the assault as indecent. 'It is for the jury to decide whether what occurred was so offensive to contemporary standards of modesty and privacy as to be indecent' (*per* Lord Ackner). If the assault is, objectively, neither clearly decent nor clearly indecent, then the jury could take into account the defendant's state of mind and any secret sexual motive he might have in order to decide whether the circumstances of the assault were indecent.

Sargeant (1997): Applying the objective test of indecency

Facts

D grabbed V (aged 16) while V was on the way home from a disco. V was forced to masturbate into a condom. V said he obeyed D's demands because he was terrified. Although D had assaulted V when he grabbed him, he had not touched him indecently in any way. D was convicted of indecent assault and appealed.

Decision

In the view of the Court of Appeal, there was clearly an assault in this case which became indecent because it was done in circumstances of indecency and would be considered by right-minded persons to be indecent. There need not be any indecent touching or threat of the same.

5.2.2 Mens rea

Kimber (1983): Recklessness as to consent

Facts

D was a psychiatric patient in a hospital. He indecently assaulted another patient who did not consent and who was severely mentally handicapped. D admitted that he thought she consented although he knew she was severely mentally handicapped.

Decision

The Court of Appeal held that the *mens rea* of indecent assault was that D either knew V was not consenting or was reckless as to V's consent. *Per* Lawton LJ: '[D's] attitude to her was one of indifference to her feelings and wishes. This state of mind is aptly described in the colloquial expression "couldn't care less". In law, this is recklessness.'

Pratt (1984): *Mens rea* in respect of indecency

Facts

D was charged with indecent assault on two 13 year old boys. The two boys had been fishing at night. D appeared wearing a stocking mask and threatened them by pretending he had a gun. D forced the boys to undress so as to reveal their private parts. As each boy undressed, the other was forced to shine a torch on him. D did not touch the boys and stood a short distance away. D claimed his only motive was to search the boys for cannabis, which he thought they had stolen from him.

Decision

The Crown Court ruled that as well as proving the existence of common law assault and objective indecency as a question of fact, it is also necessary, for a charge of indecent assault, for the prosecution to prove a *mens rea* in respect of the indecency. If there is no indecent intention, then there cannot be an indecent assault.

CHAPTER 6

THEFT

Introduction

The offence of theft is governed by ss 1–6 of the Theft Act 1968. Other offences within this Act will be covered in Chapter 7. The Theft Act 1968 codified the old common law offence of larceny, but used more modern terms to express the precise requirements for the offence. Nevertheless, the extensive case law set out below illustrates how these provisions have needed further clarification and development.

Theft is committed where the defendant dishonestly appropriates property belonging to another with the intention of permanently depriving the other of it. Hence the *actus reus* consists of appropriating property belonging to another and the *mens rea* consists of the two elements of dishonesty and the intention to permanently deprive.

The meaning of the word appropriation has exercised the courts since the enactment of the Theft Act and continues to do so (see *Hinks* (2001)). Appropriation is defined in s 3 of the Theft Act 1968 as any assumption of the owner's rights. The courts added the word 'adverse' to this definition, assuming that an appropriation which took place with the consent of the owner (such as in *Morris* where goods are taken from a supermarket shelf with the consent of the store) could not amount to theft no matter how dishonest the defendant's intentions. However, it has been confirmed in *Gomez* (1992) that consent is irrelevant in deciding whether an appropriation had taken place. This has had the unfortunate effect of rendering both theft and obtaining property by deception (s 15 of the Theft Act 1968) equally applicable as the charge in some circumstances, since in both offences the defendant comes by the property with the victim's consent. It has been argued that this cannot have been what Parliament intended in creating two separate offences in the legislation. Had Gomez been charged under s 15, this issue would not have arisen, notwithstanding that the irrelevance of consent was confirmed in *Hinks* (2001).

Other cases have considered the situation where money is withdrawn from a bank account and whether this can amount to an appropriation. This all depends on the method used to withdraw the money and whether the defendant usurped the rights of the owner of the property. Where a defendant withdraws money by cheque (either through forgery or without authorisation), he does appropriate the funds in the account because he usurps the right of the owner of a debt to demand payment of that debt by the bank. Transfers between bank accounts may also amount to appropriation, since in this case the defendant usurps the right of the owner of the balance of the account (an indefeasible title to property – *Hilton* (1997)).

It was established in the case of *Hilton* that the balance of a bank account did fall within the definition of property, as it is effectively a debt owed by the bank to the account holder which in turn is a thing in action. 'Property' is defined in s 4 of the Theft Act 1968 as including 'money and all other property real or personal, including things in action and other intangible property'. The definition expressly excludes land or things forming part of land and the courts have further excluded certain forms of intellectual property such as information (*Oxford v Moss* (1979)), human body parts (*Kelly* (1998)), and electricity (*Low v Blease* (1973)). Further clarification of the meaning of property has been necessary when the courts have been dealing with the offence of obtaining property by deception; these cases are discussed in Chapter 7.

The property must 'belong to another' which, according to s 5 of the Theft Act 1968, includes any person having possession or control over property or a proprietary interest in it. In some cases (such as those involving purchases from a shop) this has required examining a contract where property is transferred from one person to another to determine exactly who owned the property at the time of the appropriation, particularly where a contract may be void. Property entrusted to the defendant does not necessarily 'belong' to him, despite his possession or control of it, if he is under a legal obligation to deal with it in a particular way on behalf of the owner (*Clowes (No 2)* (1994)). On the other hand, the legal owner of property could appropriate that property where another has possession or control of it (*Turner* (1971)).

The *mens rea* requirement of dishonesty is not specifically defined in the Theft Act 1968, although s 2 offers three statutory 'defences' or situations where the defendant will not be deemed to be dishonest. It has been left to the courts to interpret the meaning of this term and to develop a test for determining dishonesty, which they did in *Ghosh* (1982). The jury have to apply subjective and objective tests. First, they have to decide whether the defendant was dishonest according to the standards of ordinary reasonable people. If so, then they should go on to decide whether the defendant knew that he was acting dishonestly according to the standards of ordinary reasonable people.

Finally, the defendant charged with theft must intend to permanently deprive. This is defined in s 6 of the Theft Act 1968. Someone who borrows property intending to give it back may still be deemed to intend to permanently deprive the owner of it where he returns it in such a changed state that it has lost its value or usefulness (*Lloyd* (1985)), or where he treats it as his own to dispose of regardless of the owner's rights (for example, by investing it in a risky venture – *Fernandes* (1996)).

6.1   *Actus reus* of theft

6.1.1   *Appropriation*

6.1.1.1 *With consent*

Lawrence (1972): Consent irrelevant to appropriation

Facts
A tourist, who spoke little English, arrived in London. He approached a taxi driver (D) to take him to an address. On arrival, the tourist offered D £1, but D took a further £6 from the tourist's wallet. The correct fare was 10 s 6 d. D was convicted of theft of the £6 and appealed on the grounds that the tourist had consented to him taking the money from the wallet and, therefore, he could not have appropriated it.

Decision

The House of Lords held that for the purposes of s 1 of the Theft Act 1968, it was not necessary for the prosecution to establish that the appropriation had taken place without the owner's consent. Belief or absence of belief that the owner consented to the appropriation may be relevant to the issue of dishonesty, but not to the issue of appropriation.

Dobson v General Accident Fire and Life Assurance Corp (1990): Consent irrelevant to appropriation

Facts

The plaintiff had a home contents policy which covered him against theft. When P advertised some jewellery for sale, it was bought by a rogue with stolen building society cheques. P claimed under his insurance policy, but the insurance company argued that his loss had not been caused by theft, because the appropriation took place with P's consent.

Decision

The Court of Appeal held that in order for there to be a theft, there must have been a dishonest appropriation of the items by the purchaser. Following the authority of *Lawrence* (above), the purchaser did assume the rights of the owner dishonestly and with intention to permanently deprive P of them. The fact that appropriation took place with P's consent was irrelevant.

Morris (1983): Adverse usurpation of the owner's rights

Facts

D took articles from a supermarket shelf and switched price labels with those from lower priced goods. D was detected before he got to the checkout. D was convicted of theft.

Decision

The House of Lords ruled that the true meaning of the word 'appropriation' in s 3(1) of the Theft Act 1968 meant an adverse usurpation or interference with some (although not all) of the rights of the owner, and could not be committed with the express or implied consent of the owner. Therefore, the act of switching labels, either alone or in conjunction with some other act, did constitute an appropriation. Taking articles off the shelf in a self-service supermarket did not, in itself, constitute an appropriation, because this was not an act which was adverse to the owner's rights; it was an act for which the shopper had implied authority. Furthermore, the act of switching the labels was not, in itself, an appropriation, unless it was combined with some other act which went beyond the implied authority of the owner, such as attempting to pay the lower price at the checkout.

Skipp (1975): Coincidence of 'adverse' appropriation and *mens rea* of theft

Facts

D posed as a haulage contractor and agreed to deliver two loads of oranges and onions from London to a customer in Leicester. Having collected the goods, he made off with them and did not deliver them to the customer. He had the intention to steal them from the outset.

Decision
The Court of Appeal held that an assumption of the rights of the owner did not necessarily take place at the same time as an intent to permanently deprive the owner of it. Although D intended to steal the goods from the outset, he did not appropriate the goods until they were all loaded, and probably not until they had been diverted from the route to the agreed destination. Until the goods were diverted from this destination, D was acting with the authority of the owner.

Meech (1974): Authority of owner negates appropriation
Facts
D was asked to cash a cheque for P and return the cash to P. D cashed the cheque, but organised a fake robbery by his friends in order to steal the money. D was convicted of theft.

Decision
The Court of Appeal held that the appropriation took place at the time the fake robbery took place, or was at least arranged. Until that time, although D had the intention to steal, he was acting with the authority of P.

Eddy v Niman (1981): Appropriation must be inconsistent with the owner's rights
Facts
D went into a supermarket intending to steal goods. He placed a number of items in a trolley, but changed his mind about stealing them before he reached the checkout. He abandoned the goods in the trolley and left the shop. D was acquitted at trial for theft on the grounds that there had been no appropriation.

Decision
The Queen's Bench Divisional Court held that the question to be asked about appropriation was: had the defendant done some overt act inconsistent with the true owner's rights? Since D in this case had merely taken goods from the shelf and placed them in a trolley provided by the store, he had not done any overt act inconsistent with the rights of the owner. Therefore, D had rightly been acquitted.

Fritschy (1985): Appropriation must be 'unauthorised'
Facts
D was convicted of theft of a quantity of Krugerrands. He dealt in coins for a Dutch company. D bought 70 coins for $49,000, which were to be held in Holland until they could be transferred to a Swiss bank. D told H to remove the coins from the Dutch company, claiming he had doubts about the company's financial standing. D, in accordance with H's wishes, collected the money in England, but did not take it to H's Swiss bank.

Decision

The Court of Appeal held that there was no evidence of any act by D in England which was not expressly authorised by H. Therefore, there was no appropriation in England.

Gomez (1992): Authorised act may amount to appropriation as consent irrelevant

Facts

D was an assistant at an electrical shop. He was asked by B to supply goods in exchange for two building society cheques, which D knew were stolen. D obtained authority from the manager to supply the goods, without telling him the cheques were stolen. D was convicted of theft. D appealed on the grounds that there was no appropriation, as he acted with the authority of the shop manager. The Court of Appeal allowed his appeal, but the prosecution appealed to the House of Lords.

Decision

The House of Lords held that *Lawrence* was the appropriate authority on this issue of appropriation, and the consent of the owner was irrelevant in deciding whether an appropriation had taken place. *Per* Lord Keith:

> While it was correct to say that appropriation included an act by way of adverse interference with or usurpation of the owner's rights, it did not necessarily follow that no other act would amount to an appropriation and, in particular, that no act expressly or impliedly authorised by the owner could do so ... The decision in *Morris* was correct, but it was erroneous and unnecessary to indicate that an act expressly or impliedly authorised by the owner could never amount to an appropriation.

Atakpu (1993): Appropriation took place overseas

Facts

D embarked on a scheme whereby expensive cars were hired abroad, driven to England, altered and sold to unsuspecting purchasers. D obtained a false passport and driving licence in England, hired three cars abroad and drove them to England. D was arrested on arrival at Dover by customs officers. D was charged with conspiracy to steal, but claimed that no appropriation had taken place in England and therefore the case was not triable in England.

Decision

The Court of Appeal held that if goods had once been stolen, they could not be stolen again by the same thief exercising the same rights of ownership over property. Where the thief came by property by stealing it, his later dealings with it could not be an assumption of the rights of the owner amounting to an appropriation, whether the theft took place in England or abroad. Therefore, as the cars were stolen abroad where the appropriation took place, D could not be tried for conspiracy to steal in England.

Mazo (1996): Consent to appropriation obtained by fraud

Facts

D was a maid to V. D was convicted of theft after cashing cheques totalling £37,000 made payable to her by her employer. V consented to the cheques being cashed, but the Crown alleged that she lacked the mental capacity to give valid consent. D appealed on the grounds that there could be no theft if V was the donor of a gift, and that the jury had not been properly directed on the issue of V's mental state.

Decision
The Court of Appeal held that a transaction might be theft, notwithstanding that it was done with the owner's consent, if that consent was induced by fraud, deception or misrepresentation. Whilst it was necessary to consider the state of mind of D and the circumstances of the transfer, it was also necessary to consider whether V had a sufficient degree of understanding to make a valid gift. The jury should have been directed to consider this; therefore, the appeal was upheld.

Hopkins and Kendrick (1997): Consensual appropriation and dishonesty

Facts
D was convicted of conspiracy to steal. V was an old lady cared for by D. D took control of V's affairs when she was too frail to take care of them herself. D took control of £127,500 of her assets and it was alleged that D intended to steal this property. D's behaviour included selling her stock at a disadvantageous time and transferring the proceeds to D's account, refusing access to V by her friends, and changing V's will, making D the beneficiary. D claimed that, at all times, he had the express authority of V and was acting in her interests. D appealed against conviction on the grounds that the judge had not directed the jury properly on the issue of V's consent, and claimed that the consent of V negated any dishonesty on D's part.

Decision
The Court of Appeal found that there was clearly an appropriation in this case and it would be contrary to the earlier case of *Mazo* to hold that the consent of V negates dishonesty. The jury had rightly been directed to consider whether there had been a dishonest appropriation and they concluded that there had been. There was ample evidence in this case of both an appropriation and V's mental incapacity from which the jury might conclude that the appropriation was dishonest.

Hinks (2001): Appropriation need not be unlawful

Facts
D persuaded V (a man of limited intelligence) to transfer a number of amounts of money from his bank account to hers. D claimed the money was a gift. D was convicted of theft but appealed on the ground that acquisition of an indefeasible title to property was not capable of amounting to appropriation.

Decision
The House of Lords held that taking a gift of an indefeasible title to property from a person who was easily influenced could constitute appropriation under s 3 of the Theft Act 1968. Appropriation is an objective term meaning any adoption of the owner's rights and was not dependent on the consent of the owner. There was no requirement that the appropriation was unlawful for it to constitute theft providing there was dishonesty and an intention to permanently deprive.

6.1.1.2 Appropriation and control

Pitham and Hehl (1976): Appropriation without control

Facts

M, knowing that his friend was in prison, decided to sell his furniture to the two defendants. He took the Ds to the friend's house and sold them some items of furniture. The Ds were convicted of handling stolen goods, but appealed on the grounds that their handling of the goods took place before they had been appropriated.

Decision

The Court of Appeal held that although M was not in a position to control the property, he had appropriated it by the time the Ds handled it. He had assumed the rights of the owner when he took the Ds to the house and invited them to buy the furniture. Once the appropriation was complete, the goods were stolen and therefore the Ds had handled stolen goods.

6.1.1.3 Appropriating money from bank accounts

Navvabi (1986): Use of banker's card to guarantee a cheque

Facts

D opened bank accounts in false names. He then drew 12 cheques supported by a banker's card in a casino in exchange for some gaming chips. There were insufficient funds in the bank accounts to cover the cheques. D was charged with theft. D appealed against his conviction on the ground that there had been no appropriation.

Decision

The Court of Appeal held that the use of a banker's card to guarantee a cheque drawn on an account with insufficient funds was not appropriation. The use of the banker's card to support a cheque merely gave the payee a contractual right against the bank to be paid the sum specified on the cheque. Therefore, there was no appropriation by D, neither when he gave the cheque to the payee nor when the payee presented the cheque to the bank and it was honoured, as D had not assumed the rights of the bank to that part of the bank's funds.

Chan Man Sin v AG for Hong Kong (1988): Using forged cheques

Facts

D was an accountant for two companies (H and M). Both companies held bank accounts in Hong Kong. D used forged cheques to withdraw funds from both H's and M's accounts, which he transferred to his own personal account. This caused both H's and M's accounts to go overdrawn, and they were forced to use an overdraft facility agreed with the bank. D was charged with theft of *choses in action*, that is, the debts owed by the bank to the companies. D appealed against his conviction on the ground that the bank had no right to honour the forged cheques and the transactions should have been void.

Decision

The Privy Council held that: 'One who draws, presents and negotiates a cheque on a particular bank account is assuming the rights of the owner of the credit in the account, or (as the case may be) of the pre-negotiated right to draw on the account up to the agreed figure' (*per* Lord Oliver).

Gallasso (1994): Although dishonest, no appropriation without adverse interference

Facts

D was a nurse in charge of a patient's finances. She transferred money from one of V's accounts to another and was convicted of theft.

Decision

The Court of Appeal held that: '... in deciding whether, objectively, an action amounts to an appropriation, you must not stop the camera too soon; you are not confined to a single point of time; you may look to the consequences. In this case, there was no appropriation because, looking at the complete picture, the nurse did not assume the owner's rights over the money' (*per* Lloyd LJ).

Governor of Pentonville Prison ex p Osman (1990): Unauthorised telex is an appropriation

Facts

Osman applied for a writ of habeas corpus, having been detained in custody to await his return to Hong Kong, where he was wanted on charges of theft, fraud, bribery and other offences. It was alleged that he had been bribed in Hong Kong, as chairman of a company (B), to make loans to another company (C). This involved drawing on B's bank account in New York. He was committed by magistrates in England on the basis that this amounted to theft of a debt owed by an American bank to its customer, B. Osman claimed that English courts had no jurisdiction to hear the theft case as, if any theft took place at all, it took place in New York where the bank withdrew the funds, and not in Hong Kong where D issued his instructions by telex. The court therefore had to consider where the appropriation had taken place in order to decide whether the English court had jurisdiction.

Decision

The Queen's Bench Divisional Court held that an appropriation is the adverse assumption of any of the owner's rights. This clearly includes the right of an owner of a debt to draw on the bank account in question. D assumed this right by drawing funds from B's account and by dishonestly drawing a cheque on the account without authorisation. Sending a telex instructing the bank to draw a cheque could amount to an appropriation if done without authority. Therefore, theft had been committed and took place in Hong Kong, where D telexed the American bank with his instructions. The English court therefore had jurisdiction.

Governor of Brixton Prison ex p Levin (1997): Appropriation by computer

Facts

L brought habeas corpus proceedings, having been arrested for theft. L had used a computer in Russia to gain unauthorised access to an American bank and diverted funds in false accounts. The issue arose as to whether the appropriation had taken place in America, where the accounts were held on a computer, or in Russia, where L was typing instructions on a keyboard.

Decision

The Queen's Bench Divisional Court found that the appropriation effectively took place in the USA. *Per* Beldam LJ:

> The operation of the keyboard by a computer operator produces a virtually instantaneous result on the magnetic disk of the computer, even though it may be 10,000 miles away ... The fact that [L] was physically in St Petersburg is of far less significance than the fact that he was looking at, and operating on, magnetic disks located in [the USA]. The essence of what he was doing was done there. Until the instruction is recorded on the disk, there is in fact no appropriation.

Hilton (1997): Appropriation of *chose in action*
See 6.1.2 below.

Ngan (1998): No appropriation where transfer of funds not made

Facts

D opened a bank account, the allocated number of which had previously been used by a debt collection agency and some cheques had mistakenly been credited to the account on behalf of the agency. D, knowing of this mistake, signed and sent a number of blank cheques to his sister in Scotland. She presented the cheques for payment, also knowing of the mistake. D was charged with theft but argued that the appropriation had taken place in Scotland and therefore the English courts had no jurisdiction.

Decision

The Court of Appeal held that the appropriation took place when the cheque was presented at the bank to draw upon the agency's funds. D signing the cheques was merely preparatory and did not amount to an appropriation (although it might amount to an attempted theft).

6.1.2   Property

Low v Blease (1973): Electricity not property for purposes of theft

Facts

D entered premises as a trespasser and made a telephone call. D was convicted of burglary contrary to s 9(1)(b) of the Theft Act 1968, on the basis that he had stolen electricity by using the telephone.

Decision

The Queen's Bench Divisional Court ruled that electricity is not property for the purposes of theft.

Oxford v Moss (1979): Information held on paper not property

Facts

A student obtained a copy of an examination paper, read it and then replaced it. He never intended to take the paper away or deprive the University of it. He was convicted of theft of the confidential information on the paper, which was classed as intangible property.

Decision

The Court of Appeal held that information held on a piece of paper could not amount to intangible property according to the true interpretation of s 4 of the Theft Act 1968.

Hilton (1997): A debt is property for the purposes of theft

Facts

D was chairman of a charity. He was convicted of theft, having on a number of occasions faxed instructions that sums of money from the charity's accounts be transferred to accounts of his own and of his creditors. D appealed against conviction, claiming that the credit balance on the charity's account did not constitute property for the purposes of a conviction for theft.

Decision

The Court of Appeal dismissed the appeal, holding that what was stolen in this case was the right of the charity as a creditor to recover a debt from the bank. The credit balance is therefore a debt or *chose in action*, which is property capable of being stolen. D had appropriated that property by assuming the charity's right to the balance once the transfers were made. D had appropriated the property even though the act of appropriation had the effect of destroying the property stolen.

Kelly (1998): Human corpse is not property for the purposes of theft

Facts

D was convicted of the theft of approximately 35 human body parts from the Royal College of Surgeons. D appealed on the ground that a human corpse or parts of it were not property capable of being stolen.

Decision

The Court of Appeal upheld D's conviction. The common law position that a human corpse was not property capable of being stolen was accepted and endorsed. However, where that corpse had been altered for the purpose of medical or scientific examination, it became valuable and therefore became property capable of being stolen. *Obiter, per* Rose LJ, the common law position on the possession of body parts was subject to change in the future. Where body parts had not been altered for medical examination, a future court may still decide that they were property, for example, where they were required for use in an organ transplant.

6.1.3   Belonging to another
See also 7.4.4 below.

6.1.3.1 Possession or control

Turner (1971): Possession or control amounts to 'belonging to another'

Facts

D took his car to a garage to be repaired. When the repairs were almost finished, the mechanic parked the car on the road outside the garage. D surreptitiously took the car away without telling the garage or paying for the repairs. D was charged with theft of the car, but claimed he owned the car and therefore it did not belong to another.

Decision

The Court of Appeal held that D had stolen the car because, at the time of the appropriation, it was under the possession and control of the garage. Although the garage had a lien over the car, this was irrelevant in the present case. The question rightly asked of the jury was: did the garage in fact have possession or control of the car at the time of the appropriation?

Woodman (1974): Belonging to another includes ignorant possession

Facts

D was convicted of theft of remnants of scrap metal from a disused factory site. The occupiers of the site were unaware of the existence of the scrap metal, although they had erected a barbed wire fence around the site to exclude trespassers. D claimed the scrap metal did not belong to another within the meaning of s 5 of the Theft Act 1968.

Decision

The Court of Appeal held that a person has possession of any articles or property on his land, even if he is not aware that that property exists or had forgotten that it exists.

6.1.3.2 Proprietary right or interest

Turner (1971): A lien

Facts as above.

Decision

The Court of Appeal held that although this was irrelevant to the decision in this case, the garage owner had a lien, a proprietary interest in the car. This illustrates how a number of people may 'own' property. Any number of people may have a legal or equitable interest or right in the property, and can thus be a victim of theft of that property. The term 'belonging to another' does not necessarily mean wholly owned by another.

Bonner (1970): Company property

Decision

The Court of Appeal held that the partner of a company could appropriate company property, and there was nothing in law to prevent him being convicted of theft of partnership or company property.

Kaur v Chief Constable of Hants (1981): Transfer of ownership in a purchase

Facts

D selected a pair of shoes from a rack marked £6.99. One of the shoes had a label indicating that the price was £6.99 and the label on the other shoe stated £4.99. D took the shoes to the counter without concealing either label. She was charged £4.99, which she paid, and left the store. She was convicted of theft. She appealed, contending that, at the moment that she left the shop with the shoes, the ownership of them had passed from the shop to her and therefore the property did not belong to another.

Decision

The Queen's Bench Divisional Court held that in a transaction such as this, the ownership of the property passes upon payment by the customer of the price to the cashier (s 18 of the Sale of Goods Act 1979). Therefore, in this case, the ownership of the shoes passed to D when she paid for them, and when she left the shop, they belonged to her; she did not intend to deprive the owner of them. The contract of sale was not void due to mistake, since the mistake was the cashier's in marking one shoe with the wrong price label. This was not a fundamental mistake which rendered the contract void (see *Morris* (1984)).

Williams (1979): Sterling value of currency

Facts

D bought some obsolete Yugoslav Dinar from a stamp collector's shop for £7.00. He took them to a bureau de change and exchanged them for £107 sterling. He was convicted of theft.

Decision

The Court of Appeal upheld D's conviction. The mistake of the cashier in thinking that the Dinar were still valid currency was a fundamental mistake which made the contract void *ab initio*. Therefore, D had appropriated property (the sterling) belonging to another and had rightly been convicted of theft.

Goodwin (1996): Ownership of coins in an arcade

Facts

D used a Kenyan five shilling coin, which is the same size and weight as a 50 pence coin, in gaming machines in an amusement arcade. He was convicted of going equipped for theft. D appealed on the grounds that, after he had inserted a coin of the size, shape and weight of a 50 pence coin, any coins which were then paid out by the machine no longer belonged to the amusement arcade, but were the property of D. He claimed that to hold that the coins belonged to the arcade after they had left the machines was a contravention of s 18 of the Gaming Act 1845.

Decision

The Court of Appeal dismissed D's appeal. D would have been trying to obtain property belonging to the owners of the arcade in a way in which he knew he did not have their consent, and in a way which was dishonest. Ownership of the coins had not passed and, had the arcade owners been able to prove that D used a Kenyan coin to obtain coins from the machines, they would have been able to recover their money in a civil action. Section 18 of the Gaming Act 1845 did not apply here, since there was never any gaming contract or wager in these circumstances.

6.1.3.3 Property received under an obligation

AG's Reference (No 1 of 1985) (1986): Proceeds of sale

Facts

D was the manager of a public house. He was under an obligation to sell only his employer's beer and to pay all the profit into the employer's account. (The manager was salaried.) D sold other beer in the pub and kept the profit for himself. He was charged with theft on the grounds that the money he had received from customers for the beer belonged to the employers under s 5(3) of the Theft Act 1968.

Decision

The Court of Appeal held that whether or not D's actions can constitute theft under s 5(3) depends upon whether the money received from the customers of the sale of the beer was received on account for the employers. The Court of Appeal here felt that it was not. It was money received by D on his own account for the private sale of his own beer. It may have been a breach of contract, but the remedy for this must be found in civil law, not criminal law.

Lewis v Lethbridge (1987): Sponsorship money

Facts

D obtained sponsorship for a friend who had entered the London Marathon. He received £54 in sponsorship, which he did not hand over to the charity. D was convicted of theft on the grounds that he was under an obligation to hand the proceeds of sponsorship (if not the actual notes and coins) to the charity.

Decision

The Queen's Bench Divisional Court found that the justices erred in finding that the debt owed by D could be described as proceeds of the property received. According to s 5(3) of the Theft Act 1968, the obligation is to deal with the property or its proceeds in a particular way. This suggests that D need not be under an obligation to keep in existence a fund equivalent to that which he has received. D can do whatever he likes with the money as long as, in due course, he hands over an equivalent sum to the charity.

Wills (1991): Investment of insurance money

Facts

D and his two assistants were financial advisers. They received money from clients, with instructions to invest it with an insurance company. The money was used for the business and was not invested as instructed. D was not present when the clients handed over the money and issued their instructions. When D was charged with theft, he claimed he was unaware of the obligation under s 5(3) of the Theft Act 1968.

Decision

The Court of Appeal held that:

> Whether a person is under an obligation to deal with property in a particular way can only be established by proving that he had knowledge of that obligation. Proof that the property was not dealt with in conformity with the obligation is not sufficient in itself. In order to establish liability under s 5(3), it is necessary to prove that D had knowledge of the nature and extent of the obligation to deal with property in a particular way (*per* Farquharson LJ).

Mainwaring (1981): Deposits

Facts

D was the director of a company in the UK developing houses in Spain and the south of France. People wishing to buy houses in Spain or the south of France handed over cash to D as deposits, but did not get their houses, and D dishonestly appropriated the money. D in fact used the money to pay off the company's overdraft.

Decision

The Court of Appeal held that the obligation to deal with the property in a particular way must be a legal obligation and not a moral one.

Clowes (No 2) (1994): Universal funds held by bank

Facts

D was a former director of an investment bank. Money from clients' accounts was used for the purchase of houses and luxury items. The money had been invested in the bank's 'portfolios' and the bank was authorised to buy and sell gilts with it and 'to place any uninvested sums with any bank, local authority or other body on such terms as [the bank] see fit whether bearing interest or not'. The prosecution claimed that under these terms the funds remained the property of clients. D claimed that the beneficial ownership of the money was transferred to the bank and therefore the funds did not belong to another.

Decision

The Court of Appeal held that under s 5 of the Theft Act 1968 the funds 'belonged to another' (the clients). Under the contract in question, the beneficial ownership did not pass from the clients to the bank, but a trust had been created under which the funds were to be invested or otherwise temporarily 'placed' but not to be used for D's private purchases.

Klineberg and Marsden (1999): Belonging to another under the Theft Act not necessarily same as civil law interpretation

Facts

D was director of a company which entered into an agreement to buy a timeshare development in Lanzarote and to sell the timeshares. Under the agreement, money paid by purchasers was to be transferred to the trust company to protect the purchasers until the apartments were ready for occupation. Purchasers paid £500,000 to the company, but only £233,000 was sent to the trust company. D was convicted of the theft of the purchasers' money. D appealed on the grounds that, once the money had been paid into the D's company's bank account, it no longer belonged to the purchasers, but was replaced by a *chose in action* (credit balance) belonging to the company. The prosecution claimed that, under s 5(3) of the Theft Act 1968, D's company was receiving money on account of the purchasers and was, therefore, under an obligation to retain and deal with the property or its proceeds in a particular way.

Decision

The Court of Appeal held that s 5(3) was a deeming provision whereby property or its proceeds 'shall be regarded' as belonging to another, even though, strictly speaking, in civil law, it did not. It applied to both the property and 'its proceeds'. Therefore, the judge at first instance had been right to conclude that s 5(3) applied here to place D under an obligation to the purchasers to retain and deal with the property in a particular way. Where the money paid to D by the purchasers was not transferred to a trustee company, that obligation had been breached.

6.1.3.4 Property transferred by mistake

Moynes v Cooper (1956): Overpayment by employer

Facts

D was given a pay packet which, by mistake, contained too much. He was charged with larceny.

Decision

The Queen's Bench Divisional Court found D not guilty of larceny. Under common law, the ownership of the money had passed to D, and so D could not have stolen his own property.

Comment

The Theft Act 1968 sought to remedy this problem.

AG's Reference (No 1 of 1983) (1985): Overpayment of salary

Facts

D, a policewoman, was overpaid her salary which was directly transferred to her bank account. When she realised the mistake, she dishonestly kept the money. She was charged with theft, but the judge directed an acquittal. The Attorney General referred the case to the Court of Appeal on a point of law, namely, whether under s 5(4) of the Theft Act 1968, D's actions were capable of amounting to theft.

Decision

The Court of Appeal held that although D had got property by another's mistake under s 5(4), she was not under an obligation to make restoration of the property. The property here was a *chose in action* (her right to sue the bank for the debt they owed her), but this *chose in action* was incapable of being restored to her employers. She was, however, obliged to restore the value of the *chose in action*, providing the transfer of funds was made under a fundamental mistake.

6.2   Mens rea of theft

6.2.1   Dishonesty under s 2 of the Theft Act 1968

Small (1988): A two stage test for dishonesty

Facts

D was charged with theft of a car. D admitted stealing the car, but said he had seen the car for two weeks in a stationary position parked on a corner of a road, with the doors unlocked and keys in the ignition. One tyre was flat, as was the battery. The petrol tank was empty and the windscreen wipers did not work. D thought it was abandoned property and could not be stolen. D was convicted and appealed.

Decision

The Court of Appeal allowed D's appeal. The jury should have been directed to consider:

(1)   whether, according to the standards of the ordinary reasonable and honest person, what D did was dishonest; and

(2)   if so, whether D must have realised what he was doing was dishonest by the standards of ordinary reasonable and honest people.

6.2.2   Dishonesty as a question of fact

Landy (1981): Subjective test of dishonesty

Facts

D was charged with conspiracy to defraud the customers of a bank. D used banking irregularities and malpractices in siphoning money from the bank, and must have known what was going on. D was actively engaged in ensuring that the money went to where it was siphoned and was putting customers of the bank at risk. D also concealed what was happening.

Decision

The Court of Appeal held:

> An assertion by a defendant that, throughout a transaction, he acted honestly, does not have to be weighed like any other piece of evidence. If that was the defendant's state of mind ... he is entitled to be acquitted. But, if the jury, applying their own notions of what is honest and what is not, conclude that he could not have believed that he was acting honestly, then the element of dishonesty will have been established (per Lawton LJ).

Feeley (1973): D's own state of mind

Facts

D worked in a betting shop as a manager. The employer issued a memo, stating that borrowing from tills was to stop. Knowing this, D borrowed £30 from the till and left an 'IOU' in its place. D was owed more than twice this sum by his employers. D was convicted of theft.

Decision

The Court of Appeal held that the word 'dishonesty' in s 1(1) of the Theft Act 1968 can only relate to D's own state of mind, and it is a question of fact which juries should decide. Judges should not attempt to define what 'dishonesty' means; jurors should apply the standards of ordinary decent people.

Ghosh (1982): Test of dishonesty

Facts

D was a surgeon acting as a *locum tenens* consultant at a hospital. He falsely represented that he had himself carried out surgical operations, and that money was due to him for the same, when the operations had, in fact, been carried out under the NHS by somebody else. D was convicted of obtaining property by deception.

Decision

The Court of Appeal ruled that in determining whether D was acting dishonestly, the jury had first to consider whether, according to the standards of the ordinary reasonable person, what was done was dishonest. If it was, the jury must then consider whether D himself must have realised that what he was doing was dishonest by the standards of the ordinary reasonable person.

Roberts (1987): Limited application of second part of *Ghosh* test

Facts

In a burglary, two Renoir paintings worth £51,000 were stolen. A claim was made against the insurers, and the loss adjuster offered a reward of 10% of the value of the paintings for their return. Three months later, D phoned the loss adjuster and told them that he could recover the paintings. D handed the paintings over in exchange for £10,000. D was arrested and charged with handling stolen goods.

Decision

The Court of Appeal held that the second part of the *Ghosh* test need only be put to the jury where the defendant specifically raises the defence that he did not think he was dishonest by his own standards.

Hyam (1997): Precise words of *Ghosh* test should be used

Facts

D was director of a company which owned the freeholds of a number of properties. He owned another company trading under a different name, which acted as the managing agents of the properties. His co-accused ran a decorating company. Work was carried out to the properties and D told the lessees that the work had been carried out by a number of firms and that he required payment for it. The prosecution alleged that he had acted dishonestly, because the work had, in fact, been done by D's companies at inflated prices. They further alleged that D had written the company names only on the cheque stubs, but had made the cheques out to acquaintances who cashed them and returned the money to D. D denied that he had acted dishonestly. The jury were directed on the question of dishonesty as follows: that dishonesty had to be judged according to the standards of ordinary right-minded people and according to prevailing standards. If a person realised that ordinary right-minded people regarded what he had done as dishonest, the jury had to find him dishonest. D argued this direction was inadequate.

Decision

The Court of Appeal, dismissing the appeal, advised that it was desirable that judges use the exact words of Lord Lane in *Ghosh*. In this case, although the exact words had not been used, the essential ingredients of the *Ghosh* direction were present, namely the objective element and whether D realised that reasonable and honest people would consider him dishonest.

Clarke (Victor) (1996): Applying both parts of the *Ghosh* test

Facts

D was a private investigator. He falsely claimed to be a former fraud squad officer and a court bailiff and, as a result of this representation, was hired by a group of fraud victims to investigate their case. He changed his plea to guilty when the judge indicated to the jury that the offence was proved if they found that he had made the false representations, and that he was hired as a result of those representations. D appealed against conviction on the ground that the judge had not directed the jury to consider whether he had been acting dishonestly.

Decision

The Court of Appeal, quashing D's conviction, held that the judge's indication in this case suggested that the actions of telling lies to obtain employment, irrespective of whether or not D could do the job properly or intended to do so, was obviously dishonest, and that the first part of the *Ghosh* test did not need to be left before the jury. The Court of Appeal disagreed and held that the jury had not been fully directed to consider the entire *Ghosh* test of dishonesty.

6.2.3   Intention to permanently deprive

Lloyd (1985): Borrowing and intention to permanently deprive

Facts

D was a projectionist at a cinema. During the day, he secretly borrowed films intended to be shown to the public and lent them to friends who made illegal copies of them. The copying process was done within a few hours and the films were returned to the cinema in time for the advertised performance, and were not damaged in any way. D was convicted of theft.

Decision

The Court of Appeal held that borrowing property could only amount to intending to permanently deprive the owner of it, by virtue of s 6(1) of the Theft Act 1968, if the intention of the borrower was to return the property in such a changed state that it had lost all its practical value. Since, in this case, the films could still be shown to the public, they had not lost all their practical value and therefore D could not have intended to permanently deprive the cinema of the films.

Coffey (1987): Conditional withholding of property

Facts

D was convicted of obtaining property by deception. He had obtained machinery using a worthless cheque. D had been in dispute with V, who refused to negotiate with him. D exerted pressure on V by obtaining and keeping the machinery until he got what he wanted.

Decision

The Court of Appeal held that if the jury thought that D might have intended to return the goods, even if V did not do what he wanted, they should not convict unless they were sure that D intended that the period of detention should be so long as to amount to an outright taking. To create a situation in which V would only get his property back by doing something which D wanted him to do, may be treating the property as D's own to dispose of, regardless of V's rights.

Lavender (1993): Meaning of 'to dispose of'

Facts

D was accused of stealing two doors. He had taken them from a council property undergoing repair and had used them to replace damaged doors at another council property. He argued that he had not intended to permanently deprive the council of the doors.

Decision

The Queen's Bench Divisional Court held that the words in s 6 'to dispose of' should not be defined too literally as meaning to sell or get rid of. The proper question to be considered was whether D intended to treat the doors as his own, regardless of the council's rights not to have them removed. In this case, D, in removing the doors, had clearly intended to treat the doors as his own.

Fernandes (1996): Risking loss of property amounts to 'disposing of'

Facts

D was a solicitor who transferred money from a client's account to R. The money was to be invested in a moneylending firm, of which R was a partner. The money disappeared. D knew the investment was unsafe and was convicted of theft. On appeal, the question arose as to whether s 6(1) could apply here.

Decision

The Court of Appeal held that the second limb of s 6(1) could apply in a case such as this, where a person in possession of another's property dealt with it in a way in which they knew they were risking its loss. D, in this case, can be said to have treated the money as his own to dispose of, regardless of the other's rights, and therefore intended to permanently deprive the other of it.

Marshall (1998): Reselling unexpired tickets

Facts

D obtained unexpired tickets and travelcards of London Transport and resold them. D was charged with theft.

Decision

The Court of Appeal held that the unexpired tickets remained the property of London Transport who had the sole right to sell tickets on their transport system. Therefore, the resale of the tickets by D amounted to an intention to treat the thing as his own to dispose of regardless of the owner's rights.

CHAPTER 7

OTHER PROPERTY OFFENCES

Introduction

This chapter examines the case law in relation to a number of the other property offences in the Theft Acts (TA) 1968 and 1978, as well as criminal damage. These include burglary (s 9 of the TA 1968), robbery (s 8 of the TA 1968), blackmail (s 21 of the TA 1968), and the deception offences. The cases relating to the first three of these clarify elements of the *actus reus* and *mens rea* for those offences. In the case of burglary, this has principally meant clarifying the meaning of 'entry' of premises to include any partial or whole entry which is effective for the purposes of carrying out one of the subsidiary offences intended by the defendant, and the extent to which the defendant does so as a trespasser or without the authority of the occupant or owner.

In the case of robbery, the main issue has been the extent of force (used or threatened) necessary to make out the offence, which in the case of *Clouden* (1987) amounted to very little. Finally, in the case of blackmail, the courts have had to consider what is meant by the word 'menaces' or threats used by the defendant to persuade the victim to succumb to his demands. Again these need not amount to a serious threat of violence (*Thorne v Motor Trade Association* (1937)).

The common theme of the deception offences is, of course, the fact that the defendant must deceive the victim and the cases have explored what is required by this element. The case law demonstrates that the defendant has to make a false representation, but may do this verbally by telling the victim something that is not true, or by behaving in a way which causes the victim to believe something that is not true. However the deception is carried out, the victim must actually be deceived; so if they know that the defendant's representation is false there is no deception. Further, the deception must be operative at the relevant time so that it causes the victim to part with whatever the defendant is charged with obtaining. If the victim would have parted with it notwithstanding the deception, then in law the defendant has done nothing wrong (*Lambie* (1981); *Miller* (1992)).

Once it is established that there was an operative deception, carried out intentionally or recklessly by the defendant, the nature of the criminal charge will depend on what the defendant obtained. Section 15 of the TA 1968 deals with obtaining property belonging to another with the intention to permanently deprive the other of it. The meaning of property here bears the same meaning as for theft, although it is possible to obtain land by deception. In recent years the issue before the courts has been whether obtaining a mortgage advance from a bank or building society fits within this offence. In *Preddy* (1996), the House of Lords argued that the electronic transfer of funds in this situation does not involve the transfer of any identifiable property (it does not constitute money, or a debt belonging to another) and so no offence was committed under s 15. As a result of this case, others who had previously been convicted for mortgage fraud under that section successfully appealed against their convictions (*Graham* (1996)), although there was some speculation as to whether this activity amounted to obtaining services by deception under s 1 of the TA 1978. This unsatisfactory state of affairs was eventually put right by Parliament in amending the TA 1968 to create a new offence of obtaining a money transfer by deception (s 15A).

The other deception offence in the 1968 Act is to obtain a pecuniary advantage, which is the opportunity to borrow money or to earn money. So to secure a job by making a false representation on a curriculum vitae could result in liability under this section because the defendant is given the opportunity to earn money as a result of the deception.

The TA 1978 was enacted to close gaps in the law on deception and to cover the obtaining of things other than property or evasion of liability. Hence, s 1 creates the offence of obtaining services by deception where the victim is induced to offer a service which would normally be paid for. Section 2 of the 1978 Act creates the offence of evasion of liability by deception, which involves causing the victim to discharge a debt or unduly wait for payment of a debt through an operative deception by the defendant (for example, pretending to be out when a rent collector calls to collect your rent). Section 3 of the 1978 Act creates the offence of making off without payment. This offence was designed to specifically cover situations where the defendant obtained something which could not be distinguished as property, such as food eaten in a restaurant. Once food is eaten it becomes part of the consumer's body and their body is incapable of constituting property belonging to another (*Brooks and Brooks* (1982)). Deception is not a requirement for this offence, but dishonesty is, as is an intention to permanently avoid payment.

Criminal damage is an offence under the Criminal Damage Act 1971. Whilst there has been limited case law on what constitutes damage, the principal issue with this offence has been clarifying the *mens rea* requirements. Defendants charged with this offence must firstly intend or be reckless as to whether property is damaged. Under s 1(2)(b) of the 1971 Act, they may be charged with a more serious offence if they intend or are reckless as to whether life is endangered by their actions. The meaning of recklessness in relation to this offence has been problematic. The test was subjective until 1981 when the House of Lords in *Caldwell* set out a model direction using an objective test. After much criticism, the *Caldwell* direction was overruled by the Lords in *R v G and R* (2003) (see further Chapter 19).

7.1   Burglary

7.1.1   *Enter*

Collins (1973): Substantial and effective entry

Facts

D climbed a ladder leaning against a house and looked in a bedroom window. He saw P asleep, naked on a bed. D climbed down the ladder, removed his clothes and climbed up again, stopping on the windowsill. P, thinking D was her boyfriend, invited him into the room and they had sexual intercourse. P then discovered D was not her boyfriend. D was convicted of burglary.

Decision

The Court of Appeal held that in order to be convicted of burglary, D had to have made a substantial and effective entry as a trespasser before consent was given.

Brown (1985): Complete entry not necessary to be 'effective'

Facts

D was seen, having broken the window, with the top half of his body inside the shop window, rummaging around inside the shop. His feet were on the ground outside. D was convicted for burglary.

Decision

The Court of Appeal ruled that the word 'enter' in s 9 of the TA 1968 meant 'effective' entry; it was not necessary for the entry to be complete or even substantial, so long as the entry was effective for D to carry out the ulterior offence.

Ryan (1996): Effective entry

Facts

In the early hours of the morning, D was found stuck in a downstairs window of an occupied house. D's head and arm were inside the window and the rest of his body was outside the window. The window itself was resting on his neck, trapping him. He claimed he was trying to retrieve his baseball bat, which his friend had put through the window. D was convicted of burglary, but appealed on the grounds that his action did not constitute an entry within the meaning of s 9 of the TA 1968.

Decision

The Court of Appeal held that it was clear after *Brown* (above) that is was possible to enter a building for the purposes of s 9, even where only part of the body was actually inside the building. It is irrelevant that D, in this case, was incapable of stealing anything because he was trapped by the neck through the window.

7.1.2 A building or a part of a building

Walkington (1979): Counter area of a shop is part of a building

Facts

Just before a shop closed, D went behind a counter and opened a till drawer. It was empty, so he slammed it shut. D was convicted for burglary. D claimed he had not entered as a trespasser, as he did not realise that he was not allowed to go behind the counter.

Decision

The Court of Appeal held that it is for the jury to decide whether an area physically marked out by a counter amounted to a 'part of a building' from which the general public are excluded. In this case, it was clear that the public were impliedly prohibited from entering the counter area, and D knew of this prohibition.

7.1.3 As a trespasser

Collins (1973): Knowingly or recklessly trespasses

Facts

See 7.1.1 above.

Decision

The Court of Appeal held: '... a serious offence like burglary should require *mens rea* in the fullest sense of the phrase; D should be liable for burglary only if he knowingly trespasses or is reckless as to whether he trespasses or not' (*per* Edmund Davies LJ).

Jones and Smith (1976): Exceeding authority to enter

Facts

D stole a television set from his father's house, which he had general permission to enter. He was convicted of burglary.

Decision

The Court of Appeal found that D was a trespasser if he entered premises knowing that, or being reckless whether, he was entering in excess of any permission that had been given to him to enter.

7.2 Robbery

7.2.1 Force or threat of force

Dawson and James (1976): Meaning of 'force'

Facts

Some men jostled P, who lost his balance. As a result, D was able to steal his wallet. D was convicted of robbery.

Decision

The Court of Appeal held that whether this amounted to force or not was a question to be decided by the jury. *Per* Lawton LJ: 'The choice of the word "force" is not without interest because, under the Larceny Act 1916, the word "violence" had been used ... Whether there is any difference between "violence" and "force" is not relevant.' The jury must use their common sense to decide whether D's actions amounted to force.

Clouden (1987): Bag snatching

Facts

D wrenched a woman's bag down and out of her grasp, and ran off with it. D was charged with robbery, but claimed that snatching a bag could not amount to force.

Decision

The Court of Appeal held that whether force had been used or not is a matter to be left to the jury. In this case, the jury was entitled to conclude that pulling a bag down amounted to force.

7.2.2   Immediately before or at the time of stealing

Hale (1978): Appropriation as a continuing act

Facts
D burgled V's house. Having stolen her jewellery box, D tied V up. D argued he used force after stealing, that is, after laying his hands on the jewellery box.

Decision
The Court of Appeal held: 'The act of appropriation does not suddenly cease. It is a continuous act and it is a matter for the jury to decide whether or not the act of appropriation has finished' (*per* Eveleigh LJ). Here, D was in the course of committing theft and therefore, having used force at the time of stealing, was guilty of robbery.

7.2.3   Theft must be established

Robinson (1977): Where there is no dishonesty theft is not established

Facts
D was charged with robbery from V. V's wife owed the money to D, and D claimed that V gave it to him willingly as repayment of the debt. Therefore, he claimed, the money was not appropriated dishonestly and since there was no theft, D could not be convicted of robbery.

Decision
The Court of Appeal held that if D has not committed theft because he believed he has a right to the property (a 'defence' under s 2 of the Theft Act 1968), then he could not be convicted of robbery.

7.3   Blackmail

7.3.1   Unwarranted demand

Collister and Warhurst (1955): Implied demand

Facts
The two defendants were police officers, who arrested V for importuning. D1 told V: 'This is going to be very bad for you' and V thought D was demanding money from him in return for not reporting the offence.

Decision
The Court of Appeal held that an actual demand, either express or by unequivocal gesture, is not an essential ingredient of the offence of blackmail. The menaces need not be express. If, although there has been no such express demand or threat, the demeanour of D and the circumstances are such that an ordinary reasonable person would understand that a demand for money was being made, and if the demand is accompanied by implied or express menaces so that the balance of an ordinary mind would be upset, then these two elements of the offence of blackmail have been established.

Treacy v DPP (1971): Demand by letter

Facts
In England, D posted a letter containing an unwarranted demand to V in Germany. D claimed she could not be tried for blackmail in England, because the demand was made in Germany, where V received the demand.

Decision
The House of Lords held that the offence of blackmail was made out here. Even though blackmail is a result crime (that is, it requires the acts of D to lead to certain prohibited consequences), it is sufficient if either the acts are done, or the consequences take effect, in England. In this case, D did the acts in England, even though the consequences took effect in Germany.

7.3.2   Menaces

Thorne v Motor Trade Association (1937): Meaning of 'menace'

Facts
A trade union held a 'Stop List' on which they placed the names of members who had infringed its rule against selling items at prices other than list prices. The appellant had offered a discount on items and, under the rules of the trade union, was demanded to pay a sum of money to avoid his name being put on the Stop List. The appellant claimed this rule was illegal, as it amounted to a demand with menaces.

Decision
In the House of Lords, Lord Wright held: 'I think the word "menace" is to be liberally construed and not limited to threats of violence, but as including threats of any action detrimental to or unpleasant to the person addressed. It may also include a warning that in certain events such action is intended.' *Prima facie*, this would include a threat to place a person on the Stop List in this case, unless the trade union has a reasonable cause to do so, such as the promotion of lawful business interests. The appeal was therefore dismissed.

Lawrence and Pomroy (1971): Ambiguous menaces

Facts
D had repaired the roof of V's house for £195. V was not satisfied with the work and paid £125, promising to pay the balance when the work was finished. D told V that, unless he got the balance, 'You will have to look over your shoulder before you step out of doors'. V felt threatened by this.

Decision
The Court of Appeal held that it is not necessary for the judge to give the jury any explanation of the word 'menaces'. However, in exceptional cases, where, because of special knowledge in special circumstances, what would be a menace to an ordinary person is not a menace to the person to whom it is addressed or vice versa, it is necessary to spell out the meaning of the word to the jury.

Garwood (1987): Meaning of the word 'menaces'

Facts

D accused V of burgling his house and told him he wanted something 'to make it quits' for the alleged burglary. D also seized V by the shirt and pushed him up against a wall. V paid D some money and was told not to tell his parents or the police, otherwise D would 'get' him.

Decision

The Court of Appeal held that in most cases it is not necessary to direct the jury on the meaning of the word 'menaces'. However, there are two exceptions – either where the threat would affect a person of ordinary stability, but did not affect V, or where the threat would not have affected a person of ordinary stability, but did affect V and D was aware of the likely affect of his actions. In these circumstances, the judge may direct the jury on the meaning of the word 'menaces'.

Harry (1974): Menaces must be of a fairly strong nature

Facts

D was the treasurer of a college rag committee. He sent letters to 115 local shopkeepers, asking them to buy indemnity posters for £1.50 (the money being donated to charity). The poster would protect the shopkeepers from further rag activity. A few shopkeepers complained about the letter; the local Board of Trade took the view that the letter was ill conceived, but did not regard the matter as serious. D was charged with blackmail.

Decision

The Crown Court found that there was no menace in this case. In the common sense view, the fact that there were so few complaints indicated that no menaces had been proved. *Per* Petre J: '"Menaces" is a strong word. You may think that menaces must be of a fairly strong nature to fall within the definition.'

7.3.3   Demand must be unwarranted

Lawrence and Pomroy (1971): Inappropriate demand for debt to be paid

Facts

See 7.3.2 above.

Decision

The Court of Appeal held that, *prima facie*, the means adopted to obtain payment of a debt is not the proper way and, where D does not at his trial plead that he believed the means to be proper, then the judge need not direct the jury on the issue of whether the demands were unwarranted.

7.3.4   Belief in the propriety of using menaces

Harvey (1981): Honest belief of defendant

Facts

D paid £20,000 to S for a quantity of matter which was supposed to be cannabis, but which turned out to be some other harmless matter. D kidnapped S's wife and child and threatened to rape, maim and kill them unless S returned the money. D was convicted of blackmail because the judge directed the jury that threats to commit very serious offences could never be proper.

Decision

The Court of Appeal held that s 21(1) of the TA 1968 is concerned with the honest belief of the individual defendant in each case. It does not matter what the reasonable man or anyone else other than D would believe in those circumstances. D's honest belief is what matters in any case.

7.4   Obtaining property by deception

7.4.1   Deception (false representation by words or conduct)

Adams (1993): False representation by ticking a box

Facts

D, when filling in a car hire form, was asked whether he had any previous convictions for motoring offences, and also whether he had ever been disqualified from driving. D ticked the 'No' box in answer to both questions, notwithstanding that he had been disqualified from driving for four years in the past. D was charged with obtaining services by deception and obtaining a pecuniary advantage (the insurance cover) by deception. D claimed that ticking the box was not a false representation, as it was the correct answer to one of the questions.

Decision

The Court of Appeal found that there had been a false representation. The form was badly drafted but not misleading. D should only have ticked the 'No' box if the answer to both questions had been 'no'.

Harris (1975): Representation with intention

Facts

D asked for a single room in a hotel for four nights, giving false particulars. He had no luggage, but told the manager he had stayed in the hotel before and had to spend £30 on repairs to the windscreen of his car. D went to his room, but the manager called the police. D was arrested, but claimed he never had any intention of not paying and had given false particulars in order to obtain accommodation for which he did not, at the time, have money to pay for. D was charged with obtaining a pecuniary advantage by deception (s 16 of the TA 1968).

Decision

The Court of Appeal found that D's actions in booking into the hotel constituted a representation that D was going to pay for the room. If D did not intend to pay for the room, then his representation was false and he was committing a deception by conduct.

Ray (1973): False representation by conduct

Facts

D went into a restaurant and ordered a meal. When the meal was ordered, D intended to pay for it. After eating it, D changed his mind and decided to leave without paying for it. D waited for the waiter to leave the room (about 10 minutes) and then left the restaurant. D was charged with evading liability by deception under s 16(1)(a) of the TA 1968. D's conviction was quashed in the Divisional Court on the grounds that D had not, by words or conduct, made a false representation. The prosecution appealed.

Decision

The House of Lords restored D's conviction. D had made a false representation by conduct. The court should have regard to D's conduct throughout, in order to determine whether a deception had been made. D in this case had made a representation, on entering the restaurant, that he was an ordinary customer and would pay for his meal before he left. This, at the time, was a true representation and the waiter had acted upon it. It was a continuing representation throughout the time that D was in the restaurant, which became false when D decided not to pay for the meal. D practised a false representation by remaining at the table for a short period, until the waiter left the room, before leaving the restaurant. By that deception, D had evaded his liability to pay for the meal.

Firth (1990): False representation by omission

Facts

D was a consultant gynaecologist and head of an NHS department. D also ran a private practice from home. D could agree with the NHS that he would pay for certain tests and recoup the money from his private patients. D was charged with evasion of liability by deception (s 2 of the TA 1978), having allegedly not paid for tests conducted by dishonestly failing to tell the hospital that the patients were private.

Decision

The Court of Appeal held that if it was incumbent on D to give relevant information to the hospital, and if he dishonestly and deliberately refrained from doing so, with the result that his patients or himself were not charged for the tests, then the offence is complete. It did not matter whether it was an act of commission or an omission.

Silverman (1988): False representation by silence

Facts

D charged two old ladies excessively high prices for work done to their flat. The two ladies had trusted him to charge a fair price because, in the past, he had always done so. D was charged with obtaining property by deception (s 15 of the TA 1968) on the grounds that his excessively high quotation amounted to a false representation. D appealed against his conviction.

Decision

The Court of Appeal held that, although D had put no pressure on the ladies to accept his quotation, it did amount to a false representation by silence. A situation of mutual trust had been built up over some time between the two parties. Therefore, D's silence over the excessiveness of the quotation was 'as eloquent as if he had said "What is more, I can say to you that we are going to get no more than a modest profit out of this"' (*per* Watkins LJ).

Charles (1977): Representation by writing a cheque

Facts

D was granted an overdraft of £100 by a bank and was given a cheque book and banker's card on which was printed an undertaking by the bank to honour any cheque up to £30 under certain stated conditions. D used the card to back 25 cheques for £30 each, having already exceeded his overdraft and contrary to the express instructions of his bank manager. D was charged with obtaining a pecuniary advantage by deception (s 16 of the TA 1968).

Decision

The House of Lords held that when the writer of a cheque accepted in exchange for goods, services or cash used a banker's card, he made a representation to the payee that he had authority to enter, on behalf of the bank, into the contract expressed on the card that the bank would honour the cheque. If D knew that the bank had withdrawn that authority, then the representation was false and amounted to a deception.

Gilmartin (1983): False representation by post-dated cheque

Facts

D had signed three cheques on behalf of a company he owned in payment for goods for the company. He signed a fourth cheque, which was payable to a company with whom his business had an account. All four cheques were post-dated and were signed at a time when the business was heavily overdrawn at the bank. All four cheques were dishonoured. D sold the goods he had bought with the cheques in return for cheques made out for cash. When charged under ss 15 and 16 of the TA 1968, D claimed he intended to buy back the post-dated cheques with the cash.

Decision

The Court of Appeal ruled that the drawer of a post-dated cheque impliedly represented to the payee that, on the date that the cheque was handed over, the situation was such that, when the cheque was presented, it would be honoured on or after the dated specified on the cheque. If D knew that the bank would not honour the cheque on that date, then the representation was false and could amount to a deception.

7.4.2   Deception must be operative

Ray (1973): V acts on implied false representation

Facts

See 7.4.1 above.

Decision

The House of Lords held that:

> ... if the waiter had thought that, if he left the room to go to the kitchen, [D] would at once run out, he (the waiter) would not have left the restaurant and would have taken suitable action. The waiter proceeded on the basis that the implied representation made to him (that is, of an honest intention to pay) was effective. The

waiter was caused to refrain from taking certain courses of action which, but for the representation, he would have taken (*per* Lord Morris).

Laverty (1970): Whether representation is operative determined by effect on V

Facts

D sold a car bearing false number plates to V in return for a cheque for £165. D was charged under s 15 of the TA 1968, the deception being that D made a false representation to V that he was the lawful owner of the car and entitled to sell it. The question was, did V rely on that false representation in handing over the cheque?

Decision

The Court of Appeal held that whether the false representation in any case is operative is a question of fact to be determined by the jury. 'The proper way of proving these matters is through the mouth of the person to whom the false representation is conveyed' (*per* Lord Parker CJ). In this case, no such inference could be drawn from V's evidence.

King (1986): Jury to decide whether representation is operative

Facts

D falsely claimed that he was a tree surgeon and told V that four trees in her garden were dangerous and needed felling. D offered to fell them for £470 cash. While V was withdrawing the cash, the police were informed and D was arrested and charged under s 15 of the TA 1968. D claimed that V was not induced to part with the money as a result of the deception, but as a result of the work that would have been done.

Decision

The Court of Appeal held that whether the false representation was operative in causing the obtaining of the property was an issue of fact to be decided by the jury. In this case, there was ample evidence to suggest that, if the money had been paid, it would have been as a result of the false representation made to V.

Lambie (1981): Implied operative representation

Facts

D used a credit card in a shop to pay for goods, knowing that she was well over her credit limit and that she had no authorisation to use it according to the terms and conditions of use. D was convicted of an offence under s 16(1)(a) of the TA 1968. D appealed on the grounds that the shop assistant had not relied on her false representation to accept the card in payment for the goods.

Decision

The House of Lords found that D had made a false representation that she was authorised to enter into contracts on behalf of the credit card company, binding the company to honour the voucher signed by D. This false representation induced the shop assistant to complete the transaction and to allow D to take the goods away, because, had she known that D was acting dishonestly and making a false representation regarding her authority to use the card, she would not have completed the transaction. Although the shop assistant did not expressly state this in evidence, it had to be implied. Had the reverse been true, then the shop assistant would have been an accomplice in D's fraud.

Doukas (1978): Were Vs deceived by D's representation?

Facts
D was a hotel waiter. D was charged with going equipped to steal (s 25 of the TA 1968), having been found with a quantity of bottles of wine of a type not sold by the hotel. D admitted that he sold the wine to hotel customers for his own profit.

Decision
The Court of Appeal held that it had to be proved that D's deception was operative on customers who bought the wine. A hypothetical question has to be asked of the customers, namely, 'Why did you buy this wine?' or 'If you had been told the truth, would you or would you not have bought the commodity?'. The jury must decide the answer to this question, but there is no doubt that, in this case, the hypothetical customer would answer that he would not buy the wine if he knew of D's deception. 'Indeed, it would be a strange jury that came to any other conclusion and a stranger guest who gave any other answer', because, if he was dissatisfied with the wine for any reason, he would have no recourse to the hotel (*per* Lane LJ). (See also *Rashid* (1977) where a similar principle was applied *obiter*, although D was acquitted for other reasons.)

Rozeik (1996): Responsibility of a company for employee's false representation

Facts
D was convicted of obtaining cheques by deception. The cheques were obtained from finance companies, and were obtained by D through providing false information about equipment acquired by him under hire purchase agreements. The transactions were authorised by managers at the finance companies, who may have known that the representations were false. The jury was directed to assume that the managers did know that the representations were false and to ignore the managers in deciding whether the companies had been deceived. D appealed on the ground that the managers were not deceived and therefore the companies were not deceived and there was no offence.

Decision
The Court of Appeal allowed the appeal. A company was fixed with the knowledge acquired by one of its employees, only if the employee had authority to act in the transaction in question. If the employee was a party to the fraud, then they were not acting with the authority of the company. Knowledge of the fraud acquired by the manager could not be attributed to the company. In this case, if the managers were not proved (as opposed to assumed) to be actual parties to the fraud, then their knowledge could be attributed to the companies, with the result that the companies had not been deceived.

Miller (1992): False representation operative over a period of time

Facts

D drove an unlicensed taxi between Heathrow and Gatwick airports. V was a foreign traveller who was induced to ride in the taxi because representations were made that it was properly licensed and that the charges made would be reasonable. D, in fact, charged approximately 10 times the normal fare of a licensed taxi driver. V realised that D had been lying, but felt under an obligation to pay the sum requested. D was convicted of obtaining property by deception on the ground that his lies had caused V to part with his money.

Decision

The Court of Appeal held that it was necessary to look at the whole story to see whether the deception was operative, and it was not appropriate to isolate the moment when the money was handed over. There were various deceptions committed during the course of this story which caused V to hand over the money, and it was irrelevant that, at the final moment, V suspected he was being deceived.

Coady (1996): False representation must be made before property obtained

Facts

D served himself with petrol at a self-service petrol station. He told the assistant to charge the cost of the petrol to the account of his former employer, which he no longer had authority to do. D was convicted of obtaining property by deception but appealed, claiming that the false representation had been made after the obtaining of property and therefore could not be said to have caused it.

Decision

The Court of Appeal held that the false representation must be made before the property is obtained in order for it to have been operative. In this case, the representation was made after the petrol had been obtained. It was not correct to say that D had made a general representation that the petrol would be paid for on arrival at the petrol forecourt.

7.4.3 Deception must be deliberate or reckless

Large v Mainprize (1989): Subjective recklessness applies

Facts

D was a fisherman who was required to deliver a sales note to the relevant authorities, detailing the weight of his catch at sea. His sales note was under-calculated by around 50%. D claimed that the error was made in using his calculator to convert the weight of his catch into kilograms. He was charged under an EC regulation with recklessly furnishing false information as to his catch, but was not convicted. The prosecution appealed.

Decision

The Queen's Bench Divisional Court held that the meaning of recklessness here was that laid down in *Cunningham*, that is, conscious indifference to truth or falsity or foresight of the risk that the catch would be weighed and checked against the documentation, but indifference as to the risk or willingness to run it. The justices were entitled to find that D made a simple error in this case and was not reckless as to the mistake.

Goldman (1997): *Caldwell* recklessness does not apply to deception offences

Facts
D was director of a company which sold rare coins as investments. D was convicted of fraudulent trading under s 458 of the Companies Act 1985. The prosecution claimed that he made false representations about the coins' market value and marketability. D appealed on the grounds that the jury had been misdirected on the meaning of recklessness and on the difference between recklessness and dishonesty.

Decision
The Court of Appeal held that there is no doubt that the offence of obtaining by deception can be committed recklessly or deliberately. It is not appropriate for a jury to be directed according to the *Caldwell* meaning of recklessness in relation to offences committed by deception. Where a deception has to be dishonest, it cannot also be inadvertent. It must be either deliberate or made with a conscious indifference to a risk. Dishonesty and recklessness in a deception case are separate issues, and the judge should make this clear in his summing up.

7.4.4   Property belonging to another

Preddy (1996): Electronic money transfer is not property

Facts
D had applied to building societies and other lenders for mortgages. Each application contained at least one statement by D which he knew to be false. The advances paid to D as a result of the applications totalled more than £1 million. Some had been paid by cheques, others had been paid by CHAPS (Clearing House Automated Payment System). D was convicted of obtaining mortgage loans (property) by deception. He appealed.

Decision
The House of Lords held that where a payment had been made by electronic or telegraphic transfer, no identifiable property had been transferred from payer to payee and therefore it could not be said that D had obtained 'property belonging to another'. In this case, the payment was made from one account to another, and so the payer's credit balance was extinguished and a new *chose in action* was created in the payee's account. D had obtained mortgage advances by deception, but this did not contravene s 15 of the TA 1968.

Comment
As a result of this judgment, a number of defendants who had been convicted under s 15 for similar mortgage frauds appealed against their convictions to the Court of Appeal.

Graham (1996): Mortgage advance is a service but not property

Facts

D was a solicitor who submitted a mortgage application containing false statements. The transaction was never completed but, if it had been, the advance would have been made by CHAPS. D was convicted of obtaining property by deception. On appeal, the court was asked to consider whether the alternative charges of theft or evasion of liability could have been substituted.

Decision

The Court of Appeal ruled that if the reasoning in *Preddy* now precluded a charge of obtaining property by deception, it most probably also precludes a charge of theft. If it could be shown that the *chose in action* was appropriated at a time when it belonged to another, a charge of theft could be brought. However, this is unlikely in these circumstances, since the result of D's dishonest actions is to create a new *chose in action*. There might also be a problem in identifying an appropriation. The court thought that a charge of evasion of liability, on the grounds that D had secured remission of the liability of the lender's bank to the lender, was unrealistic. D could have been charged, however, with the alternative offence of false accounting. The previous Court of Appeal case, *Halai* (1983), in which it was held that a mortgage advance could not be described as a service, was no longer good law and should not be followed.

Cooke (1997): Mortgage fraud in the light of *Preddy*

Facts

D had been convicted of mortgage fraud but, after *Preddy*, brought an appeal claiming that his conviction could not be sustained. The Crown claimed that charges of obtaining services (the mortgage advance) by deception (s 1 of the TA 1978) should be substituted.

Decision

The Court of Appeal held that in the light of negative comments made in *Graham* about the *Halai* case, the charge of obtaining services by deception could be a substitute charge in a mortgage fraud case. There was no reason to exclude the advance of a mortgage by a financial institution, provided it met with the essential criterion that a benefit be conferred, on the basis that it would be paid for.

Naviede (1997): Application of *Preddy* to credit card fraud

Facts

This was another *Preddy* appeal in which the court was asked to consider whether credit fraud could amount to obtaining services by deception. This concerned the obtaining of credit facilities from two banks.

Decision

The Court of Appeal held that although the decision in *Halai*, regarding whether a mortgage advance could be a 'service', could not be taken to have intended to lay down that no mortgage advance, no matter what terms might be attached and no matter in what circumstances the advance was made, could amount to a service. The court in *Halai* were obviously concentrating on the specific circumstances of a private individual securing a mortgage advance from a building society in order to purchase a home for their private residence. In these circumstances, the mortgage advance would not amount to a service, because a benefit would not be conferred. Although this case involved revolving credit rather than a mortgage advance, the same authorities applied. The decisions in *Graham* and *Cooke* (see above) and *Cumming-John* (1997) were not *per curiam*.

Nathan (1997): Service obtained by D on behalf of another

Facts
D, a solicitor, applied for a loan on behalf of his client (and co-accused), giving false representations as to the purpose of the loan. The loan was transferred by electronic transfer to D's client account. D was charged with obtaining property by deception. D appealed against conviction on the ground that, after *Preddy*, the telegraphic transfer of money between bank accounts cannot amount to such a charge. He also claimed that a charge of obtaining services by deception could not be substituted, because the provision of the banking facility was tendered to his client, and not to himself.

Decision
The Court of Appeal substituted D's conviction for one under s 1 of the TA 1978. The argument of the Crown that, although a new *chose in action* was created by the credit balance in the client account, it belonged to the bank until it was transferred to the client on exchange, was untenable. It belonged to both the solicitor and the bank, because the solicitor held it as a trustee for the bank. The conviction was therefore considered unsafe and quashed. There was nothing in s 1 of the TA 1978 which stated that the service had to be obtained for D himself.

Comment
As a result of the difficulties highlighted by the *Preddy* judgment and the subsequent appeals, a new offence has been created specifically to cover this type of fraud. The new s 15A of the TA 1968 (as created by the Theft (Amendment) Act 1996) creates the offence of dishonestly obtaining a money transfer for himself or another by deception. A money transfer is explicitly aimed to cover the situation where a debit is made to one account and a credit is made to another, the latter resulting from the former.

7.4.5   Dishonestly obtains property belonging to another with intention to permanently deprive

See Chapter 6 above.

7.5   Obtaining a pecuniary advantage by deception

Waites (1982): Borrowing by overdraft

Facts
D opened a bank account and was issued with a chequebook and a banker's card for guaranteeing cheques up to £50. D made no arrangements for an overdraft and used

the cheques and the card to make purchases until she was £850 overdrawn. D was charged with obtaining a pecuniary advantage. D claimed she was not allowed to borrow by way of overdraft according to s 16(2)(b) as the bank stopped her from doing so.

Decision

The Court of Appeal quashed D's conviction. The definitions in s 16(2) were exclusive and, if D's actions did not fall within them, there was no offence. The meaning of the word 'allow' in s 16 included permission to use the card, which carried with it power in the cardholder, albeit in breach of contract with the bank, to use the card beyond the limits imposed, knowing that the bank would be obliged to meet the debt created with the shopkeeper. Therefore, D had been 'allowed' to borrow by way of overdraft.

Bevan (1987): Borrowing by overdraft

Facts

D was convicted of obtaining a pecuniary advantage. He had been issued with a cheque guarantee card, but had no overdraft arrangement. The cheque card did not entitle him to overdraw without such an arrangement. D presented three cheques supported by the cheque card while his account was overdrawn. The bank was obliged to honour the cheques, but D claimed he was not 'allowed' to borrow by way of overdraft.

Decision

The Court of Appeal quashed D's conviction. A transaction completed using a cheque card was borrowing by way of overdraft. The bank had complied with the request of the payee's bank for reimbursement. The overdraft was consensual, since D had impliedly requested it and the bank, by honouring the cheques, had, albeit reluctantly, agreed. The bank had therefore allowed D to borrow by way of overdraft.

Callender (1992): Meaning of 'office or employment'

Facts

D was self-employed as an accountant. D falsely claimed that he was an associate member of the Chartered Institute of Management Accountants and a graduate of the Institute of Marketing. D was hired by B to prepare his accounts. D was charged with obtaining a pecuniary advantage by deception, but claimed that he had not obtained an 'office or employment'.

Decision

The Court of Appeal held that the phrase 'office or employment' in s 16(2)(c) was not confined to the narrow limits of a contract of service, but was to be construed in a wider sense as a matter of ordinary language. Therefore, the services given by D did amount to obtaining a pecuniary advantage by deception.

Clarke (Victor) (1996): Deception as to qualifications

See 6.2.2 above.

7.6   Obtaining services by deception

Widdowson (1986): Hire purchase agreement not a credit facility

Facts

D had been indicted for obtaining services by deception. The services on the indictment were credit facilities to assist in the purchase of a car. D claimed that he had obtained a hire purchase agreement, that this was not the same thing as credit facilities, and it did not fall within the definition of services in s 1 of the TA 1978.

Decision

The Court of Appeal held that a hire purchase agreement could not be described as credit facilities because, on making a hire purchase agreement, the company did not give any credit to the hirer, but merely the option to purchase on paying all the instalments, or to terminate the agreement at any time. Therefore, the indictment was wrong. *Per curiam*: obtaining a hire purchase agreement did fall within the definition of services in s 1 of the TA 1978.

Graham (1996); *Naviede* (1997): Mortgage advance is a service but not property

See 7.4.4 above.

Shortland (1995): 'Free' services

Facts

D opened two bank accounts in a false name, using a passport also in the false name. The bank claimed that they would not have opened the accounts if they had known he was using a false name. D was convicted of obtaining services by deception under s 1 of the TA 1978.

Decision

The Court of Appeal held that although there was no evidence that the banking services would have been paid for, the judge held it would be 'an affront to common sense' that the services would have been provided for free and that the jury should assume that they would be paid for. This statement should have been withdrawn from the jury, as the jury could not infer this with any certainty.

7.7   Evasion of liability by deception

7.7.1   *Inducing a creditor to wait or forgo payment*

Holt (1981): Intention to make permanent default

Facts

The Ds were eating in a restaurant. They planned to evade payment for their meals by pretending that the waitress had removed a £5 note which they had placed on the table. An off-duty police officer was also eating there and overheard them. The police officer prevented them from leaving after they had carried out the deception, and they were charged under s 2(1)(b) of the TA 1978. The prosecution argued that they should have been charged under s 2(1)(a) of the Act, because, had their attempt succeeded, their liability to pay would have been 'remitted' and not merely 'forgone'. This was rejected by the judge and the Ds were convicted under s 2(1)(b).

Decision

The Court of Appeal held that although there were substantial differences in the elements of the three offences in s 2(1) of the TA 1978, they had common elements in that they all required the use of deception, a liability and dishonesty on the part of D to gain some advantage in time or money. However, the elements that are unique to s 2(1)(b) of the Act are the default on the whole or part of an existing liability and an intention to make permanent default. In this case, the defendants were motivated by an intent to make permanent default and therefore they had been rightly convicted under s 2(1)(b).

Attwell-Hughes (1991): Evasion of another's liability to pay

Facts

D was the manager of a hotel. He was charged with evading his liability to pay VAT by deception. D claimed that the liability to pay VAT was that of the hotel owner and not D himself, and so the indictment was worded wrongly. The trial judge rejected this and D was convicted.

Decision

The Court of Appeal held that s 2(1)(b) of the TA 1978 envisaged an offence which might be committed by D intending to make permanent default in respect of a personal liability, or by intending to enable another to make permanent default in respect of that other's liability. Therefore, it did not matter whether, in this case, D or the hotel owner was liable; the indictment was worded correctly.

Andrews v Hedges (1981): Payment by cheque

Facts

D was charged with an offence under s 2(1)(b) of the TA 1978. His creditors had supplied him with large quantities of meat on credit terms of up to three weeks. D paid by cheque, but the cheques were not honoured due to insufficient funds. It was alleged that this caused the creditors to wait for payment.

Decision

There was no inducement to wait for payment where the parties had traded together previously, where the credit terms had been allowed and where payment by cheque was accepted in the ordinary course of dealing between the parties. Section 2(1)(b) of the 1978 Act only applied where the creditor was induced to accept a cheque instead of cash, and only then did s 2(3) operate as a matter of law to treat the creditor as having been induced to wait for payment.

7.7.2 Obtaining exemption from or abatement of a liability

Firth (1990): Future or expected liability

Facts

See 7.4.1 above.

Decision

The Court of Appeal held that the word 'existing' could be found in s 2(1)(a) and 2(1)(b), but not in s 2(1)(c) of the TA 1978. Section 2(1)(c) was meant to cover a future or expected liability, even if the alleged deception was not a continuing one.

7.8 Making off without payment

7.8.1 Making off

Brooks and Brooks (1982): Departing the spot where payment is required

Facts

The defendants, D1 and D2, had a meal with S in the upstairs room of a restaurant. D1 left the restaurant in a hurry. The manager went upstairs and D2 and S were not there, but he found S in the toilet. D2 was also found in the restaurant trying to leave, but was caught by the manager. Both Ds were charged under s 3 of the TA 1978.

Decision

The Court of Appeal held that the words 'dishonestly makes off' in s 3 of the Act should be given their ordinary meaning, and the jury should relate these words to the facts of any case. 'Making off' required departure from the spot where payment was required. However, where D was stopped before passing the spot where payment was required, the jury should be directed that that may be an attempt to commit the offence rather than the substantive offence itself (provided the other elements of an attempt are present).

7.8.2 Payment on the spot

MacDavitt (1981): Meaning of 'the spot'

Facts

D had a meal with some friends at a restaurant. After the meal, the friends left the restaurant and D stayed at the table. The bill was brought to D and, after an argument, D refused to pay it. D went towards the door but was advised not to leave as the police had been called. D stayed in the restaurant until the police arrived. D admitted he intended to leave the restaurant without paying and was charged with an offence under s 3 of the TA 1978.

Decision

The Crown Court held that 'makes off' refers to making off from the spot where the payment is required or expected. What that spot is depends on the facts in any case. In this case, the spot was the restaurant and the jury would be directed not to find D guilty, as he did not leave the restaurant (although they could find him guilty of attempt to commit the offence).

Aziz (1993): No need for a specific 'spot'

Facts

D requested a taxi driver to take him to a club 13 miles away. On arrival at the club, D refused to pay the fare of £15, claiming that the journey was only four miles. D was taken to the police station, where he ran out of the taxi but was caught by the taxi driver. D was charged with making off without payment contrary to s 3 of the TA 1978, but claimed on appeal that he had not made off from where payment was required, 'on the spot', which was the final destination of the journey.

Decision

The Court of Appeal ruled that the TA 1978 did not require that payment be made on any particular spot. 'On the spot' related to the knowledge which the customer had as to when payment should be made. In the case of a taxi, payment may be made whilst sitting in the car or standing at the window, but the fares were requested when the customer was still in the car. Therefore, D, in this case, was making off without payment from the spot where payment was required or expected.

7.8.3 As required or expected

Troughton v Metropolitan Police (1987): Payment not required where contract breached

Facts

D was convicted under s 3 of the TA 1978. A taxi driver had agreed to take D home but D, being intoxicated, had not told him his address. The driver stopped to obtain directions from someone and D accused the driver of making an unnecessary diversion. The taxi driver drove to the nearest police station.

Decision

The Queen's Bench Divisional Court found that the journey was not completed and the taxi driver had breached a contract. The taxi driver was unable to demand the fare after he had diverted from the proper route to D's destination. D was therefore not bound to pay the fare, and could not have committed the offence of making off without payment since payment was not required.

7.8.4 With intent to avoid payment

Allen (1985): Intention to avoid paying permanently

Facts

D left a hotel without paying his bill of £1,286. D was charged under s 3 of the TA 1978. D claimed he genuinely expected to pay the bill and intended merely to defer payment until he received the proceeds of certain business deals.

Decision

The House of Lords held that the words 'with intent to avoid payment' in s 3 of the Act, on their true construction, required an intention to avoid payment permanently, and an intention to defer payment did not suffice to establish the offence.

7.9 Criminal damage

7.9.1 Destroy or damage

Cox v Riley (1986): Definition of damage

Facts

D deliberately erased a computer program from a plastic circuit card of a computerised saw, in order to render it inoperable. D was convicted of criminal damage, but appealed on the ground that the property in question was not tangible and therefore could not be damaged under the Criminal Damage Act 1971.

Decision
The Queen's Bench Divisional Court found that D was rightly convicted, as erasing the computer program did constitute damage under s 1 of the Criminal Damage Act 1971. The principle that the word 'damage' should be given its ordinary dictionary meaning was upheld. Accordingly, 'damage' was defined as 'injury impairing value or usefulness' and is a question of fact and degree in each case. In this case, time and effort were required to put right the damage caused.

Gayford and Chandler (1898): Trampling grass constitutes damage

Facts
D was a trespasser who walked across a grass field belonging to V. The grass was long and D trampled it down, causing damage to the grass.

Decision
The Queen's Bench Divisional Court held that trampling down grass or other vegetation constituted damage. In this case, the damage to the grass incurred expense to the value of 6 d.

Hardman v Chief Constable for Avon and Somerset (1986): Temporary damage suffices if expense and inconvenience incurred in repairing it

Facts
The defendants were members of CND. They painted human silhouettes on a pavement in water-soluble paint specially mixed so that rainwater would wash it off. However, before this could happen, the local authority employed people to clean the pavement.

Decision
The Crown Court found that, notwithstanding the fact that the markings could be easily washed, the defendants had caused criminal damage which had incurred expense and inconvenience on the part of the local authority to put right.

Roe v Kingerlee (1986): Temporary damage

Facts
D was charged with criminal damage to a wall of a police cell. D had smeared mud on the wall and it cost £7 to clean.

Decision
The Queen's Bench Divisional Court held that whether D's actions amount to criminal damage is a question of fact and degree, and it is for the jury, applying their common sense, to decide. It is not necessary for the damage to be permanent. In this case the damage did amount to criminal damage because expense had been incurred to put it right.

Morphitis v Salmon (1990): Damage must impair usefulness or value

Facts

S erected a barrier across an access road which led to premises used by himself and M. The barrier consisted of a scaffold bar. M dismantled the barrier in order to gain access to the premises. The scaffold bar was scratched and M was charged with criminal damage.

Decision

The Queen's Bench Divisional Court found that a scratch on a metal scaffolding bar could not amount to criminal damage, because it did not impair its usefulness or value.

Roper v Knott (1898): Damage may not render property totally useless

Facts

D sold milk to V. D had watered the milk down and was charged with malicious damage to property.

Decision

The Queen's Bench Divisional Court held that the damage does not have to render the property totally useless. If the value of the property has been impaired, the damage constitutes an offence. D had deliberately and intentionally caused the damage and therefore was rightly convicted.

7.9.2   Recklessness

R v G and R (2003): *Caldwell* overruled

See Chapter 19 below.

Comment

The House of Lords in this case finally overruled *Caldwell* and the objective test of recklessness has been abolished. The objective test, in their view, caused manifestly unjust results, especially in a case such as *G and R* where the defendants were children who were less capable of appreciating a risk that may have been obvious to the ordinary reasonable adult. The test for recklessness in a case of criminal damage is now a subjective test as laid down in *Cunningham* (1957).

7.9.3   Without lawful authority

Jaggard v Dickinson (1980): Drunken mistake as to authority

Facts

D, who was drunk, went to a house which she mistakenly thought belonged to her friend. She broke into the house believing, correctly, that had it been her house, the friend would have consented to her doing so. D was convicted of criminal damage but appealed, claiming that, despite her drunkenness, she was entitled to rely on the defence in s 5(3) of the Criminal Damage Act 1971 (where D believes she has a lawful excuse for causing the damage).

Decision

The Queen's Bench Divisional Court held that D could rely on her intoxication to negative her *mens rea*, notwithstanding that she had been charged with a basic intent crime. This was because Parliament specifically intended the defence to be subjective, that is, the court should consider the defendant's actual state of belief, not the state of belief that ought to have existed. An honest belief is honestly held, even if it stems from intoxication. (See further Chapter 11.)

Denton (1982): Dishonest intent irrelevant to charge of criminal damage

Facts

D worked at a cotton mill. He set fire to some machinery and the mill was damaged in the fire. D was charged with arson. He claimed that he believed he had the owner's consent, as he thought the owner had asked him to set fire to the machinery in order to make a fraudulent insurance claim.

Decision

The Court of Appeal held:

> ... one has to decide whether or not an offence is committed at the moment that the acts are alleged to be committed. The fact that somebody may have had a dishonest intent which, in the end, he was going to carry out, namely, a claim from the insurance company, cannot turn what was not originally a crime into a crime. There is not unlawfulness under the [Criminal Damage] Act 1971 in burning a house. It does not become unlawful because there may be an inchoate attempt to commit fraud contained in it; that is to say it does not become a crime under the 1971 Act, whatever may be the situation outside the Act (*per* Lord Lane CJ).

Hill and Hall (1989): Honest belief in necessity of damage to protect property

Facts

The Ds were charged with possession of an article (a hacksaw blade) with intent to damage property. The Ds were members of CND, who were, as part of a campaign, going to cut part of the perimeter fence of a US naval base in England. The Ds claimed a defence on the basis of an honest belief that damage was justified as the property was in need of protection. They believed that the purpose of the naval base was to monitor the movements of USSR submarines and, if war broke out, the base would be the subject of a nuclear strike, resulting in the devastation of the surrounding area which included the Ds' property and that of their friends and neighbours.

Decision

The Court of Appeal ruled that the judge had to decide whether the defendants' actions did amount to protection of property which they honestly believed to be in immediate danger. The judge here had rightly concluded that the proposed act was too remote from the eventual harm from which the property was being protected.

Lloyd (1992): Consent to damage provides lawful authority

Facts
D parked his car in a private car park without permission. The car was clamped. D removed the clamp illegally (without paying the levy) and removed the car from the car park. D was charged with criminal damage to the padlocks of the wheel clamp. D claimed he had lawful authority to cut the padlocks off because they were a trespass to his car.

Decision
The Queen's Bench Divisional Court held that even if the clamps were a trespass to the car, D consented to the risk of being clamped and so was not in a position to complain when it occurred. D had suffered, at worst, a civil wrong, the remedy for which he should have sought in the civil courts. Self-help, using force, was only to be contemplated when there was no other reasonable alternative. Therefore, D had no lawful excuse for causing criminal damage.

Blake v DPP (1993): Consent of God not lawful authority

Facts
D was a vicar demonstrating against the use of military force by the allies in Iraq and Kuwait. D used a marker pen to write a Biblical quotation on a concrete pillar outside the Houses of Parliament. D was convicted of criminal damage, but claimed he had a defence under s 5(2)(a) of the Criminal Damage Act 1971, because he was carrying out the instructions of God and therefore had consent to damage property, which meant he had lawful authority to commit the damage.

Decision
The Queen's Bench Divisional Court held that a belief, however genuine, powerful or honestly held, that he had the consent of God and therefore consent of the law of England to damage property, did not afford D the excuse of lawful authority. The appeal was dismissed.

7.9.4   With intent to endanger life

Dudley (1989): Lives need not actually be endangered

Facts
D set fire to an occupied house by throwing a firebomb at it. The occupants of the house were able to put the fire out quickly and little damage was caused. D was convicted of causing damage being reckless as to life being endangered.

Decision
The Court of Appeal held that the fact that lives are not actually endangered is irrelevant if it was D's intention to endanger lives, or if D was reckless as to the same.

Parker (1993): Lives need not actually be endangered

Facts
D was a lodger in a semi-detached council house. D set fire to a sofa in the house one evening and then left. Both houses were unoccupied at the time, but the occupiers of

the attached property returned an hour later and found their living room filled with smoke through the air vents in the party wall. D was convicted of criminal damage under s 1(2) of the Criminal Damage Act 1971. D claimed on appeal that, since no life was actually endangered, no offence under s 1(2) was committed.

Decision

The Court of Appeal held that it was not necessary to establish that life actually was endangered. Had the parliamentary draftsmen intended that to be the case, they would have worded s 1(2) differently. The fact that D created an obvious risk that life would be endangered was all that was needed to prove that D had committed the offence.

Webster (1995): Intention that lives be endangered as a result of D's actions

Facts

D pushed a heavy piece of stone off of a railway bridge onto a passenger train below. The stone landed on the rear bulkhead of a carriage and a corner of the stone penetrated the roof. Passengers were not physically injured, but were showered with debris from the roof of the carriage. D was convicted of criminal damage under s 1(2) of the Criminal Damage Act 1971. D appealed on the ground that the judge misdirected the jury in relation to endangering lives.

Decision

The Court of Appeal upheld D's conviction. If D had intended that the stone itself would crash through the roof of the train and thereby endanger the lives of the passengers (or was reckless whether it did), s 1(2) of the Criminal Damage Act 1971 would not apply. However, if D intended (or was reckless) that the stone would damage the roof so that debris from it would fall upon passengers, he was guilty of an offence under s 1(2). Consequently, the judge had misdirected the jury, who must have found that the former intention was present in this case. However, since D must also have been reckless as to the danger of debris falling from the roof onto passengers, D was guilty of an offence under s 1(2).

CHAPTER 8

SELF-DEFENCE

Introduction

In some circumstances the law allows a defendant to inflict unlawful force on another where it is necessary to do so in order to protect themselves or others from harm, to protect property from damage, or to prevent crime. This defence is therefore sometimes called the 'necessary' defence. Not surprisingly, given that a defendant who successfully pleads this defence is acquitted, the courts have set out a number of restrictions on the circumstances in which they will allow the defendant to offend with such impunity.

It is a basic requirement that the force used by the defendant must be justified as necessary. This means that the defendant must show that the circumstances in which he acted must be sufficiently and imminently threatening (*Devlin v Armstrong* (1971)). This threat must not be created by the defendant himself (*Malnik v DPP* (1989)) and the force used in response must be reasonable in the view of the defendant and proportionate to the threat (*Clegg* (1995); *Martin* (2000)). Proportionality may also be judged subjectively (*Owino* (1995)). That said, in some of the cases below, the courts have allowed the defendant to 'strike the first blow' so that they do not have to wait for their attacker to apply force towards them, and there is no duty to retreat from the threatening situation.

8.1 Force justified where necessary and reasonable

8.1.1 The threatening circumstances must be imminent

Devlin v Armstrong (1971): Danger not imminent

Facts
During a riot, D urged others to build barricades and throw petrol bombs at police, claiming that such actions were necessary to prevent people from being assaulted and property damaged.

Decision
The Court of Appeal of Northern Ireland found D guilty of inciting a riot, as she did not anticipate an imminent danger. 'The plea of self-defence may afford a defence where the party raising it uses force, not merely to counter an actual attack, but to ward off or prevent an attack which he has honestly and reasonably anticipated. In that case, however, the anticipated attack must be imminent ...' (*per* MacDermott LJ).

AG's Reference (No 2 of 1983) (1984): Anticipation of imminent threat to persons or property

Facts
After D's shop was looted during a riot, D made 10 petrol bombs to use as a defence to future rioters.

Decision

The Court of Appeal held that D's petrol bombs were in his possession for a lawful object, if D's 'object was to protect himself or his family or his property against imminent apprehended attack and to do so by means which he believed were no more than reasonably necessary to meet the force used by the attackers' (*per* Lord Lane CJ).

Beckford (1987): Pre-emptive strike does not negative defence

Facts

D, a police officer, while investigating a domestic dispute at a house, shot and killed a man who ran out of the back of the house.

Decision

The Privy Council found D not guilty of murder. *Per* Lord Griffiths:

> (1) A person has a right to protect himself from attack and to act in the defence of others if force is necessary and reasonable. (2) A man about to be attacked does not have to wait for his assailant to strike the first blow or fire the first shot: circumstances may justify a pre-emptive strike. (3) The test to be applied for self-defence is that a person may use such force as is reasonable in the circumstances as he honestly believes them to be in the defence of himself or another.

Malnik v DPP (1989): If risk can be avoided it is not imminent

Facts

D, an adviser to the owner of some stolen cars, went to visit the suspected car thief, who was known to be violent. Accordingly, D armed himself with a martial arts weapon, being arrested en route.

Decision

The Court of Appeal found D guilty of possession of an offensive weapon. Unlike the police, D did not have a necessary defence, because the risk of violence could have been avoided and indeed was created by D.

8.1.2   No duty to retreat from threatening circumstances

Julien (1969): Must demonstrate unwillingness to fight

Facts

D was involved in a quarrel with V, who was armed with a chopper. D threw a milk bottle at V, causing his head to bleed.

Decision

The Court of Appeal found D guilty of assault occasioning actual bodily harm. There is no duty upon D to 'take to his heels and run … but what is necessary is that [D] should demonstrate by his actions that he does not want to fight' (*per* Widgery LJ).

Field (1972): Need not retreat before threat arises

Facts

D was warned of an impending fight with V, but refused to retreat. When confronted by V, D said he did not want to fight. V and another attacked D, who thrust a knife at V, causing his death.

Decision

The Court of Appeal found D not guilty of murder. There is no duty to retreat until the parties were, at any rate, within sight of each other; D need not avoid a place for fear of being attacked. By the time D said he wished no fight, D could not have retreated without risking injury.

Bird (1985): Evidence of attempted retreat may be probative

Facts

At a party, D was slapped by V and a struggle ensued, during which D struck V with a drinking glass, causing V to lose his sight.

Decision

The Court of Appeal found D not guilty of unlawful wounding by reason of self-defence. There is no duty to retreat when faced with an unjust attack, but evidence that D attempted to retreat was probative as to whether D's actions constituted justified force.

Gay (1996): Jury may consider how D could have got away

Facts

D was knocked down by police who were using force on a crowd during a march. D then picked up two sticks and banners and threw them 'to make the police go back'.

Decision

The Court of Appeal found D guilty of rioting. There is no duty to retreat from the use of force, but 'one of the factors for [juries] to take into account is how easily the self-defender could have got away from his attacker' (*per* Curtis J).

8.2   Force justified where proportionate

8.2.1   The reaction must be proportionate and reasonable

Palmer (1971): D's view of reasonableness

Facts

D was carrying a gun and went with a group to buy an illegal narcotic. After a dispute with the suppliers, D and his group fled without paying and a chase ensued, during which one of the pursuers was shot and killed.

Decision

The Privy Council found D not guilty of murder. *Per* Lord Morris:

> If an attack is serious so that it puts someone in immediate peril, then immediate defensive action may be necessary ... If there has been an attack so that defence is reasonably necessary, it will be recognised that a person defending himself cannot weigh to a nicety the exact measure of his necessary defensive action. If a jury thought that, in a moment of unexpected anguish, a person attacked had only done what he honestly and instinctively thought was necessary, that would be most potent evidence that only reasonable defensive actions had been taken.

AG for Northern Ireland's Reference (No 1 of 1975) (1977): Meaning of reasonable

Facts

D, a soldier, had shot and killed a retreating man, whom D thought to be a member of the IRA.

Decision

The House of Lords held that a jury would convict D if the prosecution proved beyond reasonable doubt that the accused did not use force as was reasonable in the circumstances. *Per* Lord Diplock, whether D's actions were reasonable depended on:

(1) the circumstances as believed by the accused;
(2) the 'shortness of the time available to him for reflection';
(3) 'what was the highest degree at which a reasonable man could have assessed the likelihood' that the retreating man, if permitted to escape, would engage in homicidal acts of terrorism.

Shannon (1980): Act must be defensive in manner

Facts

D stabbed V with a pair of scissors while being dragged downwards by D's hair.

Decision

The Court of Appeal found D not guilty of manslaughter. The stabbing would be justified if 'essentially defensive in character', but would not be justified if D 'lost his temper' and stabbed 'by way of revenge, punishment, retaliation or pure aggression' (*per* Ormrod LJ).

Scarlett (1993): Subjective belief in reasonableness of force

See 3.1.1 above.

Clegg (1995): No defence where danger has passed

Facts

D was a soldier on duty in Northern Ireland. He shot and killed the driver of a stolen car whilst on patrol, claiming that he had fired four shots in self-defence. The fourth shot had been fired after the car had passed and, on this basis, his defence of self-defence at his trial for murder failed. He appealed.

Decision

The House of Lords held that:

> Since the danger had already passed when Private Clegg fired his fourth shot, there could be no question of self-defence and, therefore, no question of excessive force in self-defence ... There is no rule that a defendant who has used a greater degree of force than necessary in the circumstances should be found guilty of manslaughter rather than murder ... so as far as self-defence is concerned, it is all or nothing. The defence either succeeds or fails. If it succeeds, the defendant is acquitted. If it fails, he is guilty of murder (*per* Lord Lloyd).

Comment

Sedley J held in *Armstrong-Braun* below that '*Owino* (1995) ... reasserts the law as previously understood and, to this end, reads *Scarlett* down'. Therefore, *Scarlett* may be confined to its facts.

Owino (1995): Honest belief in reasonableness of force

Facts

V was injured by her husband D, who alleged that V's bruising was caused only by reasonable force used in restraining her and in preventing her from assaulting him.

Decision

The Court of Appeal found D guilty of assault causing bodily harm. *Per* Collins J:

> ... proportionality is not determined on the basis of what was objectively reasonable. ... The jury have to decide whether a defendant honestly believed that the circumstances were such as required him to use force to defend himself from an attack or a threatened attack. In this respect, a defendant must be judged in accordance with his honest belief, even though that belief may have been mistaken. But the jury must then decide whether the force used was reasonable in the circumstances as he believed them to be.

Armstrong-Braun (1998): Subjective test for reasonableness of force

Facts

D, a county councillor, entered a construction site to preserve an endangered animal's habitat. D used a wooden stake to interfere with construction machinery and told worker V he was committing a crime. V became angry and chased D who struck him once with the stake on his arm.

Decision

The Court of Appeal found D guilty of battery. D's response was disproportionate and unreasonable. *Per* Brooke LJ: '... the force used by the defendant accused of battery in self-defence should be assessed in an objective sense as to whether it was reasonably necessary in the circumstances, as the defendant subjectively believed them to be.' *Per* Sedley J: '... what is done in answer to the perceived threat is to be judged by a judicial appraisal of its reasonableness in all the circumstances which, by definition, include the defendant's honest belief as to the danger he is in.'

Culverhouse (1996): Direction on reasonableness unnecessary where no self-defence

Facts

D and V punched and choked each other during a fight, then D slashed V's forehead with a knife.

Decision

The Court of Appeal found D guilty of assault causing grievous bodily harm. Where there is no evidence of circumstances giving rise to self-defence, there will be no '... misdirection, because the judge omitted to direct the jury to consider the appellant's state of mind in the context of the reasonableness or otherwise of the self-defence' (*per* Kay J).

Speede and Baptiste (1996): Direction on reasonableness essential

Facts

V was stabbed in the hand by D1 and D2, who then jumped out of a window. They alleged that V had threatened them with a knife.

Decision

The Court of Appeal found D1 and D2 not guilty of affray. The trial judge will commit a 'material misdirection' where he fails to provide 'a careful direction on the possible significance of the subjective perception of each appellant as to the risk to which he claimed to have been exposed' (*per* Forbes J).

Martin (2002): Personal characteristics not relevant in assessing reasonableness of force

Facts

D shot two people engaged in burgling his house. V was killed and the other was wounded. D was charged with murder. As D suffered from a paranoid personality disorder which affected his perception of the risk to his safety posed by the burglars, he pleaded the defences of self-defence and provocation at his trial. Both defences failed and D was convicted of murder.

Decision

The Court of Appeal held that the defences of provocation and self-defence are distinguishable. Whilst for the purposes of provocation D could rely on his psychiatric disorder which affected the degree of self-control that could reasonably be expected of him, this could not be relied upon in applying the test of the reasonableness of force in relation to self-defence. However, D's conviction for murder was reduced to manslaughter by reason of diminished responsibility.

CHAPTER 9

MISTAKE

Introduction

The cases in this chapter have developed the defence afforded to the defendant where his mistaken perception of an element of the offence may affect his liability. In some cases a mistake may actually negative an essential element of the offence and result in the defendant's acquittal. In these cases the mistake is excusatory in that the prosecution fails to prove the complete offence. In other cases a mistake may offer the defendant a defence to an offence that is proved and is therefore justificatory. The offence is proved but we can excuse the defendant's conduct in the circumstances because he was operating under a mistaken view of the situation. The category into which a defendant's mistake falls depends on the nature of the mistake and the type of offence he is charged with.

As a matter of policy the courts have been adamant that a mistake of law does not afford any defendant a defence, since criminal law must operate on the assumption that all citizens know what the law is. This rule applies to a mistake as to whether the defendant's conduct was unlawful under the criminal law. Where the defendant has made a mistake as to his position in civil law, the courts have tended to view this as a mistake of fact. For example, in *Smith* (1974), the defendant's mistake as to who owned the fixtures in his rented home was a mistake of fact and afforded him a defence when he was charged with criminally damaging them. This is an example of the defence operating in an excusatory way.

The defendants in *Morgan* made a mistake of fact in relation to whether the victim in that rape case consented or not. Since the offence of rape involves the perpetrator having sexual intercourse with the victim, 'knowing' or being reckless as to whether she consents, a mistaken perception that she does consent will negative the *actus reus* of the offence and the defendant must be acquitted. The House of Lords in that case argued that a mistaken belief that a woman consents should not even be called a 'defence' strictly speaking, since in fact it is a justification of the defendant's conduct. The requirement is simply that the defendant honestly held that belief. Note that the defendants in that case were convicted because the Lords were of the view that the mistaken belief was so unreasonable that it could not have been honestly held. The belief did not have to be reasonable in the circumstances, but its manifest unreasonableness in that case suggested that the defendants could not honestly say that they held that belief. It is interesting to note that some commentators have argued that an honestly held mistaken belief in the need to kill another for the purposes of self-defence may breach the victim's right to life under the Human Rights Act 1998. The courts have not yet had the opportunity to consider this issue in a particular case.

In other cases the defendant may be mistaken as to whether he has a defence for his conduct, rendering otherwise unlawful conduct lawful. This commonly arises in relation to self-defence, where the defendant mistakenly believes that he needed to commit a crime to prevent injury or damage to property. In these circumstances the courts will allow the defendant to plead the excusatory defence where his mistaken belief is honestly held (*Williams (Gladstone)* (1984)). However, they have drawn the line at an honest mistaken belief in the need for self-defence where that mistaken view is induced by the consumption of alcohol. So *O'Grady* (1987) was not afforded a defence because his honestly held belief was not reasonable.

9.1　Mistake of law

9.1.1　*Ignorance of the law excuses no one*

Arrowsmith (1974): Ignorance of the law is no defence

Facts

In the past, when D had previously distributed leaflets to British soldiers *contra* to the Incitement to Disaffection Act 1934, the DPP had declined to prosecute. The DPP then decided to prosecute.

Decision

The Court of Appeal found D guilty of inciting to disaffect. Mistake of law would not avail D, except in regard to sentencing mitigation.

Grant v Borg (1982): 'Knowingly' includes knowledge of the law

Facts

D was a non-patriate with limited leave to remain in the UK. D remained in the UK beyond the time limit and was charged with 'knowingly ... remain[ing] beyond the time limited by the leave', *contra* to the Immigration Act 1971.

Decision

The House of Lords found D not guilty of the Immigration Act 1971 offence (on other grounds). *Per* Lord Bridge:

> The principle that ignorance of the law is no defence in crime is so fundamental that to construe the word 'knowingly' in a criminal statute as requiring not merely knowledge of the facts material to the offender's guilt, but also knowledge of the relevant law, would be revolutionary and ... wholly unacceptable.

Financial Services Authority v Scandex Capital Management (1997): Mistake as to foreign law no defence

Facts

A Danish company was carrying on investment business in the UK in contravention of the Financial Services Act 1986.

Decision

The Court of Appeal found D guilty of violating the Financial Services Act. A mistake of foreign law does not constitute a mistake of fact, but rather 'would be a mistake of English law' and thus no defence (*per* Millett LJ).

9.2   Mistake of fact

9.2.1   Mistake as to the actus reus

Tolson (1889): Reasonable and honest belief

Facts

D remarried five years after last seeing her husband, believing him lost at sea. In fact, he had deserted her and was still alive.

Decision

The Crown Court found D not guilty of bigamy, as she believed 'in good faith and on reasonable grounds' that her husband was dead.

Thabo Meli (1954): Mistake as to condition of V

See 13.4.1 below.

Church (1965): Mistake as to condition of V

See 3.1.3 above.

Smith (DR) (1974): Honest mistaken belief suffices

Facts

During his tenancy, D built some panelling to conceal some wires. D removed the panelling when his tenancy ceased.

Decision

The Court of Appeal found D not guilty of criminal damage. Although the property was *de jure* the landlord's, D honestly but mistakenly believed that the damaged property was his own. *Per* James LJ: '... provided that the belief is honestly held, it is irrelevant to consider whether or not it is a justifiable belief.'

Morgan (1976): Honest mistaken belief suffices

Facts

See 5.1.5 above.

Decision

The House of Lords found D guilty of aiding and abetting rape; the companions were guilty of rape. Mistake as to V's consent must be honest, but need not be reasonable. Reasonableness is relevant only for evidentiary purposes, not for liability itself. *Per* Lord Hailsham:

> [1] Once one has accepted ... that the prohibited act in rape is non-consensual sexual intercourse, and that the guilty state of mind is an intention to commit it, it seems to me to follow as a matter of inexorable logic that there is no room for either a 'defence' of honest belief or mistake, or of a defence of honest and reasonable belief or mistake. Either the prosecution proves that the accused had the requisite intent or it does not. [2] Since honest belief clearly negatives intent [for the offence of rape], the reasonableness or otherwise of that belief can only be evidence for or against the view that the belief and therefore the intent was actually held ...

9.2.2   Mistake of fact as to a defence

Williams (Gladstone) (1984): Honestly held belief suffices

Facts
D saw a man assaulting a youth, who was calling for help. The man was, in fact, effecting a lawful arrest of the youth, albeit falsely claiming to be a police officer. After asking for and not obtaining a warrant card, D struggled with and punched the man.

Decision
The Court of Appeal found D not guilty of assault occasioning bodily harm. There will be no assault if D honestly believed that he was preventing an unlawful assault. *Per* Lord Lane CJ:

> The reasonableness or unreasonableness of the defendant's belief is material to the question of whether the belief was held … at all. If the belief was in fact held, its unreasonableness, so far as guilt to innocence is concerned, is neither here nor there. It is irrelevant.

O'Grady (1987): Mistake and intoxication

Facts
D was heavily intoxicated when he struck and cut V, causing his death, on the mistake of fact that V was attacking him with a glass.

Decision
The Court of Appeal found D guilty of murder:

(1)   So far as self-defence was concerned, reliance could not be placed on a mistake of fact induced by voluntary intoxication.

(2)   *Per curiam*, a sober man who mistakenly believes he is in danger of immediate death at the hands of an attacker is entitled to be acquitted of both murder and manslaughter, if his reaction in killing his supposed assailant was a reasonable one.

Comment
The reasonableness element is required for a mistake of fact as to the defence of duress, but not for a mistake of fact as to the defence of justified force. See Chapter 12.

Beckford (1987): Honest belief in need for self defence
See 8.1.1 above.

Scarlett (1993): Honest belief
See 3.1.1 above.

Morrow, Geach and Thomas (1994): Mistaken belief not reasonable

Facts
M, G and T planned and carried out an anti-abortion demonstration outside a clinic, causing severe distress to some patients.

Decision
The Court of Appeal found M, G and T guilty of offences under the Public Order Act 1986. Notwithstanding the sincere and deeply held opinions of the defendants, there

was sufficient evidence upon which the court could conclude first, that the appellants were guilty of disorderly behaviour and secondly, that such conduct was not reasonable.

Hipperson v DPP (1996): Mistake as to necessity of action

Facts

D broke into the Atomic Weapons Establishment compound on Hiroshima Day, allegedly to prevent the crime of genocide.

Decision

The Court of Appeal found D guilty of causing criminal damage. *Per* McCowan LJ: 'There is no suggestion [that D was] acting under a mistake of fact, and I am clear that [D was] not. They were acting under a sincerely held mistake of law as to what constitutes the crime of genocide.'

CHAPTER 10

MENTAL DISORDER

Introduction

Defences relating to the defendant's mental disorder rest on the assumption that a person should only be convicted on the basis of acts voluntarily committed, and that the mental disorder (providing it fits within the requisite definition) rendered the defendant unable to act voluntarily. In this sense defences of mental disorder negative the *mens rea* of any offence and are therefore justificatory.

In order to claim that his mental disorder affords him a defence, the defendant must establish that he was 'insane' in the legal sense. Where his disorder does not fit within the legal definition of insanity, the courts have been willing to afford him the defence of automatism, that is a defence that his body was acting without any control of his mind. The issues in these cases have arisen largely from the difficulties that defendants have had in fitting their mental disorder within the legal definition of insanity set out in the case of *M'Naghten* in 1843. This definition is clearly out of date and does not recognise many mental disorders now known to psychiatrists. Indeed, the definition is reminiscent of an age where psychiatrists believed insanity was caused by a physical malfunction within the body. Hence the law's insistence that insanity must arise from a 'disease' of the mind which caused a defect of reason. This definition urgently needs reform and has resulted in very few defendants being able to claim the defence. Although diminished responsibility defines mental abnormality in a more inclusive way (see Chapter 2), it is only a defence to murder and therefore of no help to mentally disordered offenders charged with other offences.

The requirement for a 'disease' of the mind has resulted in the courts considering a number of physical disorders which have rendered the defendant unable to control their actions. Hence, a person acting during an epileptic seizure may be deemed to be 'insane' in a legal sense as their defect of reason is caused by an internal, organic factor (*Sullivan* (1984)). The same issue has arisen in relation to diabetic defendants who commit their offence during a 'black out' caused by a malfunction in their blood sugar levels. The requirement that insanity be caused by an internal factor has resulted in the rather odd situation that a diabetic suffering a hyperglycaemic episode may be deemed insane for legal purposes, whereas a diabetic suffering a hypoglycaemic episode must rely on the defence of automatism. This is because hyperglycaemia, or excessively high blood sugar levels, tend to be caused by the inherent defect in the ability of the pancreas to convert blood sugar into insulin. Hypoglycaemic episodes (excessively low blood sugar levels) on the other hand are usually caused by the intervention of an external factor such as where the defendant takes too much insulin or does not eat. The outcome of both defences is the same; the defendants will be acquitted on the basis that their mind was incapable of forming the *mens rea* for the offence. However, for a diabetic in the former situation, being labelled 'insane' may not just be personally offensive but also results in compulsory hospitalisation.

The courts have been reluctant to afford a defence where the consumption of alcohol plays a part in their 'mental disorder'. Where intoxication affects the condition of diabetes or epilepsy, the courts are minded to view this as a self-induced mental disorder and will not afford a defence (*Quick* (1973)). They are similarly dismissive of alcoholism, refusing to recognise it as a mental disorder unless the impulse to drink is involuntary (see Chapter 11).

10.1   Insanity

M'Naghten (1843): Definition of insanity

Facts

D was charged with the murder of the Prime Minister's Private Secretary. He claimed he was insane and, in particular, that he had an obsession with morbid delusions.

Decision

The Court of Appeal held that:

> ... to establish a defence on the ground of insanity, it must be clearly proved that, at the time of the committing of the act, the party accused was labouring under such a defect of reason, from a disease of the mind, as not to know the nature and quality of the act he was doing, or, if he did know it, that he did not know he was doing what was wrong (*per* Lord Tindall CJ).

10.1.1   Disease of the mind

Kemp (1957): Impairment of mental faculties

Facts

D suffered from arteriosclerosis, which caused unconsciousness. Whilst unconscious, he attacked his wife with a hammer.

Decision

The Court of Appeal held that the physical state of the brain is irrelevant in deciding whether D had a disease of the mind; rather, the court has to decide whether the mental faculties of reason, memory and understanding are impaired or absent.

Sullivan (1984): Epilepsy and insanity

Facts

D had attacked P in the later stages of an epileptic seizure. He was charged with inflicting grievous bodily harm. When the trial judge ruled that this amounted to insanity rather than automatism, D changed his plea to guilty. He appealed, claiming that he should have been able to raise the defence of automatism.

Decision

The House of Lords held that in order to raise the defence of insanity, D had to be suffering from a 'disease of the mind'. The term 'mind' meant the mental faculties of reason, memory and understanding. If the effect of the disease was to impair these faculties so severely as to cause D to not know what he was doing or that what he was doing was wrong, then he is 'insane' in the legal sense. It did not matter whether the disease of the mind was organic or functional, or whether the impairment was permanent or transient and intermittent, provided it existed at the time of the commission of the offence. *Per curiam*, the defence of non-insane automatism (for which the verdict is not guilty) may be available where the temporary impairment of the faculties is caused by an external factor, rather than an internal factor.

Hennessy (1989): Hyperglycaemia, internal cause and insanity

Facts

D was a diabetic charged with driving a car whilst disqualified. D pleaded not guilty, claiming that he had failed to take his proper dose of insulin because he was in a state of stress, anxiety and depression. He was suffering from hyperglycaemia and claimed that he was in a state of automatism. The trial judge ruled that the appropriate defence was insanity and D changed his plea.

Decision

The Court of Appeal ruled that stress, anxiety and depression are not themselves external factors of the kind capable in law of causing a state of automatism since they were neither unique nor accidental factors. Hyperglycaemia is caused by the inherent defect (diabetes) and, if not corrected by insulin, is an internal factor causing a disease of the mind; therefore, insanity is the appropriate defence.

Burgess (1991): Somnambulism, internal cause and insanity

Facts

D attacked his friend. He claimed that he was acting unconsciously while sleep walking and that he should be acquitted on the grounds of non-insane automatism. The jury instead returned the verdict of not guilty by reason of insanity. D appealed.

Decision

The Court of Appeal held that whatever the cause of D's somnambulism, it was an internal cause and was, therefore, a disease of the mind, which rightfully resulted in a verdict of not guilty by reason of insanity. Although sleep walking is not regarded by medical experts as a mental disorder and although sleep is a normal condition, sleep walking, especially involving violence, is not normal. It is a disease of the mind caused by an internal factor.

10.1.2 D did not know what he was doing or that his actions were wrong

Windle (1952): D must know actions are legally wrong

Facts

D killed his wife by giving her an overdose of aspirin. She had been mentally ill for some time and often talked of committing suicide. D claimed in his defence that he was insane, suffering from a form of communicative insanity known as *folie a deux*, where, having been constantly attending to a person of unsound mind for a long period of time, D himself became mentally ill. D therefore claimed that he did not know at the time that his actions were legally wrong.

Decision

The Court of Appeal held that D must not know that his actions were legally wrong. It is not enough that he knew his actions were morally wrong. 'Therefore, there is no doubt that, in the *M'Naghten* Rules, "wrong" means contrary to the law, and not "wrong according to the opinion of one man"' (*per* Lord Goddard CJ).

Sodeman (1936): 'Irresistible impulse'

Facts

D took V for a ride on his bike, strangled her, tied her hands behind her back, stuffed some clothing into her mouth and left her for dead. V died from suffocation. D had committed three other similar murders. At trial he pleaded the defence of insanity, and medical evidence was adduced to suggest that D was suffering from irresistible impulses to do what he did.

Decision

The Privy Council held that the *M'Naghten* Rules made it clear that, where a man knew he was doing wrong, but was forced to do the act by an 'irresistible impulse' produced by a disease of the mind, he could rely on the defence of insanity.

10.2   Automatism

Bratty v AG for Northern Ireland (1961): Meaning of involuntary act

Facts

D killed a girl in his car by strangulation with her stocking. He claimed he was suffering from psychomotor epilepsy at the time and did not know what he was doing. D was convicted of murder when the trial judge refused to leave the defence of insanity to the jury and the jury rejected the defence of insanity.

Decision

The House of Lords ruled that if the defence of insanity is rejected by the jury, D is entitled to raise the defence of automatism as an alternative. Proper evidence must be adduced; however, to establish that D was acting under non-insane automatism:

> No act is punishable if it is done involuntarily, and an involuntary act in this context means an act which is done by the muscles without any control by the mind such as a spasm, a reflex action or a convulsion; or an act done by a person who is not conscious of what he is doing, such as an act done whilst suffering from concussion or done whilst sleep walking (*per* Lord Denning).

An act is not involuntary simply because a person does not remember it, or because D could not control his impulse to do it.

Broome v Perkins (1987): Hypoglycaemia and automatism

Facts

D was charged with driving without due care and attention. He had driven his car erratically five or six miles along a familiar route. D was a diabetic and claimed he was suffering hypoglycaemia at the time, and remembered nothing after the very start of his journey.

Decision

The Queen's Bench Divisional Court found that D should have been convicted. If, during some of the erratic driving, D's actions were voluntary and if, occasionally, D's mind had exercised some control over his limbs so that his actions were not automatic, then he was not acting under automatism and was not entitled to a defence.

Bingham (1991): Hypoglycaemia, external cause and automatism

Facts

D was charged with the theft of a can of coke and some sandwiches from a shop. D was a diabetic and claimed that, at the time of leaving the shop without paying for the goods, he was suffering from hypoglycaemia and was unaware of what he was doing. The trial judge had refused to leave the defence of automatism to the jury.

Decision

The Court of Appeal held that hypoglycaemia is not caused by the disease of diabetes but by the treatment of it, in the form of too much insulin or not enough food to counter-balance the insulin. In most cases this would not give rise to the defence of insanity, but might give rise to an acquittal on the basis that D lacked *mens rea* and was acting under automatism.

Quick (1973): Self-induced automatism

Facts

D, a nurse, assaulted a patient. D claimed he could not remember doing so because, being a diabetic, he had taken insulin but had not eaten sufficient food and had drunk quantities of whisky and rum. D pleaded not guilty on the ground of automatism. The trial judge ruled that he could only plead the defence of insanity, so D changed his plea to guilty and appealed.

Decision

The Court of Appeal found that D was suffering from a mental abnormality caused by hypoglycaemia. This was not caused by the internal factor of his diabetes, but by his use of insulin prescribed by his doctor. This was an external factor and therefore caused a bodily disorder, not a disease of the mind, and automatism was the appropriate defence. However, *per* Lawton LJ: '... a self-induced incapacity will not excuse ... nor will one which could have been reasonably foreseen as a result of either doing or omitting to do something, for example, taking alcohol against medical advice after using certain prescribed drugs or failing to have regular meals while taking insulin.' The appeal was allowed.

Bailey (1983): Automatism and basic intent crimes

Facts

D, a diabetic, went to visit his ex-girlfriend and her new partner, V. D took insulin and a mixture of sugar and water, but ate nothing. He then assaulted V. He told the police he had hit V to teach him a lesson for associating with his girlfriend. D pleaded not guilty to a charge of wounding V, claiming that he acted in a state of automatism caused by hypoglycaemia.

Decision

The Court of Appeal held that self-induced automatism (unless caused by intoxication) could provide a defence to a basic intent crime. The jury must decide whether D's conduct, in view of his knowledge of the likely results of his actions, was sufficiently reckless. There was no conclusive presumption that it was reckless conduct for a person to fail to take food after a dose of insulin.

AG's Reference (No 2 of 1992) (1994): Total loss of voluntary control

Facts

D was a lorry driver who was charged with two counts of causing death by reckless driving. D had been driving for six hours when his lorry hit a stationary vehicle on the hard shoulder of the motorway and killed two people. D claimed a defence of 'driving without awareness', D being in a state of automatism at the time.

Decision

The Court of Appeal ruled that automatism is only available as a defence where there is a total loss of voluntary control. Impaired or reduced control was not sufficient to afford a defence. In this case, D had still been in some control of the lorry at the time as he was able to steer it and was partially aware of what was going on on the road ahead.

Marison (1996): Foreseeability of risk of hypoglycaemic episode

Facts

D was a diabetic who had regularly had hypoglycaemic episodes, including whilst driving his car, and these episodes caused him to lose consciousness without warning. In the incident in question, D's car veered to the wrong side of the road and collided with another car, killing the driver of that car. D was convicted of causing death by dangerous driving, after the judge ruled that D must have been aware of the risk of having a hypoglycaemic episode whilst driving. D appealed on the ground that the judge's ruling was wrong.

Decision

The Court of Appeal found that, although D became an automaton at the time of the accident, he could not use automatism as a defence. This was because, as a driver, he was in a dangerously defective state due to his diabetes and had already committed the offence of dangerous driving before the accident took place. The hypoglycaemic episode was reasonably foreseeable and therefore the judge's ruling was correct.

T (1990): Rape as an external factor

Facts

D was arrested and charged with armed robbery together with two men. On arrest, she was passive and indifferent, and could only recollect parts of the preceding events. Later, when D was transferred to prison, it was revealed that she had been raped three days before her arrest and a psychiatrist diagnosed her as suffering from post-traumatic stress disorder and being in a dissociative state. Further, she was said to have committed the offence during a psychogenic fugue and was not acting with a conscious mind or will. D pleaded the defence of automatism, but the prosecution contended that she had recalled some of the events surrounding the crime and had exercised partial control over her actions in using a weapon.

Decision

The Crown Court held that this was the first case in which the 'external' event causing the malfunction of the mind was a rape. However, such an incident would have a severe effect on any young woman and therefore the rape would suffice as the external triggering condition. The malfunction of the mind here (due to post-traumatic stress disorder) was not a disease of the mind and, although there was only partial loss of control throughout the incident, D acted as if she were in a dream. Therefore, the defence of automatism could rightly be put before the jury.

CHAPTER 11

INTOXICATION

Introduction

A defendant may wish to argue that, through intoxication, they were unable to control their actions and that therefore they were acting 'involuntarily'. The courts' response to this has been mixed, but they are generally reluctant to afford any defence to a person who voluntarily gets themselves drunk before committing a crime. This explains their response in some cases that 'a drunken intent is nevertheless an intent' (*Sheehan and Moore* (1975)). It is ironic that given the air of disapproval of drunkenness in the courts' *dicta* on intoxication, the more drunk you are the more likely you are to have a defence. A number of cases have explored this issue. While it is a matter of degree in the circumstances of each case, the defendant is more likely to succeed with a defence if he is so drunk that his mind is incapable of forming *mens rea* (*Stubbs* (1989)), although this does not necessarily mean that the defendant has to be fully unconscious (*Sooklal (Narine) v Trinidad and Tobago* (1999)).

Once the degree of intoxication is established, the court will then consider to what extent it can provide a defence. The House of Lords in *Majewski* (1977) set out a basic rule that intoxication may be a defence to a specific intent crime, but never a defence to a basic intent crime. A specific intent crime is one which, according to the substantive criminal law, can only be committed with intention. Basic intent crimes are those where recklessness will suffice for the *mens rea* to be proved. Specific intent crimes require the proof of a subjective *mens rea*, that is, that the defendant intended the consequence or actually foresaw it as a highly probable or virtually certain consequence of their actions (see Chapter 1). If their drunkenness prevented such intention or high level of foresight, then they may be said not to have formed the necessary *mens rea* and should be acquitted. On the other hand, recklessness requires foresight of merely probable consequences and the rationale behind denying the defendant a defence in relation to these crimes is that intoxication is less likely to render the defendant unable to have this lower standard of foresight. Many of the cases have discussed which crimes are specific intent crimes and which merely require basic intent.

11.1 Levels of intoxication

Sheehan and Moore (1975): Drunken intent no defence

Facts

The Ds suspected V of stealing. They bought a can of petrol, went to V's house and V was later found dead, having been doused with petrol and set alight. Both Ds claimed they were intoxicated at the time and lacked the necessary *mens rea*.

Decision

The Court of Appeal held that:

... the mere fact that the defendant's mind was affected by drink, so that he acted in a way in which he would not have done had he been sober, does not assist him at all, provided the necessary intention is there. A drunken intent is nevertheless an intent (*per* Lane LJ).

Stubbs (1989): Extreme drunkenness required

Facts

D stabbed V during a fight outside a pub. D was charged under s 18 of the Offences Against the Person Act 1861. D offered to plead guilty to the lesser offence of s 20 of the Act on the grounds that he was intoxicated at the time and could not remember what he had done.

Decision

The Court of Appeal held: 'A defence of drunkenness really requires to be very extreme before it should be allowed to influence the Crown to say they will accept a plea to s 20' (*per* O'Connor LJ). The plea should therefore not have been accepted by the prosecutor in this case.

Bowden (1993): Intoxication irrelevant where *mens rea* exists

Facts

D was convicted of wounding with intent. D claimed a defence of intoxication due to drink and drugs. The jury were directed as to the meaning of intent and that 'you may, when drunk, intend things that you would not intend were you sober'.

Decision

The Court of Appeal held that if D formed the necessary *mens rea*, then intoxication is irrelevant and cannot be pleaded as a defence. The jury should be directed that the mere fact that D's mind was affected by drink, so that he acted in a way which he would not otherwise have done if sober, would not afford him a defence.

Brown (1998): Level of drunkenness required

Facts

D was convicted of causing grievous bodily harm contrary to s 18 of the Offences Against the Person Act 1861. D was intoxicated at the time of the assault. D appealed against his conviction on the grounds that the judge had misdirected the jury as to the effect of the intoxication on D's capacity to form intent.

Decision

The Court of Appeal held that in a case requiring proof of specific intent it is necessary to inform the jury that they must take into account that D was drunk and if, because he was drunk, they considered that he did not intend to cause the requisite harm he was entitled to be acquitted. It is not enough to simply say a drunken intent is still an intent.

Comment

This case appears to be saying that the extent of drunkenness required for the defence is a matter of degree, to be determined by its effect on D's ability to form intent. So there is no need for D to be so drunk as to be unconscious, providing he is drunk enough to lack the ability to form intent.

Sooklal (Narine) v Trinidad and Tobago (1999): Degree of intoxication required

Facts

D was convicted for the murder of V. D pleaded the defence of intoxication. The judge directed the jury that they should acquit D if, through drunkenness, they considered that he lacked the intent required for murder.

Decision

The Privy Council held that in this case there was no evidence that intoxication caused D to lack the specific intent for murder, particularly since, as he admitted at trial, he was able to give the police a lucid account of his actions. The degree of intoxication fell far below that which would preclude the formation of the specific intent required for murder.

Groark (1999): Intoxication and intent

Facts

D, after consuming 10 pints of beer, assaulted V. D was charged with wounding with intent (s 18 of the Offences Against the Person Act 1861), but claimed that he knew what was happening and that he hit V in self-defence. The judge gave no direction to the jury on the possible relevance of voluntary intoxication and the element of intent. D was convicted and appealed, claiming that the judge should have directed the jury that his intoxication may have been relevant.

Decision

The Court of Appeal held that if there was evidence of drunkenness which might give rise to a defence to a specific intent crime, the jury should normally be directed to consider that a drunken intent is, nevertheless, an intent, but to be sure that D did have the necessary intent. However, where D did not contend that he was unable to form the necessary intent, it was up to defence counsel whether they had any objection to the issue of drunkenness being raised. In this case, there had been no issue about whether the necessary intent was formed and the judge was therefore correct in not directing the jury on that issue.

Richardson (1999): Intoxication relevant to issue of foresight

Facts

D was a university student who had been drinking in the student union bar. On returning to D's flat with friends, some horseplay ensued and D lifted V over the edge of the balcony and dropped him. He fell 10–12 feet and suffered injuries. D was charged under s 20 of the Offences Against the Person Act 1861. D claimed that V consented to the horseplay and that his fall was an accident. D was convicted and appealed, claiming that the judge acted inappropriately in directing the jury that they should judge D's intention on the basis of a reasonable sober person.

Decision

The Court of Appeal allowed the appeals. The judge should have directed the jury to consider D's drunken state of mind when deciding whether D had the requisite foresight of risk to satisfy the *mens rea* requirements of the offence.

11.2   Involuntary intoxication

Kingston (1994): No defence where *mens rea* formed

Facts

P invited a 15 year old boy to his flat and gave him a drink containing a soporific drug, which sent him to sleep. D was also given a 'laced' drink and he indecently assaulted the boy. D claimed he remembered nothing after arriving at P's flat until he awoke at home the next morning.

Decision

The House of Lords held that involuntary intoxication did not constitute a defence, although it could be used in mitigation. If it could be proved that D had the necessary intent to commit the offence, then intoxication was no defence, even though intoxication was induced by a third party. If D was unable to form the necessary *mens rea* due to involuntary intoxication, he must be acquitted.

11.3   Voluntary intoxication

Allen (1988): D unaware of strength of alcohol

Facts

D drank a large quantity of wine, which made him intoxicated. He claimed he did not realise that the wine had a high alcohol content. D was convicted of buggery and indecent assault.

Decision

The Court of Appeal ruled that where D knows he is drinking alcohol, it is irrelevant whether he knows the precise nature or strength of the alcohol. Drinking does not become involuntary simply because D did not know the precise nature or strength of the alcohol he was drinking.

Hardie (1984): Soporific drugs

Facts

D took several Valium tablets without knowing what effect they might have on him. He later started a fire in an occupied house. D was convicted of criminal damage with intent to endanger life. He claimed that he had no *mens rea* as a result of taking the drug.

Decision

The Court of Appeal held that, although Valium was a drug and D had taken it deliberately (and not for medical purposes), it was wholly different from the kind of drugs liable to cause unpredictability and aggression. *Per* Parker LJ:

> ... if the effect of the drug is merely soporific or sedative, the taking of it, even in some excessive quantity, cannot in the ordinary way rouse a conclusive presumption against admission of proof of intoxication for the purposes of disproving *mens rea* in ordinary crimes, such as would be the case with alcoholic intoxication or incapacity or automatism resulting from the self-administration of dangerous drugs.

11.3.1 Crimes of specific intent

Beard (1920): Intoxication no defence to rape as basic intent crime

Facts

In the course of committing a rape, D killed his victim. He was charged with murder (under the murder felony rule which then existed). It was established that D intended to commit the rape and was, therefore, deemed to have intended the death which ensued.

Decision

The House of Lords held that:

> [D's] drunkenness was irrelevant, as it did not affect his formation of *mens rea* for rape. However, where specific intent is an essential element of the offence, evidence of a state of drunkenness, rendering D incapable of forming such an intent, should be taken into consideration, in order to determine whether he had in fact formed the intent necessary to constitute the particular crime (*per* Lord Birkenhead).

Majewski (1977): Specific intent means 'direct intent'

Facts

During a fight at a pub, D attacked the landlord, two others and several police officers. D was charged with assault occasioning actual bodily harm and assaulting a police officer in the execution of his duty. D claimed that he had taken a quantity of drugs and alcohol during the previous 48 hours, and he did not know what he was doing when he committed the assaults.

Decision

The House of Lords held that intoxication could only be a defence to crimes of specific intent. Specific intent meant 'direct' intent: '... the prosecution must, in general, prove that the purpose for the commission of the act extends to the intent expressed or implied in the definition of the crime' (*per* Lord Russell).

Caldwell (1982): Criminal damage as a basic intent crime

Facts

D quarrelled with his employer, the owner of a hotel. D got drunk and set fire to the hotel while it was occupied. D was charged with intentionally or recklessly causing criminal damage (to which he pleaded guilty) and with causing criminal damage with intent to, or being reckless as to, whether lives are endangered. D pleaded the defence of intoxication.

Decision

The House of Lords held that intoxication is only a defence to crimes which require proof of intention (specific intent crimes). It is not a defence to crimes which can be committed recklessly (basic intent crimes). The offence in s 1(2) of the Criminal Damage Act 1971 is a basic intent crime. However, classification into crimes of 'specific' and 'basic' intent is irrelevant where being reckless as to whether a particular harmful consequence will result from one's act is a sufficient *mens rea* (*per* Lord Diplock).

Comment

The prominent crimes of specific intent are: murder; wounding or causing grievous bodily harm with intent (s 18 of the Offences Against the Person Act 1861); theft; handling stolen goods; burglary; robbery; attempted offences; and indecent assault (see *Court* (1989) 5.2.1 above).

11.3.2 Crimes of basic intent

Majewski (1977): Intentional intoxication provides sufficient *mens rea* in basic intent crimes

Facts

See 11.3.1 above.

Decision

The House of Lords found that intoxication is no defence in a crime of basic intent. *Per* Lord Elwin-Jones:

> If a man, of his own volition, takes a substance which causes him to cast off the restraints of reason and conscience, no wrong is done to him by holding him answerable criminally for any injury he may do while in that condition. His course of conduct in reducing himself by drink and drugs to that condition in my view supplies the evidence of *mens rea*, of guilty mind, certainly sufficient for crimes of basic intent. It is a reckless course of conduct and recklessness is enough to constitute the necessary *mens rea* in assault cases ... The drunkenness is itself an intrinsic part of the crime, the other part being the evidence of the unlawful use of force. Together they add up to criminal recklessness.

Caldwell (1982): Criminal damage is a basic intent crime

Facts

See 19.2 below.

Decision

The House of Lords held that if the crime can be committed recklessly, then intoxication cannot be a defence. In order to prove recklessness in criminal damage cases, the jury must consider two questions:

(1) did D commit an act which created an obvious risk?; and

(2) when D committed the act, did he either give no thought to the possibility of there being a risk or, having recognised it, did he go on and take it? The objective element in the test precludes intoxication from being a defence to basic intent crimes to which *Caldwell* recklessness applies.

Comment

Although the test of recklessness laid down in *Caldwell* has been overruled in *G & R* (see 19.2 below), this does not alter the fact that criminal damage is a basic intent crime for which the defence of intoxication is not available.

Fotheringham (1989): Rape is a crime of basic intent

Facts

D and his wife went out, leaving V, a 14 year old babysitter, to look after their children. D's wife told V to sleep in the matrimonial bed. When D and his wife returned home,

D got into his bed and had sexual intercourse with V without her consent. D claimed that he was drunk and had mistaken V for his wife. At D's trial for rape, the judge told the jury to disregard D's voluntary intoxication in considering whether his belief that V was a consenting woman (that is, his wife) was reasonable. D was convicted and appealed.

Decision

The Court of Appeal found that D's voluntary intoxication was no defence in any crime of basic intent. Since rape is an offence where recklessness (at least as to the consent of V) will suffice as a *mens rea*, it is clearly a basic intent offence. D therefore could not use his voluntary intoxication in relation to the issue of consent to claim that his belief was reasonable.

C (1992): Indecent assault is a basic intent crime

Facts

D, whilst drunk, inserted his fingers into a child's vagina. He was charged with indecent assault, but claimed that he could not remember the offence because he was drunk. The judge told the jury to ignore this, as voluntary intoxication was not a defence to a charge of indecent assault. D was convicted, and appealed on the grounds that, after the decision in *Court*, indecent assault is now a specific intent crime (see Chapter 5).

Decision

The Court of Appeal ruled that the decision in *Court* (1989) had been based on facts where the indecency of D's actions was ambiguous. The House of Lords in that case stated that, where there was such ambiguity, the jury had to consider D's intention (that is, whether he intended to commit an indecent assault). However, in this case there was no ambiguity regarding the indecency of the assault, so there was no requirement to consider D's intention. In such a case, the House of Lords in *Court* had not changed the position that indecent assault is a crime of basic intent, and so voluntary intoxication is no defence.

Kellett (1994): 'Allow' indicative of basic intention

Facts

D was the owner of a pit bull terrier which escaped from her flat and was found in a public place without a lead or a muzzle. At the time, D was drunk. D was charged with an offence contrary to s 1(7) of the Dangerous Dogs Act 1991. D claimed that, as she was intoxicated, she had not 'allowed' her dog to be in a public place. On appeal, the prosecution claimed that she could not use the defence of voluntary intoxication, since the word 'allow' suggested an element of *mens rea*, and that the offence was one of basic intent.

Decision

The Queen's Bench Divisional Court held that the word 'allow' did indeed import some element of *mens rea*, since D could not allow something of which she was unaware or could not prevent. The offence was therefore one of basic intent, and she was, therefore, unable to plead the defence of voluntary intoxication.

Comment

The prominent crimes of basic intent are: manslaughter; wounding or inflicting grievous bodily harm (s 20 of the Offences Against the Person Act 1861); assault occasioning actual bodily harm (s 47 of the Offences Against the Person Act 1861); rape; indecent assault (see *C* (1992) above); common assault; criminal damage; and deception offences.

11.4   Drunken mistake

O'Grady (1987): Intoxicated mistaken self-defence is no defence

Facts

D had killed a friend whilst heavily intoxicated. He had thought his friend was attacking him and responded with what he thought were minor blows in self-defence. He was convicted of manslaughter, but pleaded the defence of intoxicated mistaken self-defence.

Decision

The Court of Appeal held that there is no defence of intoxicated mistaken self-defence, regardless of whether D is charged with a crime of basic or specific intent. The issue of mistake must be considered separately from that of intent and intoxication. If D mistakenly believed that his force was necessary to defend himself and that mistake was induced by voluntary intoxication, then the defence must fail. (See also *Williams (Gladstone)* 9.2.2 above.)

O'Connor (1991): Intoxicated mistaken self-defence may be defence to specific intent crime

Facts

D had been drinking heavily and killed V during an argument. D was charged with murder, but claimed he had acted in what he believed to be self-defence.

Decision

The Court of Appeal held that where D, through self-induced intoxication, formed a mistaken belief that he was using force to defend himself, a plea of self-defence must fail (as *per O'Grady*). Therefore, the judge need not direct the jury on intoxication, as it affected the plea of self-defence. The judge should, however, have directed the jury on intoxication, as it affected D's ability to form specific intent.

Jaggard v Dickinson (1980): Drunken mistake as to authority

See 7.9.3 above.

11.5   Intoxication causing mental abnormality

Tandy (1989): Alcoholism as a mental abnormality

Facts

D was an alcoholic who killed her daughter after drinking almost a whole bottle of vodka, rather than her usual drink of vermouth. She was charged with murder, and raised the defence of diminished responsibility as a result of her alcoholism.

Decision

The Court of Appeal ruled that in order for a craving for a drink in itself to produce an 'abnormality of mind' induced by the disease of alcoholism, the alcoholism had to have reached such a level that D had suffered from brain damage causing gross impairment of her judgment and emotional responses, or the craving had to be such as to render D's impulse to drink involuntary, because she was no longer able to resist. If D had simply resisted an impulse to drink, it was not an involuntary impulse and the defence of diminished responsibility was not available. In this case, D was unable to plead diminished responsibility on the grounds that the evidence showed that her impulse to drink was not involuntary, as she had left some vodka in the bottle.

11.6   Dutch courage

Gallagher (1961): Dutch courage intoxication no defence

Facts

D was a psychopath suffering from a disease of the mind. He was liable to outbursts of violent behaviour when he drank alcohol. He decided to kill his wife, bought some alcohol, drank it and killed her. He was charged with murder and raised the defences of intoxication and insanity.

Decision

The House of Lords held that:

> If a man, whilst sane and sober, forms an intention to kill and makes preparation for it, knowing it is a wrong thing to do, and then gets himself drunk so as to give himself Dutch courage to do the killing, he cannot rely on this self-induced drunkenness as a defence to a charge of murder, nor even reducing it to manslaughter ... The wickedness of his mind before he got drunk is enough to condemn him (*per* Lord Denning).

CHAPTER 12

DURESS AND NECESSITY

Introduction

The defences of duress and necessity are often referred to as a concession to human frailty. This means that they are excusatory defences; they excuse the defendant's conduct which is otherwise unlawful. The grounds for excusing the conduct are that the defendant was compelled to act as he did because of a threat to his or another's life or because of a threat of serious injury. This threat may be issued by another person (duress) or it may arise out of the situation that the defendant finds himself in (necessity or duress of circumstances).

Duress may excuse any crime except murder. The rationale behind this is that a defendant who intentionally kills another because his own life is threatened has been faced with a stark choice; he can save his own life or that of his victim. The courts take the view that in this situation the defendant has a moral duty to sacrifice his own life in order to save that of his victim and failure to do so renders the defendant a 'coward and a poltroon' (*Howe and Bannister* (1987)) to whom the law will offer no defence. They have also extended this rule to attempted murder (*Gotts* (1992)) on the same moral argument.

Where duress is available as a defence, there are restrictions on its application. The threat must be a serious one, as a result of which the defendant must fear death or serious injury to himself or another. Furthermore, the threat of this serious harm must be imminent in the sense that it affords the defendant no time to escape from the threat or take steps to prevent the harm happening. The courts have not allowed the defence where the defendant may have sought protection from the police (*Heath* (2000)), or where the defendant has had the opportunity to escape (*DPP v Tomkinson* (2001)), or where the time has elapsed since the issue of the threat and it no longer carries such weight. Nevertheless, the courts have given a generous interpretation of imminence where the defendant seeks to escape from a perceived implicit threat even where it is unlikely to be carried out immediately (*Abdul Hussein* (1999); *Safi* (2004)). In these unusual circumstances, the threat is so great and the death or serious injury so certain that that is sufficient to render it 'imminent'. No matter how serious or imminent a threat may be, the courts drew the line at a threat issued by the defendant towards himself (*Rodger* (1998)).

In order for the imminent threat to afford a defence, it had to have been operative on the defendant. This means it had to actually compel the defendant to commit the offence and his will must have been 'overborne' (*DPP v Lynch* (1975)). Effectively, the defendant in this situation feels he has no choice but to commit the crime and that is the basis on which the courts will excuse his 'human frailty' in choosing the criminal course of action. The cases have discussed whether the defendant's perception that he has no choice but to commit the crime ought to be reasonable. The test is indeed objective, the jury must decide whether the ordinary reasonable person would have acted in the same way had they been in the defendant's shoes. This ordinary reasonable person may share the sex, age and certain other personal characteristics of the defendant (such as sexuality – *Graham* (1982)) but the courts have been reluctant to go too far in assigning the reasonable person with too much of the defendant's persona. The restrictive nature of cases such as *Hegarty* (1994) and *Bowen* (1996) contrast with the approach to objectivity taken in relation to provocation (see Chapter 2).

The courts have also been restrictive in affording the defence of duress to defendants who voluntarily put themselves in a situation where they are likely to receive threats. This has included joining a criminal gang or a violent organisation such as the IRA (*DPP v Lynch* (1975)), but has also been extended recently to defendants who use illicit drugs and get themselves into debt with their supplier (*Harmer* (2002)). The rationale here is that if you lay yourself open to threats as a result of your activities or lifestyle, then you cannot expect the law to protect you from criminal liability for your actions.

The defence of necessity may also be termed the defence of duress of circumstances. This arises where it is the situation that the defendant finds himself in that threatens death or serious injury rather than another person. Therefore, all the above rulings and restrictions on the issue of duress apply.

12.1 Duress

Lynch (1975): Definition of duress

Facts
The defendant was charged with the murder of a policeman in Northern Ireland. D was charged as an accessory because, although he was not directly involved with the shooting, he had driven the armed gunmen to the scene of the crime and away again. D pleaded the defence of duress, alleging that he had been ordered by M (a well known ruthless gunman in the IRA) to take part in the crime. There was evidence that if D had not obeyed M's orders, D would have been shot.

Decision
The House of Lords held:

> ... the decision of the threatened man whose constancy is overborne so that he yields to the threat is a calculated decision to do what he knows is wrong, and is therefore that of a man with a 'guilty mind'. But he is at the same time a man whose mind is less guilty than is his who acts as he does, but under no such constraint (*per* Lord Morris).

12.1.1 Threat

Lynch (1975): Threat of death or serious injury

Facts
See 12.1 above.

Decision
The House of Lords held that: 'If someone is really threatened with death or serious injury unless he does what he is told to do ... must the law not remember that the instinct and perhaps the duty of self-preservation is powerful and natural? I think it

must' (*per* Lord Wilberforce). '... Nobody would dispute that the greater the degree of heinousness of the crime, the greater and less resistible must be the degree of pressure' (*per* Lord Morris).

Howe and Bannister (1987): Proportionality between the threat and the crime

Facts

Two defendants participated with others in torturing, kicking, punching and sexually abusing a man. The man was then strangled to death by one of the others. The Ds claimed they acted under duress at the orders of, and through fear of, a man called Murry, who was known to be violent and sadistic.

Decision

The House of Lords held that: '... some degree of proportionality between the threat and the offence must, at least to some extent, be a prerequisite of the defence ...' (*per* Lord Hailsham).

Valderrama-Vega (1985): Threat of death or serious injury need not be only threat

Facts

D imported a quantity of cocaine into London from Columbia. He claimed he did so under duress from a Mafia-type organisation in Columbia, who would have killed or seriously injured him or his family if he had not carried out the smuggling. He was also under severe financial pressure and had been threatened with disclosure of his homosexual inclinations.

Decision

The Court of Appeal held that, although a threat of serious injury or death is a necessary prerequisite of the defence, it need not be the sole or only threat to D, and the jury are entitled to look at the effect of all threats on D, as long as one of them is a threat of death or serious injury.

12.1.2 Threats and the defendant

Graham (1982): Two stage test on effect of threat on D

Facts

D was a practising homosexual living in a ménage à trois with another man (K) and D's wife. D was taking drugs for anxiety, which made him vulnerable to bullying. K was a violent man, jealous of D's wife. One night after D had been drinking heavily, K put an electric flex around the wife's neck, pulled it tight and asked D to pull the other end. D did and the wife was killed. D claimed he complied with K's demand because of his fear of K and partly due to the drugs he was taking.

Decision

The Court of Appeal held that there were two questions for the jury to consider:

(1) (a subjective question) Was D impelled to act as he did because, as a result of what he reasonably believed, the person issuing the threat had said or done, he

had good cause to fear that if he did not do the act, that person would kill him or cause him serious injury?;

(2) (an objective question) Would a sober person of reasonable firmness, sharing the characteristics of the defendant, have responded to whatever D reasonably believed the person said or did, by taking part in the killing?

The fact that D's will to resist a threat had been eroded by the voluntary consumption of drink or drugs is not relevant to the test.

Horne (1994): D's characteristics irrelevant to objective test

Facts

D was an employee of the DSS, who conspired with others to make fraudulent claims for Income Support. D pleaded the defence of duress, claiming that one of his co-conspirators had pressurised him with telephone calls and visits to his home. Although he had not directly been threatened with violence, the co-conspirator had hinted that his brother 'might sort him [D] out'. D had sought to use psychiatric evidence relating to the effect of the duress at trial.

Decision

The Court of Appeal held that : '... if the standard for comparison was a person of reasonable firmness, it must be irrelevant for the jury to consider any characteristic which showed that he was not such a person, but was pliant or vulnerable to pressure' (*per* Russell LJ). To consider D's characteristics would undermine the objective nature of the test.

Hegarty (1994): Personality disorder irrelevant to objective test

Facts

D was charged with robbery and he pleaded the defence of duress. D claimed that some men had attacked him and threatened violence against his family if he did not carry out the robberies. D sought to introduce evidence at trial of his mental instability. D had a history of mental illness and was described as 'emotionally unstable' and in a 'grossly elevated neurotic state'.

Decision

The Court of Appeal found that D's emotionally unstable or grossly elevated neurotic state was not a relevant characteristic to consider in the test for duress. The test of whether D's will was overborne is not purely subjective. The jury has also to consider the response of a sober person of reasonable firmness 'sharing the characteristics of the defendant'. They could take into account the age, sex and physical health of D, but not a personality disorder such as that experienced by D in this case.

Bowen (1996): Characteristics relevant to the objective test

Facts

D was charged with obtaining services by deception, but claimed he was forced to do so by two men who had threatened to harm his family if he did not carry out the offence. At trial, D pleaded duress on the basis that he was abnormally suggestible and that a psychiatrist had testified that his IQ was only 68. D was convicted, but appealed on the ground that the judge had failed to direct the jury to consider D's characteristics in applying the objective test.

Decision

The Court of Appeal ruled that:

(1) The mere fact that [D] is more pliable, vulnerable, timid or susceptible to threats than a normal person could not be characteristics with which it is legitimate to invest the reasonable/ordinary person for the purpose of considering the objective test.

(2) [D] may be in a category of persons who the jury may think less able to resist pressure than people not within that category. Obvious examples are age ... possibly sex ... pregnancy, where there is added fear for the unborn child ... recognised mental illness or psychiatric condition, such as post-traumatic stress disorder leading to learned helplessness ... (*per* Stuart-Smith LJ).

Where D wished to show that he was suffering from a mental illness, mental impairment or other recognised psychiatric condition, which may have made him more susceptible to threats, psychiatric evidence was admissible. Where D wished to submit that he had a characteristic listed in (2) above, then he had to make that clear to the judge, who could rule at that stage whether medical evidence was admissible. In this case, the fact that D was abnormally suggestible was irrelevant. His low IQ, which fell short of mental impairment or defectiveness, was not a characteristic which made people less courageous or able to withstand threats and pressure. The judge therefore had directed the jury sufficiently – they could only consider D's age and sex.

Flatt (1996): Drug addiction as self-induced characteristic irrelevant

Facts

D was charged with possession of drugs with intent. He pleaded the defence of duress, claiming that he was addicted to crack cocaine and owed his dealer £1,500. He claimed the dealer had told him to look after some drugs for him or he would shoot D's grandmother and girlfriend. D was convicted and appealed, claiming that the judge should have directed the jury to consider his drug addiction in applying the objective test.

Decision

The Court of Appeal held that drug addiction was a self-induced condition and not a characteristic. Furthermore, there was no evidence that the drug addiction caused D to be less able to withstand threats or pressure. The appeal was dismissed.

Emery (1993): History of abuse relevant to capacity to withstand duress

Facts

D was convicted of cruelty to her child, who died aged 11 months. D claimed that, after years of violence towards her by the father of the child, she had developed learned helplessness and was unable to withstand pressure or threats from him.

Decision

The Court of Appeal held that the history of violence towards D caused her inability to withstand the duress and therefore was relevant evidence. Evidence could be allowed 'to give an expert account of the causes of the condition of dependent helplessness, the circumstances in which it might arise and what level of abuse would be required to produce it' (*per* Taylor LCJ).

Hurst (1995): Mere speculation of a characteristic inadmissible

Facts
D was charged with an offence relating to the importing of cocaine. She raised the defence of duress, and sought to call evidence from a psychiatrist that her ability to withstand the duress had been affected by her sexual abuse as a child.

Decision
The Court of Appeal found that the expert evidence she sought to adduce could not be viewed as anything but mere speculation and was, therefore, rightly excluded.

12.1.3 *Imminence of the threat*

Hudson and Taylor (1971): Defence not available where D had opportunity to escape

Facts
Two girls were convicted of perjury in a criminal case where they were witnesses for the prosecution. They claimed they had been threatened with violence unless they committed perjury in court.

Decision
The Court of Appeal held that : '... in the present case, the threats ... were likely to be no less compelling because their execution could not be effected in the court room, if they could be carried out ... the same night ...' (*per* Widgery LJ). A defendant should not be able to plead duress if he had the opportunity to extricate himself from danger, or an opportunity to seek protection from the police. However, in deciding whether such an opportunity was reasonably open to D, the jury should have regard to his age and circumstances and to any risks to him which may be involved in the course of action relied upon.

Heath (2000): Avenue of escape
See 12.1.6 below.

Howe and Bannister (1987): No escape where official protection would be ineffective

Facts
See 12.1.1 above.

Decision
The House of Lords held that:

> ... if duress is introduced as a merciful concession to human frailty, it seems hard to deny it to a man who knows full well that any official protection he may seek will not be effective to save him from the threat of death under which he has acted (*per* Lord Griffiths).

Abdul-Hussein and Others (1999): Threat need not be immediate providing it is operative

Facts

The Ds were Shi'ite Muslim fugitives from Iraq. They had been living in Sudan, but had outstayed their right to residence and feared deportation back to Iraq, where they thought they would be executed. In Sudan, they boarded a plane bound for Jordan, but hijacked it by threatening the crew with imitation knives and grenades. The plane eventually landed at Stansted airport and, after eight hours of negotiation, they released the passengers and crew and surrendered. They were charged with hijacking but raised the defence of necessity. The judge ruled that the defence should not be left to the jury because the threat was not sufficiently immediate.

Decision

The Court of Appeal held that the defence should have been available. It is generally available for the offence of hijacking, although the terror induced in passengers should be balanced against the threat that the Ds were avoiding. The imminent danger to D had to operate on his mind at the time the offence was committed, so as to overbear his will. D did not have to be under threat of immediate execution, provided his mind was so affected that his will was overborne. 'If Anne Frank had stolen a car to escape from Amsterdam and had been charged with theft, the tenets of English law would not, in our judgment have denied her a defence of duress of circumstances, on the ground that she should have waited for the Gestapo's knock on the door.' The Court of Appeal again called for urgent codification of this defence in order to set out its precise requirements and parameters (see also *Rogers*, 12.2 below).

Safi (2004): Honest belief in imminence of threat

Facts

D and others hijacked a plane as it left Afghanistan until it eventually arrived at Stansted Airport. D claimed to be an opponent of the Taliban regime and that he and his family were at risk of capture, torture and execution by that regime. Therefore he pleaded the defence of duress of circumstances to his charges relating to the hijacking, since he had acted under the imminent threat of death or serious injury. The judge directed the jury that for the defence to succeed there must be evidence that there was or might have been such an imminent threat. D claimed that the proper direction should have been whether D reasonably believed in the existence of such a threat.

Decision

The Court of Appeal ruled that the judge had misdirected the jury. The correct test for establishing the defence of duress was established in *Graham* and contained both subjective and objective elements. First, the jury must consider whether D was compelled to act as he did because of his reasonable belief that he faced death or serious injury, and then secondly, whether a reasonable person in the same circumstances would have acted in the same way.

12.1.4   The threat may be directed at D or some other person

Conway (1988): Threat of death or serious injury to another

Facts
D was parked in his car with two passengers. One of the passengers, T, was wanted by the police. Two police officers approached the car and asked to speak to T. T told D to drive away, which he did at great speed and in a reckless manner. D was charged with reckless driving, but pleaded the defence of duress of circumstances on the basis that T had narrowly avoided being shot by two men a few weeks before and, when two plain-clothed officers approached the car, he thought they were going to shoot T. He claimed he only realised they were policemen after he had dropped T off at a safe location.

Decision
The Court of Appeal held that necessity will only be a defence to the charge of reckless driving where D was under duress of circumstances; that is, where he was constrained by circumstances to avoid death or serious injury to himself or another person.

Martin (1989): Threat to D's wife suffices

Facts
D was charged with driving whilst disqualified. D's wife had suicidal tendencies and had previously attempted to take her own life. D's son had overslept and was going to be late for work. To avoid the son losing his job, D drove him to work (despite being disqualified), because the wife was distraught and was threatening suicide.

Decision
The Court of Appeal allowed D to plead the defence of duress of circumstances because there was a threat of death or serious injury directed against the wife, provided D acted reasonably and proportionately in order to avoid the threat.

Ortiz (1986): Threats to family suffice

Facts
D, a Columbian, came to England with his wife and child on holiday. C asked D to courier drugs for him, threatening to cause serious harm to the wife and child if D did not agree to be a courier. D took possession of the drugs and was arrested when the police found them.

Decision
The Court of Appeal found that threats against D's wife and child would suffice for duress. Threats do not have to be solely directed at D.

12.1.5   The threat must be operative

Bell (1992): Offence stopped after threat ceased to be operative

Facts
D drove a car with excess alcohol in his bloodstream. He was being pursued. As a result, he ran over V. D was convicted of driving with excess alcohol, but appealed on the grounds that he should have been able to plead the defence of duress.

Decision

The Queen's Bench Divisional Court held that the defence of duress was made out where fear engendered by threats caused a person to lose complete control of his will. D was allowed the defence of duress of circumstances because he was in terror when he drove off in his car. Also, he had stopped driving as soon as he was safe from pursuit; so he had only committed the offence while the threat was operative.

DPP v Tomkinson (2001): No duress where offence continues after threat ceases to be operative

Facts

D was convicted of drink driving under s 5 of the Road Traffic Act 1988. She claimed that it had been necessary to commit the offence because she was in fear of physical attack from her husband and that her behaviour was reasonable in the circumstances. Her defence was successful but the prosecution appealed.

Decision

The Queen's Bench Divisional Court found that when D left the house she was not under any effective threat of violence. Further, she had driven 72 miles from her home and a considerable time had elapsed after the threat by the time she was arrested.

Davis (1994): Was D's reaction to the threat reasonable?

Facts

D was charged with driving with excess alcohol. He had been suffering stress and anxiety. He accepted an invitation for a meal with a male acquaintance. After the meal, he was subjected to an unwelcome homosexual advance by the acquaintance. He ran out of the flat and drove away. At the trial, the magistrates had applied a subjective test in deciding it was more likely than not that the events had caused D to lose control of his will. D was acquitted and the prosecution appealed.

Decision

The Queen's Bench Divisional Court held that, although the defence of duress was subjective, there were objective elements after the test laid down in *Graham* (1982) (see 12.1.2 above). The magistrates had overlooked the objective question of whether a reasonable sober person would have responded to the threats in the same way. Since D had only been in fear in the flat, he had not been in fear for his life or of serious injury, and the magistrates had not found that he was still in fear whilst driving two miles down the road before he was stopped. In these circumstances, had the magistrates applied an objective test, it would have been impossible to conclude that the threat, such as it was, was still operative when D was driving the car.

Pittaway (1994): Time elapsed between threat and crime

Facts

D had recently divorced her husband, who had been violent towards her. She formed a new relationship with P. After an argument at a party, she had an angry exchange of words with P, who issued threats towards her. D ran to her house, which was about 200 yards from the party, but hid in her car instead. After about five minutes, she drove about 200 yards before being stopped. P was not in the vicinity at the time that she drove the car. D was charged with driving with excess alcohol. She claimed that, after her marriage she was frightened of men and that, as a result of the threats issued by P, she feared immediate violence. She was acquitted and the prosecution appealed.

Decision
The Court of Appeal allowed the appeal. The magistrates had failed to apply the objective test, concentrating on the effect on D of a man behaving violently towards her. They had not considered whether there was good cause for her to fear immediate violence, and they had not considered whether the threat was still operative after five minutes of sitting in the car, unpursued by P. A conviction was ordered.

Cole (1994): Nexus between threat and crime must be established

Facts
D was charged with robbery. He pleaded the defence of duress, claiming that his inability to repay moneylenders had caused them to threaten him, hit him with a baseball bat and threaten his girlfriend and child. The trial judge directed the jury that duress was only available if the threats were directed at the commission of the offence charged, and the threat in this case related to a debt and not to the consequences of not committing a robbery. D changed his plea and appealed against conviction.

Decision
The Court of Appeal held that there were two distinct defences: duress by threats and duress of circumstances. The former applied when the person issuing the threat nominated the crime. D could not rely on this as the moneylenders had not forced D to commit the robbery to meet their demands. Regarding duress of circumstances, it was necessary to establish a nexus between the imminent peril and the criminal course of action. In this case, the imminent peril was lacking and the connection between the robbery and the consequences of not paying the moneylenders was not sufficiently proximate so that the threats were not operative.

12.1.6   *Where D places himself in a position open to threats*

Sharp (1987): Voluntary membership of a criminal gang negates defence

Facts
D joined a gang of robbers, knowing they used firearms. He participated in a robbery of a post office, but claimed that another member of the gang had threatened to kill him if he did not participate in the robbery.

Decision
The Court of Appeal held that:

> ... if a person can avoid the effects of duress by escaping from the threats without damage to himself, he must do so ... It seems to us part of the same argument ... to say that he must not voluntarily put himself in a position where he is likely to be subjected to such [threats] ... Where a person has voluntarily, and with knowledge of its nature, joined a criminal organisation or gang, he cannot avail himself of the defence of duress (*per* Lord Lane CJ).

Shepherd (1988): Whether D anticipated criminal activities by joining gang

Facts

D joined a gang of thieves. Their practice was to go into shops and, while one distracted the shopkeeper, the others would steal items from the shop. D claimed that, after the first offence, he wanted to give up, but he and his family had been threatened with violence if he did not carry on.

Decision

The Court of Appeal recognised the exclusion from the defence laid down in *Sharp* (see above), but were concerned with the breadth of the exclusion. The defence is still a concession to human frailty and D may have been faced with a choice between two evils. In some cases, there is no excuse. Members of paramilitary groups, gangs of armed robbers or thieves must be taken to anticipate what may happen to them if their nerve fails. The jury must ask themselves whether D could be said to have taken the risk of violence or threats simply by joining a gang, that is, did D appreciate the nature of the gang and the attitudes of those in charge of it, and then consider whether D had voluntarily submitted himself to threats.

Ali (1995): Anticipation of violence negates defence

Facts

D robbed a building society of £1,175, threatening cashiers with a gun. He was charged with robbery. At his trial he raised the defence of duress, claiming that he had been addicted to heroin. He had agreed to sell heroin on behalf of his violent dealer and hand the proceeds to him. He had, in fact, used the heroin himself. The dealer threatened to shoot him and, on the day before the robbery, had given D a gun and told him to commit a robbery to get the money or he would be killed. D was too scared to go to the police and so he carried out the robbery. The judge asked the jury to consider whether D had voluntarily placed himself in a position where he knew he would be open to being forced to commit crimes under threats from the dealer. D was convicted and appealed on the grounds that the judge should have phrased the question in terms of him knowing that the dealer would force him to commit armed robbery, as opposed to 'a crime'.

Decision

The Court of Appeal held that, if a defendant voluntarily participated in criminal offences with a person whom he knows to be violent and likely to require him to perform other criminal acts, he cannot rely on the defence of duress when the other person does so. The judge's direction had been clear. If D had had no reason to anticipate violence, he could rely on the defence. However, if he knew of a propensity to violence in those with whom he was working, then he could not rely on duress.

Heath (2000): Debt to drug dealer amounts to voluntary exposure to risk of threat

Facts

D was a heroin addict who owed his supplier £1,500. The supplier threatened D with violence but offered to discharge £1,000 of the debt if D agreed to take a consignment of cannabis to Bristol. D was arrested on his journey and charged with possession of a class B drug. D pleaded the defence of duress.

Decision

The Court of Appeal found that D could not rely on the defence of duress because, although he was not a member of a criminal gang, becoming indebted to a drug dealer he had voluntarily exposed himself to the risk of unlawful violence. Further, an avenue of escape was available to him by asking for police protection from the dealer. Any reasonable person in D's situation would have done so.

Harmer (2002): Debt to drug dealer amounts to voluntary exposure to risk of threat

Facts

D was stopped by customs officials having illegally imported quantities of cocaine into Dover. D was charged with importation of a class A drug. At trial D raised the defence of duress. He claimed he was addicted to cocaine and had incurred debts with his supplier who had threatened him with violence if he did not import the drugs.

Decision

The Court of Appeal found that D could not rely on the defence of duress. He had voluntarily become indebted to the supplier of drugs and therefore had exposed himself to unlawful violence.

12.1.7   Duress as a defence to murder

Lynch (1975): Secondary party to murder may plead duress

Facts

See 12.1 above.

Decision

The House of Lords held that it is open to a person charged with second degree murder to plead the defence of duress, although the defence is not available to the principal offender. There was a manifest difference between allowing an aider and abettor to do so. The principal chooses between saving his own life and taking another innocent life. However, an accessory decides to save his own life at a time when the loss of another life is not a certainty and the innocent life may be saved, or the principal may fail to kill him.

Abbott (1977): Principal in charge of murder cannot plead duress

Facts

D was ordered by M to kill a girl. He claimed that, if he had not obeyed, he feared his mother would be killed. D dug a hole for the girl's body and held her while another man stabbed her. She was left to die in the hole while D and the others filled it.

Decision

The Privy Council confirmed the rule that a principal in a charge of murder cannot plead the defence of duress. *Per* Lord Wilberforce, dissenting:

There is no let-out for any principal in the first degree, even if the duress be so dreadful as would be likely to wreck the morale of most men of reasonable courage and even were the duress directed not against the person threatened, but against other innocent people (in this case, the appellant's mother), so that considerations of mere self-preservation are not operative. That is indeed a blueprint for heroism.

Howe and Bannister (1987): Duress not available to any party to a charge of murder

Facts
See 12.1.1 above.

Decision
The House of Lords held that a defendant who sacrifices an innocent life to save their own is not justified in pleading duress and is a 'coward and a poltroon' (*per* Lord Hailsham). There is no firm basis on which to base a distinction between principals and accessories in a charge of murder. Therefore, duress should not be available to a charge of any degree of murder.

Gotts (1992): Duress no defence to attempted murder

Facts
D, aged 16, had been ordered by his father to kill his mother (who was separated from the father). D claimed that, if he did not kill his mother, his father had threatened to shoot him. D stabbed his mother in the street, but was restrained by a passer-by from inflicting any further injuries and, although seriously injured, the mother survived. D was convicted of attempted murder.

Decision
The House of Lords ruled that the defence of duress is not available to the charge of attempted murder. There is no justification in law or morality or logic to afford defence to an attempted murderer and not to a murderer. Indeed, the intent required for attempted murder is greater than that for murder, and it is pure chance that D was charged with a murder which was attempted and not actual.

12.2 Necessity and duress of circumstances

Dudley and Stevens (1884): Necessity is no defence

Facts
Two defendants and a cabin boy were cast away at sea in an open boat, 1,600 miles from land. They drifted in the boat for 20 days. When they had gone eight days without food and six days without water, and fearing that they would all soon die, the Ds killed the cabin boy, whom they judged as most likely to die first, and they ate his flesh and drank his blood for four days. They were then rescued by a passing ship. The Ds were convicted of murder, but they claimed killing the cabin boy was necessary for their survival and that the cabin boy would have died anyway.

Decision
The Queen's Bench Divisional Court found that in this case necessity was no defence. *Per* Lord Coleridge CJ: '... a man has no right to declare temptation to be an excuse ...

nor allow compassion for the criminal to change or weaken in any manner the legal definition of the crime.' As tough as this decision was, necessity is no defence in English law. However, the death penalty passed on both defendants at trial was commuted to six months' imprisonment.

O'Toole (1971): Public interest requires no defence of necessity

Facts
D was an ambulance driver. Answering an emergency call, he drove in excess of the speed limit (which did not apply to ambulances driving to an emergency). D collided with a car and was convicted of dangerous driving. D was disqualified from driving and appealed against sentence.

Decision
The Court of Appeal found that necessity was no defence in this case. *Per* Sachs LJ:

> ... courts must recognise that a balance must be maintained in the interest of the public between the essential element of not unnecessarily impeding the answering of calls of humanity in emergencies, and that of not involving road users in unnecessary risks. Great care has to be applied in determining on which side of the line a case falls.

The sentence was reduced to an absolute discharge.

Woods v Richards (1977): Necessity no defence to police officers in road traffic offences

Facts
D was a police driver. He answered an emergency call but got stuck in a queue so he pulled over to the hard shoulder, which he intended to use thinking it was clear. He collided with a broken-down vehicle there and caused damage. D was convicted of driving without due care and attention and was sentenced as any other driver would have been.

Decision
The Queen's Bench Divisional Court found that necessity was no defence in this case. No authority supported the contention that a special standard was to be adopted for police drivers, and nothing in the wording of s 3 of the Road Traffic Act 1972 enabled an exception to be made in the case of a police driver. Whether the defence of necessity existed depended on the degree of emergency or alternative danger to be averted. Natural sympathy with police drivers did not enable the court to re-write the requirements of the offence.

Southwark LBC v Williams (1971): To allow defence of necessity would open floodgates

Facts
The defendants, who were homeless, entered an empty house owned by the local authority and squatted there. They were sued for trespass.

Decision
The Court of Appeal held that:

If homelessness were once admitted as a defence to trespass, no one's house could be safe. Necessity would open a door which no man could shut. It would not only be those in extreme need who would enter. There would be others who would imagine that they were in need or would invent a need so as to gain entry.

Per Edmund-Davies LJ: 'It appears that all the cases where a plea of necessity has succeeded are cases which deal with an urgent situation of imminent peril'.

Martin (1989): Necessity is a defence where there is duress of circumstances

Facts
See 12.1.4 above.

Decision
The Court of Appeal held that:

English law does, in extreme circumstances, recognise a defence of necessity. Most commonly, this arises as duress, that is, pressure on the accused's will from the wrongful threats or violence of another. Equally, however, it can arise from other objective dangers threatening the accused or others. Arising thus, it is conveniently called 'duress of circumstances' (*per* Simon Brown J).

Willer (1986): Defence of duress of circumstances exists in English law

Facts
D was convicted of reckless driving. He had driven slowly on the pavement in order to escape from a gang of youths, who intended to use violence on him. D claimed the defence of necessity, but the trial judge ruled that it was not available, so D changed his plea to guilty.

Decision
The Court of Appeal held that, regardless of whether necessity had been established or was available, the defence of duress of circumstances was applicable while the threat existed and should have been left to the jury.

Conway (1988): Duress of circumstances threatening death or serious injury
See 12.1.4 above.

Cichon v DPP (1994): Difference between defences of necessity and duress

Facts
D owned a pit bull terrier, which he took out into a public place without a muzzle because it had kennel cough and it would be cruel to muzzle a coughing dog. He was convicted of an offence under the Dangerous Dogs Act 1991 having been denied the defence of necessity.

Decision
The Queen's Bench Divisional Court held that there was a distinction between the defence of duress, where D's will was overborne, and necessity, where D's freely

adopted conduct was justified. The question in this case was whether the defence of necessity was available to D where he could show that he broke the law to avoid serious harm to the dog. The 1991 Act was introduced to protect the public and it did not allow a person to make a value judgment between what was good for the dog and what was good for the public. Therefore, the statute itself denied the defence to D.

Harris (1994): Duress of circumstances only available in exceptional cases

Facts
D, a police officer, was driving a car for police purposes and failed to stop at a red traffic light. He was covertly following another car which he believed to contain persons planning to carry out an armed robbery. He was therefore in an unmarked car and failed to stop at the red light in order to maintain contact with the other car. He collided with another car. He pleaded necessity to a charge of driving without due care and attention.

Decision
The Queen's Bench Divisional Court found that D could not rely on the defence of necessity. The defence of duress of circumstances may be available to a charge of reckless driving, but the present offence, which required D merely to wait a few seconds at the junction and edge forward carefully, could not attract the defence. The defence would only arise in exceptional cases where D had acted reasonably and proportionately to the necessity of the situation.

Pommell (1995): Defence not available where D could have desisted from committing the offence

Facts
D was convicted under the Firearms Act 1968 of possessing a prohibited weapon and ammunition without a firearms certificate. He pleaded necessity as a defence, on the ground that, the night before he had taken the gun away from someone who was threatening to shoot some other people. He had intended to take the gun to the police that day. At his trial the judge had denied him the defence on the ground that he had not gone immediately to the police.

Decision
The Court of Appeal held that the principle behind the defence of duress (or duress of circumstances) was to allow, in some situations, someone to disobey the letter of the law to prevent 'a greater evil befalling himself'. This does not apply where D commendably breaks the law in order to prevent another from committing the 'greater evil'. In order to plead the defence of duress of circumstances, he should have 'desisted from committing the crime as soon as he reasonably [could]' (*per* Kennedy LJ). Although all cases on the defence of necessity had so far concerned road traffic offences, there is no reason why, being closely related to the defence of duress, the defence should not be available in relation to all crimes except murder and attempted murder.

Rogers (1998): Objective test in *Graham* must be applied

Facts

D had an argument with his wife, who ran to a neighbour. D feared the neighbour would attack him, although the neighbour had no history of violence. D drove his car with excess alcohol and was stopped by the police. D raised the defence of necessity and was acquitted. The prosecution appealed, raising the question of whether the defence could be pleaded where there was no direct threat of violence towards D.

Decision

The Queen's Bench Divisional Court held that this was another case where, at trial, the objective test laid down in *Graham* (see 12.1.2 above) had not been applied. The magistrates in this case had not asked whether it was reasonable for D to act in the way that he did in those circumstances. *Per curiam*, the difficulties which had arisen in cases where magistrates had not applied the objective test could be attributed to the fact that the parameters and requirements of this defence had not been set out clearly in statutory form. Instead, they had had to plough through copious case law. The magistrates in this case had not had the benefit of seeing the judgment in *Baker and Wilkins* (below), which set the law out clearly. The court called for the codification of the defence as soon as possible.

Baker and Wilkins (1997): Threat of psychological injury not sufficient

Facts

B and W had had a relationship, during which they had a child. After their separation, W was given access to the child for short visits. On one occasion, W did not return the child, fearing that it had been abused. W told B that he was going to run away with the child. D went to W's house and, on hearing the child crying, broke in through the door. D was charged with criminal damage. D claimed the defence of necessity in the light of the refusal to return the child and the threat to run away with it. D was denied the defence at trial because there was no immediate risk of death or serious injury.

Decision

The Court of Appeal found that the defence was not available, as there was no risk of immediate death or physical injury. The need to avoid serious psychological injury was not accepted as a sufficient threat.

Rodgers (1998): Threat of D's own suicide not sufficient

Facts

D was convicted of escaping from prison. He had previously been convicted of murder and was serving a life sentence. He had just been informed that the tariff of his sentence was going to be increased, as a result of which he became depressed and suicidal. D claimed that had he not escaped from prison he would have committed suicide. The trial judge did not allow him to plead the defence of duress of circumstances.

Decision

The Court of Appeal ruled that the defence of duress of circumstances was only available where the circumstances causing the duress were external to D. In this case, it was only D's subjective thought processes and emotions which operated as the duress. It is contrary to the public interest to extend the defence that far.

Cairns (1999): Threat need not be real or actual

Facts

D was driving his car late at night when V climbed on the bonnet and laid there with his face up against the windscreen. D was frightened, but thought it was best to drive on. D claimed he had also been frightened by friends of V who, in order to try and stop him from lying on the car, followed D, shouting and gesturing. D drove on for a significant distance before V fell off the car, and D drove over him. V fractured his spine and was paralysed. D was charged with s 20 of the Offences Against the Person Act 1861, but raised the defence of necessity. The judge directed the jury that the defence was only available where D's action was 'actually necessary to avoid the evil in question'. D was convicted and appealed.

Decision

The Court of Appeal held that the jury should be concerned with D's perception of the threat which he faced, and to consider whether his actions were reasonable and proportionate in the circumstances. They did not have to consider whether the threat was real or actual. Therefore, the judge had wrongly directed the jury.

Re A (Children) (Conjoined Twins: Surgical Separation) (2001): Conjoined twin threatens life of other twin

See 1.1.1 above.

CHAPTER 13

CAUSATION

Introduction

For some offences it is a necessary element of the *actus reus* that the defendant caused a particular result. In these result crimes it is not always a straightforward assessment as to whether it was the defendant's conduct that caused the result, especially where, in a chain of events, the actions of other individuals or other circumstances intervene and contribute to the result. In establishing legal causation (that is, causation sufficient to render the defendant criminally liable for the result) an intervening act which breaks the chain of causation (a *novus actus interveniens*) will negate the defendant's liability, since it may be said that the intervening event or act legally caused the result and not the defendant. Not all intervening acts will break the chain of legal causation since the defendant's actions need only be a significant causal factor, not the only or last causal factor.

The case law in this area identifies two types of intervening act which may be said to break the chain of causation. The first type is where the victim of the offence does something in response to the defendant's actions which causes injury or death to themselves. For example, where the victim seeks to escape from the defendant and jumps out of a moving car, in a factual sense they may be said to have caused their own death through their actions. The courts are unlikely to view such behaviour by an innocent victim frightened by the defendant as a factor which breaks the chain of legal causation unless the victim behaved in a way which was wholly unexpected or unforeseeable by the defendant. Furthermore, the defendant must take his victim as he finds him (the 'thin skull rule') so that if the victim has a physical or emotional weakness which makes them more susceptible to injury, the defendant cannot claim that he did not intend or foresee the degree of harm he actually caused. This rule also applies where the victim refuses medical treatment on religious or other grounds (*Blaue* (1975)).

The second group of cases involve the situation where a new event intervenes in the factual chain of causation after the defendant's initial actions. This may be the intervention of medical practitioners in treating the victim's injuries or some other unexpected event. The courts have been reluctant to allow the actions of a medical practitioner to break the legal chain of causation (*Malcherek* (1981); *Cheshire* (1991)) unless the actions of the medical practitioners are highly negligent or 'palpably wrong' (*Jordan* (1956)). Where they are, the defendant's actions may not have been serious enough to cause the death of the victim, but rather the negligent medical treatment did so. In the case of intervening events, where a catalogue of tragic events occur, possibly unforeseen by the defendant, and factually cause the end result of the crime, the courts have preferred to take the view that the defendant's initial act 'continued' throughout these events and therefore liability can be established (*Miller* (1983); *Le Brun* (1991)).

13.1   Factual causation

13.1.1   Lack of factual connection vitiates actus reus

White (1910): No offence of murder where D did not cause death

Facts

D intentionally put cyanide of potassium into V's drink of nectar, but V died of a heart attack before drinking all of the poison, which was of insufficient quantity to cause death regardless.

Decision

The Court of Appeal found D not guilty of murder:

(1)   D did not cause V's death; therefore, no *actus reus* and no murder.
(2)   D was guilty of attempted murder.

13.2   Legal causation

13.2.1   Legal causation as sine qua non

Cato (1976): Possession of heroin causes death

See 3.1.2 above.

Pagett (1983): D's act need not be the sole cause

Facts

D shot at the police and used V's body as a human shield from police gunfire. V died from wounds sustained by three bullets fired by police. D was charged with manslaughter.

Decision

The Court of Appeal found D guilty of manslaughter, having caused V's death. *Per* Goff LJ:

> [1] [D's] act need not be the sole cause, or even the main cause, of the victim's death, it being enough that his act contributed significantly to that result. [2] ... a reasonable act performed [by V] for the purpose of self-preservation, being of course itself an act caused by [D]'s own act, does not operate as a *novus actus interveniens*.

Cheshire (1991): D's actions a significant cause

Facts

D shot V in the leg and stomach. Two months later, after the wound was no longer life threatening, a rare complication developed through medical mistreatment of the tube inserted in V's throat, and V choked to death.

Decision

The Court of Appeal found D guilty of murder:

(1)   'Even though negligence in the treatment of [V] was the immediate cause of his death, [exculpation follows only if] ... they regard the contribution made by [D's] acts as insignificant' (*per* Beldam LJ).

(2)   Where medical treatment seeks to repair harm done by D's acts, 'it will only be in the most extraordinary and unusual case that such treatment' will amount to a *novus actus interveniens.*

AG's Reference (No 3 of 1994) (1997): Foetus part of mother for causation purposes

See 1.1.1 above.

Kennedy (1998): Joint cause of death

See 3.1.2 above.

Commissioners of Police for the Metropolis v Reeves (1999): Contributory negligence and causation

Facts

V was held in custody, attempting to hang himself twice. The same day as a previous attempt, V hung and killed himself with his shirt through cell bars, having been left unsupervised for a few minutes.

Decision

The House of Lords found the defendant to be contributorily negligent, having breached his duty of care:

(1)   '... given the admitted breach of duty of care, the defence of *novus actus interveniens* cannot assist the commissioner. The deceased's suicide was the precise event to which the duty was directed and, as an *actus*, it was accordingly neither *novus* nor *interveniens*' (*per* Lord Jauncey). Accordingly, nor does a defence of *volenti non fit injuria* succeed.

(2)   V's 'voluntary choice was the cause of his loss ... To qualify as an autonomous choice, the choice made must be free and unconstrained – that is, voluntary, deliberate and informed. If the plaintiff is under a disability, either through lack of mental capacity or lack or excess of age, the plaintiff will lack autonomy and will not have made a free and unconstrained choice' (*per* Lord Hobhouse).

(3)   'The act of the deceased was accordingly a substantial cause of his own demise and any damages recoverable by the plaintiff should be reduced to reflect this [viz, 50/50]' (*per* Lord Hoffmann).

13.3   Novus actus interveniens

13.3.1   Innocent intervention

Michael (1840): Actions of 'unconscious agent' do not break chain of causation

Facts

D gave his child's nurse a large dose of laudanum to administer to the child, saying that it was medicine. Although the nurse left the dosage untouched on her mantelpiece, the laudanum was retrieved by the nurse's five year old child, and fatally administered to D's child.

Decision

The Crown Court found D guilty of murder. D caused the child's death, intentionally achieving the result of murder, albeit through 'an unconscious agent', rather than through an innocent adult as originally planned.

Commissioners of Police for the Metropolis v Reeves (1999): Contributory negligence and causation

See 13.2.1 above.

13.3.2 Involuntary and justified self-preservation

Roberts (1971): Reasonably foreseeable behaviour by V

See 4.3.2 above.

Daley (1979): Reasonably foreseeable behaviour by V

Facts

D threw stones at V, who fled, tripped and was killed by the fall.

Decision

The Privy Council found D guilty of manslaughter. Where injuries are sustained as a result of an escape occasioned by fear that was caused by D, and reasonably foreseeable, D will be said to have caused the result.

Williams and Davis (1992): Proportionality between D's threat and V's actions

Facts

V was picked up as a hitchhiker by driver A and passenger D. V was told to hand over his money, but jumped out of the car travelling at 30 mph, eventually dying of head injuries.

Decision

The Court of Appeal found W and D not guilty of manslaughter. In determining foreseeability, the nature of D's threat must be proportionate to the resulting action of V. *Per* Stuart-Smith LJ:

> The jury should consider two questions: first, whether it was reasonably foreseeable that some harm, albeit not serious harm, was likely to result from the threat itself; and, secondly, whether the deceased's reaction in jumping from the moving car was within the range of responses which might be expected from a victim placed in his situation. The jury should bear in mind any particular characteristic of the victim and the fact that, in the agony of the moment, he might act without thought and deliberation.

Pagett (1983): D's act need not be the sole cause

See 13.2.1 above.

PD (1996): Civil law principles of causation do not apply in criminal law

Facts

D and V were drinking companions. D accused V of molesting D's child. V was slashed by D, who later dressed the cuts. V died two days later, but may have intentionally opened the wounds or failed to staunch the blood from the wounds, apparently leaving a suicide note.

Decision

The Court of Appeal found D guilty of murder. Civil law principles of causation should not be imported into the criminal law. Criminal causation should be determined by asking 'Were the injuries inflicted by the defendant an operating and significant cause of death?' (*per* Rose LJ).

M (Richard) (A Juvenile) (2000): Test for causation is objective

Facts

D (who was aged 16) was among a group of people who broke into V's room. V jumped out of the window and was seriously injured. D was convicted of causing grievous bodily harm and appealed on the grounds that the trial judge had failed to direct the jury appropriately on whether D foresaw the risk of V acting in the way she did.

Decision

The Court of Appeal ruled that the test for causation is objective – would the reasonable man (as defined in *DPP v Camplin*) have foreseen V's conduct as a natural result of D's actions? Subjective foresight in this case would only have been relevant to the *mens rea* of the offence, not the issue of causation.

13.3.3   Medical treatment

Jordan (1956): 'Palpably wrong' medical treatment caused death

Facts

D stabbed V, who died eight days later in hospital. At the time of death, the wound had almost healed. V's medical treatment included a second dose of a drug to which V was evidently intolerant, and intravenous doses of liquid which waterlogged V's lungs.

Decision

The Court of Appeal found D was not guilty of murder. The medical treatment was 'palpably wrong' (*per* Hallett J), and would have 'precluded' a jury from holding that death was caused by D's action.

Smith (1959): Original wound still an operating cause of death

Facts

During a fight, D twice stabbed V, piercing V's lung and causing a haemorrhage. V was dropped twice by a third party carrying V to the medical station, where doctors treated him unaware of the haemorrhage, and performed artificial respiration. V died within two hours of the stabbing.

Decision

The Court of Appeal found D guilty of murder. *Per* Lord Parker CJ: '… if, at the time of death, the original wound is still an operating cause and a substantial cause', then death resulted from the wound, 'albeit that some other cause of death is also operating'. Only where 'the original wounding is merely the setting in which another cause operates' does death not result from the wound. 'Only if the second cause is so overwhelming as to make the original wound merely part of the history' does a *novus actus interveniens* arise.

Malcherek (1981): Discontinuance of treatment

Facts

D stabbed V, causing a critical abdominal wound. V was put on a life support machine, which was subsequently switched off after doctors decided that brain death had occurred, albeit without complying with standard criteria for establishing brain death.

Decision

The Court of Appeal found D guilty of murder. *Per* Lord Lane CJ: the 'discontinuance of treatment', such as mechanical life support, 'does not break the chain of causation between the initial injury and the death'. The evidence established that the original wound was the 'continuing, operating and indeed substantial cause' of V's death, although 'it need not be substantial to render the assailant guilty'.

Comment

The court held, *obiter*, that it preferred the decision in *Smith* (above) to that of *Jordan* (above), the latter being 'a very exceptional case'.

Cheshire (1991): Medical treatment not a significant cause

See 13.2.1 above.

Airedale NHS Trust v Bland (1993): Withholding of treatment causing death is lawful

Facts

B existed in a persistent vegetative state (PVS), requiring ventilation, nutrition and hydration by artificial means. B never consented to the termination of such artificial means by the hospital, which would cause death. The hospital sought a judicial reference as to liability.

Decision

The House of Lords argued that it was not unlawful for doctors to withdraw life supporting medical treatment, including artificial feeding through a nasogastric tube, from a patient in a PVS who had no prospect of any recovery, notwithstanding that such discontinuance would cause the patient's death within a matter of weeks. *Per* Lord Goff, withdrawal of treatment causing death:

> ... may be lawful, either because the doctor is giving effect to his patient's wishes by withholding the treatment or care, or even, in certain circumstances, in which (on principles [enumerated below]) the patient is incapacitated from stating whether or not he gives his consent. But it is not lawful for a doctor to administer a drug to his patient to bring about his death, even though that course is prompted by a humanitarian desire to end his suffering, however great that suffering may be.

Four safeguards guide a lawful withdrawal of treatment:

(1) Every effort should be made at rehabilitation for at least six months after the injury.

(2) The diagnosis of irreversible PVS should not be considered confirmed until at least 12 months after the injury, with the effect that any decision to withhold life-prolonging treatment will be delayed for that period.

(3) The diagnosis should be agreed by two other independent doctors.

(4) Generally, the wishes of the patient's immediate family will be given great weight.

13.3.4 Refusal to accept medical treatment

Blaue (1975): D takes V as he finds him

Facts

D stabbed V, who thereby required but refused a blood transfusion, which V was told would permit recovery, by reason of her religious beliefs as a Jehovah's Witness.

Decision

The Court of Appeal found D guilty of manslaughter. *Per* Lawton LJ: '... those who use violence on other people must take their victims as they find them.' Thus, V's refusal of a blood transfusion did not break the causal connection between D's act and V's death.

Comment

The principle applied is referred to as the 'thin skull' rule.

13.4 Contemporaneity

13.4.1 Contemporaneity applies to actions as a whole

Thabo Meli v R (1954): Causation established over a series of acts

Facts

D1 and D2 conspired to murder V, eventually striking V over the head. Believing V dead, they rolled his body over a cliff, after which V died of exposure while unconscious.

Decision

The Privy Council found D1 and D2 guilty of murder. Their actions were indivisible, belonging to a single series of acts which culminated in V's death and therefore not requiring contemporaneity between *actus reus* and *mens rea* at every moment of the chain of events resulting in the death of V.

Comment

The principle of contemporaneity requires that the *actus reus* and *mens rea* must coincide temporarily to incur criminal liability.

Church (1965): Causation through a series of acts

See 3.1.3 above.

Miller (1983): Causation through a 'continuous act'

Facts

D, a squatter, lit a cigarette and fell asleep on a mattress, which caught fire. Awaking to the fire, D went to the next room and fell asleep. The house was damaged by fire and D was charged with arson.

Decision

The House of Lords found D guilty of arson in breaching his duty to prevent further damage caused by his accidental actions. *Per* Lord Diplock, the events commencing with D's dropping of the cigarette and ceasing when the damage by fire was complete amounted to a 'continuous act' of D.

Le Brun (1991): Causation established where lapse of time between D's actions and death

Facts

D was walking with his wife; the two argued. D struck her on the chin and dragged her along the pavement to avoid detection, during which time her head struck the pavement and she later died.

Decision

The Court of Appeal found D guilty of manslaughter. Where the unlawful application of force and the eventual act causing death were part of the same sequence of events, the fact that there was an appreciable interval of time between the two did not serve to exonerate the appellant from liability. The act which caused death and the necessary mental state to constitute manslaughter need not coincide in point of time.

PD (1996): Civil law principles do not apply in a criminal case

See 13.3.2 above.

CHAPTER 14

COMPLICITY

Introduction

This chapter covers the development of the law relating to the criminal liability of secondary parties (or accomplices) to an offence. Whilst a defendant may not actually perform that act which results in the criminal offence charged, they may have participated in the offence to an extent great enough to afford them liability for it. The general rule is that secondary parties to a crime can be liable to the same degree as the principal offender (the person who actually commits the acts required for the substantive offence) and may be punished to the same degree, whether or not this appropriately reflects the extent of their contribution to it. Indeed, *Concannon* (2002) mounted a challenge to this rule under the Human Rights Act 1998, claiming that it breached his right to a fair trial under Art 6 of the European Convention on Human Rights. The Court of Appeal were dismissive of the challenge though, on the basis that Art 6 allows a defendant to complain of procedural unfairness in English law, but not to complain of unfairness resulting from the substantive criminal law.

Accomplices may contribute to a criminal offence in a number of ways. They may aid and abet an offence; that is, provide some assistance to the principal offender, encourage the offender or procure the offence (that is, facilitate its commission). Presence at the scene of the crime is not necessary but mere presence without any form of encouragement (such as innocently witnessing a crime taking place) will not result in liability (*Clarkson and Carroll* (1971)). Liability as a secondary party commonly arises in the cases where a group of defendants embark on a joint unlawful enterprise. The courts have had to balance the need to prevent group criminality as a matter of policy on the one hand with the need not to extend liability to a defendant who is marginally involved in the offence on the other. This is particularly so where the principal offender commits an act which the defendant argues was not part of the original enterprise. The courts have developed the *mens rea* of complicity to deal with this situation, so that if the defendant could have foreseen the principal's actions happening as part of the joint enterprise, then he will be liable (*Powell and English* (1997)).

A defendant may escape liability as a secondary party if he withdraws from participation of the crime at any point during its commission. However, the courts have asserted that it is not enough to silently make the decision to withdraw, he must communicate that with the other parties to the crime (*Becerra* (1975)).

14.1   General

14.1.1   Defining 'aiding, abetting, counselling or procuring'

AG's Reference (No 1 of 1975) (1975): Meaning of procure

Facts

A surreptitiously laced D's drinks with double measures of spirits, knowing that D would be driving home. D drove with an excess quantity of alcohol in his body and was thereby criminally liable.

Decision

The Court of Appeal held that A need not share an intention with D to commit the offence, nor positively encourage D, for A to be liable for procuring an offence:

(1)   The words 'aid, abet, counsel or procure' (*per* Lord Widgery CJ), under s 8 of the Accessories and Abettors Act 1861, should be given their ordinary meaning.

(2)   Aiding, abetting, or counselling almost inevitably involves a meeting of the minds of principal and secondary offender(s).

(3)   Procuring need not involve a meeting of the minds. 'To procure means to produce by endeavour.'

Comment

Under the common law, 'principal' refers to the person committing the derivative offence; 'accessory' refers to the person aiding, abetting, counselling or procuring the 'principal' in the commission of the offence.

Blakely and Sutton v DPP (1991): Procuring recklessly

Facts

B and S laced D's drink with vodka in order to preclude D from driving home, since B and S thought D would not knowingly drive with an excess of alcohol. However, D left before they could inform him of the lacing.

Decision

The Court of Appeal found B and S not guilty of procuring the offence:

(1)   The use of the word 'recklessness' is best avoided when considering the *mens rea* of a procuring offence.

(2)   Procuring an offence cannot be committed by inadvertent recklessness, but by 'contemplat[ing] that his act would or might bring about or assist the commission of the principal offence; he must have been prepared, nevertheless, to do his own act, and he must have done that act intentionally' (*per* McCullough J). *Per* Bingham LJ: '... procure is understood as importing the notion of intention or at least willing acceptance of a contemplated result.'

14.2   Minimal conduct

14.2.1   Presence at crime irrelevant

Howe (1987): All parties carry the same liability for the offence

Facts

H and B, together with others, tortured and sexually assaulted Z, who was eventually strangled to death. The events were repeated on a second occasion, except this time, H and B themselves strangled V to death with a shoelace. They claimed duress as a defence to both the first killing as accessories and the second killing as principals, on the basis that M controlled their actions.

Decision

The House of Lords found H and B guilty of murder:

(1) Presence at the scene of the crime is irrelevant as to establishing complicity to an offence.

(2) 'Where a person has been killed and that result is the result intended by another participant, the mere fact that the actual killer may be convicted only of the reduced charge of manslaughter for some reason special to himself does not ... result in the compulsory reduction for the other participant' (per Lord MacKay).

(3) For a charge of murder, the defence of duress is not available to either principal or accessory.

Clarkson and Carroll (1971): Mere presence without encouragement is not an offence

Facts

D1 and D2 heard a woman being raped in another room in their military barracks, entered that room and remained there.

Decision

The Court of Appeal found D1 and D2 not guilty of aiding and abetting rape:

(1) Mere presence at the scene of an offence and failure to intervene is not ipso facto sufficient for liability as an aider and abettor.

(2) Per Megaw LJ: 'It must be proven that [D] intended to give encouragement; that he wilfully encouraged [it] ... and there must also be encouragement in fact ...'

Allan (1963): Silent presence without encouragement no offence

Facts

D was present at the scene of an affray. Though totally passive, D silently nursed the intention to join the affray if his favoured side so required.

Decision

The Court of Appeal found D not guilty of making an affray without evidence of encouragement. Per Edmund-Davies J: 'As Cave J said in Coney (1882), "Where presence is prima facie not accidental, it is evidence, but no more than evidence, for the jury", and it remains no more than evidence for the jury, even when one adds to presence at an affray a secret intention to help.'

Wilcox v Jeffery (1951): 'Knowing' presence amounts to encouragement

Facts

D was forbidden by statute to work in the UK. C was in the audience at a concert given by D, having met D earlier at the airport and later written a favourable review of the performance in C's magazine.

Decision

The Court of Appeal found C guilty of aiding and abetting D's contravention of immigration laws. Knowing D to be contravening the law, C's presence amounted to encouragement.

14.2.2 Derivative or participative liability?

Bourne (1952): Participation under threat results in liability

Facts
D terrorised his wife into submitting to buggery with a dog. D was not present at the time of the act.

Decision
The Court of Appeal found D guilty of aiding and abetting bestiality. Though the wife could have set up a plea of duress, it did not follow that 'no offence had been committed'; rather, she lacked *mens rea* due to threats (*per* Lord Goddard CJ).

Cogan and Leak (1976): Secondary liability where principal acquitted

Facts
L terrorised his wife into submitting to sexual intercourse with C, who believed she was consenting.

Decision
The Court of Appeal found C not guilty of rape; L was guilty of procuring rape. *Per* Lawton LJ: '... the act of sexual intercourse without the wife's consent was the *actus reus*; it had been procured by L, who had the appropriate *mens rea*, namely his intention that C should have sexual intercourse with her without her consent.'

Chan Wing-Siu (1984): Foresight by secondary party

Facts
Three men went to V's flat to commit a robbery, armed with knives. V was stabbed to death.

Decision
The Privy Council found all three defendants were guilty of murder. *Per* Sir Robin Cooke: '... a secondary party is criminally liable for acts by the primary offender of a type which the former foresees, but does not necessarily intend. The criminal culpability lies in participating in the venture with that foresight.'

Millward (1994): Procuring as 'causing' principal offence

Facts
D sent an employee out in a tractor with a defective trailer, resulting in an accident and the death of another motorist.

Decision
The Court of Appeal found D guilty of procuring the offence of causing death by reckless driving. *Per* Scott Baker J: '[D] caused [the employee] to drive that vehicle in that condition, just as Leak had caused Cogan to have sexual intercourse with his wife.' (See *Cogan and Leak* above.)

Wan and Chan (1994): Foresight of events beyond scope of agreement

Facts
W and C believed that V had stolen C's valuable watch, and allegedly arranged for V to be assaulted. V was badly beaten up.

Decision
The Court of Appeal found W and C not guilty of procuring the infliction of grievous bodily harm. The attackers went beyond the scope of what W and C had asked them to do, and the jury never considered whether W and C had foreseen that the infliction of grievous bodily harm by the attackers was a substantial risk, as *per Chan Wing-Siu* (above).

Powell and English (1997): Foresight in a joint unlawful enterprise

Facts
Powell: A, B and C went to purchase drugs from a dealer, V, at his house. V was shot dead. The Crown could not prove which of the three men fired the gun, but all three knew that someone (Powell) was armed.

English: D and E were assaulting a police officer with a wooden post, when E (English) stabbed and killed the officer.

Decision
The House of Lords found A and B guilty of murder; D was not guilty of murder. *Per* Lord Hutton:

> [1] ... where two parties embark on a joint enterprise to commit a crime, and one party foresees that, in the course of the enterprise, the other party may carry out, with the requisite *mens rea*, an act constituting another crime, the former is liable for that crime if committed by the latter in the course of the enterprise. [2] ... it is sufficient to found a conviction for murder for a secondary party to have realised that, in the course of the joint enterprise, the primary party might kill with intent to do so or with intent to cause grievous bodily harm.

If the jury considered that E's use of the knife was not foreseen by D, then D is not guilty of murder. 'As the unforeseen use of the knife would take the killing outside the scope of the joint venture, the jury should also have been directed ... that [D] should not be found guilty of manslaughter.'

Comment
Per Lord Steyn (Lord Mustill concurring): '... the legislature [should] undertake reform ... namely, that a killing should be classified as murder if there is an intention to kill or an intention to cause really serious bodily harm, coupled with awareness of the risk of death.'

Reardon (1999): Reasonable foresight of principal's actions

Facts
D was in a bar with others, one of whom (M) shot two people. V1 died instantly, but V2 did not. The bodies were dragged outside, but when M realised that V2 was still

alive, he asked D to lend him a knife. M then went outside and fatally stabbed V2. D was charged with the murder of both victims. D was convicted after the jury were directed that, if D handed over the knife realising or contemplating that M would kill or cause really serious injury, then D was responsible for the consequences and, if M had killed two people, then D would be guilty of both murders. D appealed, claiming that what M did with the knife was outside his contemplation and therefore not part of any common purpose between D and M.

Decision

The Court of Appeal held that the test to be applied was whether when D handed the knife over to M, he could reasonably foresee acts of the type that D did in fact carry out. It was clear in this case that, whichever victim M stabbed first, the fatal stabbing of at least V2 was contemplated by D when he handed over the knife. D must have realised that, if V1 was found still breathing, M would have fatally stabbed him too. Therefore, M's act was one foreseen by D, even if he did not intend the knife be used in that way.

Uddin (1999): Actions outside scope of joint unlawful enterprise

Facts

After a road rage incident, V got out of his car and was confronted by four youths. The youths began attacking V. Later, two other youths joined the group and a witness saw six youths attacking, some using billiard cues as weapons. Eventually, the youths ran off. V died three days later from his injuries, the most serious of which was a stab wound near the base of the skull. D, one of the youths, was convicted of murder, but appealed, claiming that he had not foreseen the use of a knife as a possibility in the joint enterprise.

Decision

The Court of Appeal held that where several persons join to attack a victim in circumstances which show that they intend to inflict serious harm and, as a result of the attack, V sustains fatal injury, they are jointly liable for murder. However, if such injury, inflicted with that intent, is shown to have been caused solely by the actions of one participant (of a type entirely different from actions which the others foresaw as part of the attack), then only that participant is guilty of murder.

In deciding whether actions are of such a different type, the use by that party of a weapon is a significant factor. If the character of that weapon (that is, its propensity to cause death) is different from any weapon used or contemplated by the others, and if it is used with specific intent to kill, the others are not responsible for the death unless it is proved that they foresaw the likelihood of such a weapon being used. If others in the joint enterprise use a weapon which could be regarded as equally likely to inflict a fatal injury, the mere fact that a different weapon is used is immaterial.

Gilmour (2000): Acts beyond contemplation of joint unlawful enterprise

Facts

A petrol bomb was thrown into a house where six people were sleeping. A fire broke out and three of the occupants of the house were killed. D was charged with murder, and at the trial the judge found that D knew the house was occupied and was going to be petrol bombed by the two others, even though D himself merely sat in a car at the scene in order to drive the others away. The judge also found that D was aware of the intent of the others to cause grievous bodily harm to the people in the house. D was convicted of murder and appealed.

Decision

The Court of Appeal held that to establish that D was an accessory to a crime of specific intent, it is necessary to prove that he realised the principal's intentions. Where the principal departed from the contemplated joint enterprise and perpetrated a more serious act of a kind not foreseen by the accessory, then the accessory is not liable for the unforeseen acts. In this case, the principal carried out the very act contemplated by both parties and therefore the secondary party is also guilty of murder.

Concannon (2002): Secondary liability for offence and Art 6 of the European Convention on Human Rights

Facts

D and another went to V's flat. D had suggested that they should rob V. On arrival at the flat, the door was open so they went in. D asked V for money for drugs and punched V. The co-accused stabbed V to death. D claimed he was not present when the stabbing occurred and did not know that the co-accused had a knife. The judge directed the jury that as long as D foresaw the possibility that, in pursuit of a common purpose, the co-accused might stab another with murderous intent, it is sufficient for D's conviction for murder. D appealed, claiming it was unfair under Art 6 of the European Convention of Human Rights that D, who did not actually inflict the fatal wounds, was convicted of murder when he did not intend that V should die or suffer serious bodily injury.

Decision

The Court of Appeal dismissed D's appeal. The ingredients of the offence of murder are long-hallowed judge-made law, although Parliament had intervened from time to time regarding provocation and diminished responsibility. Parliament had elected not to do so regarding the liability of secondary parties. Arguments of fairness regarding the substantive criminal law are not the same as arguments regarding procedural fairness under Art 6. The personal culpability of every individual convicted of murder is not identical, but provided the criminality of D was established in accordance with legally prescribed criteria for murder, D was guilty of murder if he was convicted after a fair trial; his sentence was prescribed by law. It is for Parliament to decide when and, if so, what amendments to the law on homicide are appropriate.

14.3   Withdrawal of participation

14.3.1   Withdrawal of participation must be timely and reasonable

Becerra (1975): Withdrawal must be more than mental change of intention

Facts

D broke into a house with B and C, intending to commit burglary. D gave a knife to B to use if necessary. When V came down to investigate the noise, D said 'There's a bloke coming, let's go', and jumped out of the window. B stabbed and killed V.

Decision

The Court of Appeal found D guilty as an accessory to murder. *Per* Roskill LJ:

> To vitiate complicity, there must be 'something more than a mere mental change of intention and physical change of place ... there must be timely communication ... [that is,] such communication, verbal or otherwise, that will serve unequivocal notice upon the other party to the common unlawful cause that if he proceeds upon it he does so without the further aid and assistance of those who withdraw' (citing Sloan JA, *Whitehouse* (1941)).

Bentley (1998): Effective withdrawal

Facts

D1 and D2 were on top of a warehouse, when confronted by a police officer, V, who was shot by D2, but got away and detained D1, removing weapons from him. D2 then fatally shot V.

Decision

The Court of Appeal found D1 not guilty of murder. There was reasonable doubt that D1 believed the criminal enterprise was over upon being detained by V. *Per* Lord Bingham:

> ... for much of the time after [D's] initial seizure [by V], he was not physically held, and he agreed that he had been free to run away if he had wanted to, but this was in itself evidence of potential significance supporting the suggestion that, for him, the criminal enterprise was over.

Mitchell (1998): Communication of withdrawal unnecessary where violence is spontaneous

Facts

D1 and D2 started a fight in a restaurant, which continued outside with V and the restaurant workers. Others joined the fighting. V was badly beaten. D1 dropped a stick, ceased to fight, and then walked away. D2 picked up the stick and again beat V, who later died.

Decision

The Court of Appeal ordered a retrial. *Per* Otton LJ:

> Communication of withdrawal is a necessary condition for disassociation from pre-planned violence. It is not necessary when the violence is spontaneous. Although absent from any communication, it may, as a matter of evidence, be easier to persuade a jury that a defendant, who had previously participated, had not in fact withdrawn ... A secondary party is still guilty of murder if he participates in a joint venture, realising that, in the course thereof, the principal party might use force with intent to kill or cause grievous bodily harm.

CHAPTER 15

ATTEMPTS

Introduction

Attempted offences are inchoate or incomplete offences. This means that the defendant began to commit the offence and got so far but for some reason never completed its commission and the victim was not harmed in any way. The cases in this chapter have examined how far the courts can justifiably hold the defendant liable where the full offence is not committed and no harm is caused. Until 1981, the law on this issue was developed at common law. However, the Criminal Attempts Act 1981 codified the law on inchoate liability. The common law cases are set out below because the courts have considered them in approaching the interpretation of the provisions of the Act.

The danger of inchoate offences is that, if the defendant does very little towards carrying out the *actus reus* of the substantive offence but has the intention to do so, liability may be incurred for a 'thought crime'. Therefore, the courts have attempted to draw up a benchmark of the minimum level of actions on the part of the defendant to give rise to liability. In common law, the defendant had to have 'crossed the Rubicon and burnt his boats' (*Stonehouse* (1978)) or got to a stage in the *actus reus* where there was no going back. The statute set the benchmark out as doing acts which were 'more than merely preparatory', which the courts have interpreted as 'embarking on the crime proper' (*Gullefer* (1987); *Geddes* (1996)). This means that in each case the court must examine the defendant's behaviour and decide whether he had merely prepared to commit the offence or whether he had begun to do something which fell within the *actus reus* of the offence. An examination of how far the defendant still had to go to complete the offence may also indicate whether liability is justified (*Jones* (1990)).

Attempts have to be carried out with full intention to commit the substantive offence (although this may be inferred from foresight of virtually certain consequences – *Walker and Hayles* (1990)). This is because it is inconceivable that a defendant might attempt to commit a crime recklessly; he must have intended that the substantive offence would be carried out had he got that far. That said, recklessness as to the circumstances of the offence may suffice. For example, in a case of attempted rape where the defendant attempted but failed to have sexual intercourse with the victim but was reckless as to whether she consented or not (*Khan* (1990)), he may still be guilty of an attempted rape. This does not weaken the *mens rea* of the inchoate offence since the recklessness refers to a circumstance and not to whether the substantive offence happens or not.

Two further issues have arisen. First, where a defendant begins an attempted offence but then decides to abandon his attempt. This has been treated as a simple *actus reus* issue. If the defendant abandons the attempt before he has done anything more than merely preparatory, then he has not committed the inchoate offence. If his abandonment occurs after he has embarked on the crime proper, then his withdrawal of intent does not affect his liability (*Haughton v Smith* (1975)). Secondly, the courts have had to consider whether it is justifiable to hold a defendant liable for attempting a crime that it is impossible to commit. In common law this depended on why the offence was impossible. Where it was impossible because the circumstances for an offence did not physically exist (such as where a pickpocket places his hand in an empty pocket), or where the attempt is impossible because the substantive 'offence' is not a crime (such as where a defendant attempts to handle goods which are not in fact stolen), the courts felt it was inappropriate to find liability. However, where the offender failed in his attempt to commit a crime due to his own incapacity (such as a rapist who fails to have sexual intercourse due to his impotence), then liability could be established.

Section 1(2) of the Criminal Attempts Act 1981 appears to establish liability for impossible attempts whatever the reason for impossibility. The House of Lords had the opportunity to examine this section in *Anderton v Ryan* (1985) and concluded that Parliament cannot have intended to provide for liability for an attempt which is objectively impossible but which the defendant thought was possible. However, in the later case of *Shivpuri* (1987), the House of Lords revisited this issue and overruled their previous decision on a more literal interpretation of the Act. This now provides the current authority for the fact that the Act establishes liability for any form of impossible attempt.

15.1   *Mens rea* of attempts

15.1.1   *With intent*

O'Toole (1987): Recklessness will not suffice for an attempt

Facts

D was charged with attempted arson.

Decision

The Court of Appeal held that, although recklessness would suffice for the completed offence, only intention would suffice for the charge of attempting the offence.

Mohan (1976): Recklessness will not suffice

Facts

D, in response to a police officer's signal to stop, slowed his car down, but then accelerated and drove the car at the police officer. The police officer stepped aside and D continued on his journey. D was charged with attempt to cause bodily harm by wanton driving at a police constable. The jury were directed that it had to be proved that D deliberately drove wantonly, realising that such wanton driving would be likely to cause bodily harm.

Decision

The Court of Appeal held that intent is an essential ingredient of the offence of attempt and therefore only intent will suffice as the *mens rea* of attempted crimes. Although recklessness would often suffice as the mental element for the complete offence, attempt was a separate and often more serious offence with its own separate *mens rea*.

15.1.2 'With intent' includes 'oblique intent'

Walker and Hayles (1990): Intent includes foresight of highly probable consequences

Facts

During a fight, the Ds had thrown V over a third floor balcony. V was not killed. The Ds appealed against conviction for attempted murder on the ground that the judge had misdirected the jury on the necessary mental element for attempted murder.

Decision

The Court of Appeal, following *Nedrick* (1986) (see 1.2.2 above), held that intent to kill, as the mental element for attempted murder, could be inferred by the jury from evidence that D foresaw the death as a virtually certain or highly probable consequence of his actions.

15.1.3 Mens rea of attempted murder

Whybrow (1951): Intent to kill only will suffice

Facts

D built an electric device and gave an electric shock to his wife as she was taking a bath.

Decision

The Court of Appeal held that, although intent to cause grievous bodily harm was sufficient *mens rea* for the complete offence of murder, only an intent to kill would suffice for attempted murder. For the latter, an intent to kill was required because 'the intent becomes the principal ingredient of the crime'.

15.1.4 Recklessness and attempts

Khan (1990): Recklessness as to consent will suffice

Facts

D attempted to have sexual intercourse with a girl without her consent, but failed. D appealed against his conviction for attempted rape, on the ground that the judge wrongly directed the jury that recklessness as to whether the girl consented was sufficient *mens rea* for the offence.

Decision

The Court of Appeal held that recklessness as to whether the girl consented was sufficient *mens rea*. Per Russell LJ:

> The offences of rape and attempted rape are identical in all respects, except that in the former, sexual intercourse takes place, and, in the latter, it does not. Therefore, the *mens rea* of both offences is identical, namely, an intention to have sexual intercourse, plus a knowledge of or recklessness as to the woman's absence of consent.

Comment

The Court of Appeal is not stating that recklessness will suffice as the mental element for the attempted crime *per se*, but that intention is required in relation to the attempted act, and recklessness will suffice as to the surrounding circumstances.

Millard and Vernon (1987): Recklessness as to circumstances will suffice

Facts

The Ds were convicted of attempting to damage property. They were football supporters who repeatedly pushed against a wooden wall on a stand at a football ground. The prosecution alleged that they were trying to break it. The Ds denied this.

Decision

The Court of Appeal ruled that where the substantive offence consists simply of an act leading to a result (the *actus reus*), together with a *mens rea* relating to that result, full intent is required to prove an attempt to commit that substantive offence. However, where the substantive offence consists of a *mens rea* relating to the result, as well as a *mens rea* relating to some other circumstance, then on a charge of attempting that substantive offence, recklessness will suffice as a *mens rea* relating to the other circumstance.

AG's Reference (No 3 of 1992) (1994): Recklessness as to endangering lives suffices

Facts

D was charged with attempted arson with intent to endanger lives or with recklessness as to whether lives are endangered, under s 1(2) of the Criminal Damage Act 1971.

Decision

The Court of Appeal held that for a charge of attempted arson under s 1(2) of the Criminal Damage Act 1971, it was sufficient to prove an intent to cause damage by fire and recklessness as to whether lives are endangered thereby.

15.2 *Actus reus* of attempts

15.2.1 *Proximity test under common law*

Eagleton (1855): Proximity required for an attempt

Decision

Per Parke B: 'Acts remotely leading towards the commission of the offence are not to be considered as attempts to commit it; but acts immediately connected with it are ...'

Stonehouse (1978): D 'must cross the Rubicon and burn his boats'

Facts

D, in England, insured his own life for his wife's benefit, and then faked his own death by drowning overseas. D was charged with attempting to obtain insurance money by deception. The trial judge directed the jury that D's conduct did amount to an attempt, instead of that it could amount to an attempt.

Decision

The House of Lords found that the acts of D were sufficiently proximate to the complete offence of obtaining property by deception to be capable in law of amounting to an attempt. D must have 'crossed the Rubicon and burnt his boats' (*per* Lord Diplock).

Comment

The *actus reus* is now codified in s 1 of the Criminal Attempts Act 1981, which states that, 'if ... a person does an act which is more than merely preparatory to the commission of the offence, he is guilty of attempting to commit the offence'.

15.2.2 More than merely preparatory

Widdowson (1986): Acts remotely connected to offence are merely preparatory

Facts

D wanted to acquire a van on hire purchase and was given a hire purchase form which was to be used to make credit checks. D gave the name and address of a neighbour, knowing himself to be uncreditworthy. However, he accidentally signed the form with his own name. D was charged with attempting to obtain services by deception.

Decision

The Court of Appeal found that D's act, in giving false particulars on the form, was merely preparatory to obtaining hire purchase services because, if the hire purchase company had responded favourably to the proposal, it still remained for D to seek a hire purchase agreement with them. Also, D's acts could not be described as immediately, rather than remotely, connected with the specific offence alleged to have been attempted. Accordingly, there could be no conviction.

Boyle and Boyle (1987): Common law may assist in meaning of 'more than merely preparatory'

Facts

D was charged with attempted burglary. D damaged the door of a house with a view to entering the premises as a trespasser, and with intent to steal therein. D claimed that his acts were merely preparatory.

Decision

The Court of Appeal ruled that, in deciding whether the act was more than merely preparatory to the commission of an offence, the court was entitled to look back at the common law and see the tests that were then applied. There was ample evidence that D intended to enter the house to steal and so commit the offence of burglary; in breaking down the door, he did a more than preparatory act.

Rowley (1992): Did D do all he could to complete the offence?

Facts

D left notes in public places offering incentives to boys, designed to lure them for immoral purposes. The notes themselves were not indecent. D was convicted of attempting to incite a child aged under 14 to commit an act of gross indecency. D appealed.

Decision

The Court of Appeal found that the notes went no further than to seek to arrange a preliminary meeting with the boys. No proposition or incitement to the offence emanated from D. This act is not more than merely preparatory, even assuming that the intention of D was to commit an act of gross indecency. An attempted incitement may have taken place had D sent a letter to a boy which actually suggested committing an act of gross indecency, but where the boy never actually received it. In that situation, D would have done all he could towards inciting the boy.

Geddes (1996): Had D actually tried to commit the offence?

Facts

D was seen in the lavatory block of a school, carrying a rucksack. He had no connection with the school and no right to be there. Later, D's rucksack was found near the lavatory block, containing a large kitchen knife, some rope and a roll of masking tape. A cider can belonging to him was found inside a lavatory cubicle. D was convicted of attempted false imprisonment.

Decision

The Court of Appeal held that the line between acts which were merely preparatory and those which might amount to an attempt was not clear or easy to recognise. There was no rule of thumb test, but each case required an individual exercise of judgment on the facts. The statutory test could accurately be paraphrased as a test, *per* Lord Bingham LCJ: '... to ask whether the available evidence, if accepted, could show that a defendant had done an act which showed that he had actually tried to commit the offence in question, or whether he had only got ready or put himself in a position or equipped himself to do so.' In this case, there was little doubting D's intention, as he had clearly made preparations and equipped himself for the offence, but had not confronted or communicated with any pupil at the school and therefore had not committed acts which were more than merely preparatory.

Tosti (1997): Application of *Geddes* test

Facts

D was seen late at night, examining the padlock on the door of a barn. He saw that he was being watched and ran off. Later, his car was found parked nearby, containing oxyacetylene equipment. Two other cars were parked nearby with their engines still warm. D was convicted of attempted burglary. He appealed.

Decision

The Court of Appeal dismissed the appeal holding that, in short, the question was whether it could be said that D, in providing himself with the oxyacetylene equipment, driving to the scene, approaching the barn and examining the padlock, had committed acts which were more than merely preparatory and amounted to acts done in the commission of an offence. The court applied the guidance in *Geddes* (above), and found that there was sufficient evidence of acts which were more than merely preparatory for the question to be left to the jury.

Nash (1999): Invitation more than merely preparatory to procurement

Facts

Two letters addressed to 'Paperboy' were found by a paperboy and a papergirl in the street. They contained an invitation to commit an act of indecency with the sender. A third letter was found addressed to 'Paperboy', offering the recipient a job and requesting a urine sample. The letters were taken to the police. D was arrested and his home searched. The police found a typewriter bearing the same typeface as the letters and another letter similar to the three others. D was convicted of attempting to procure an act of gross indecency. He appealed.

Decision

The Court of Appeal followed their earlier guidance given in *Geddes* and found that the letter did contain an overtly sexual invitation, and therefore did amount to an attempted procurement. However, the third letter contained an invitation which was less unequivocal and was not sufficient to amount to an attempted procurement.

Toothill (1998): Holistic approach to attempted burglary

Facts

D was arrested outside V's house. He had knocked at her door and asked for directions and was later spotted by V standing in her garden, apparently masturbating. D was arrested in the garden near a knife and a glove and with a condom in his pocket. He was charged with attempted burglary with intent to commit rape. At the trial, the judge ruled that it was enough to show that D's acts were more than merely preparatory. D appealed, arguing that the jury needed to find evidence of both attempt to burgle and attempt to commit rape.

Decision

The Court of Appeal held that it is an inappropriate and misleading approach to inchoate offences to look at the offence as an undivided whole. In this case, the *actus reus* of the offence was entering the property as a trespasser with intent to commit one of the offences listed in s 9(2) of the Theft Act 1968. The attempt relates to the act and not to the intention. D went beyond what was merely preparatory in this case when he knocked on V's door to ask for directions.

15.2.3 Embarked on the crime proper

Gullefer (1987): Preparatory acts end when D embarks on the crime proper

Facts

During a greyhound race, D attempted to stop the race by climbing on to the track in front of the dogs. He did this because the dog on which he had placed a bet was losing and he had hoped to recover his stake. However, the stewards decided not to stop the race and D was convicted of attempted theft. D appealed on the ground that his acts were merely preparatory.

Decision
The Court of Appeal held that D could not, at the stage of jumping on to the track, be said to be in the process of committing theft, and had not committed acts which were more than merely preparatory to the offence of theft. The *actus reus* of attempt is satisfied 'when the merely preparatory acts come to an end and the defendant embarks upon the crime proper. When that is will depend, of course, upon the facts in any particular case' (*per* Lord Lane LCJ).

Jones (1990): No need to commit last act possible
Facts
D bought a shotgun, sawed off the end of the barrel and test fired it. Several days later, D climbed into the back of F's car and asked F to drive to a secluded place. D then took the sawn off shotgun from his bag and pointed it towards F. The safety catch of the gun was on. F grabbed the end of the gun, threw it out of the window and escaped.

Decision
The Court of Appeal ruled that, 'more than merely preparatory' could not mean that D had necessarily committed the last act within his power towards the commission of the offence. Although it was necessary to come close to committing the substantive offence, there may be some acts left to perform before the substantive offence is committed. In this case, although D had still to remove the gun's safety catch, put his finger on the trigger and pull it, he had performed sufficient acts which were more than merely preparatory and was, therefore, correctly convicted of attempted murder.

Campbell (1991): Application of *Gullefer* test
Facts
D planned to rob a post office. He drove to the post office on a motorcycle, walked towards the post office in his motorcycle helmet carrying an imitation gun and a threatening note, which he planned to hand over to the cashier. D was arrested before he entered the post office and was convicted of attempted robbery.

Decision
The Court of Appeal approved the *Gullefer* test as representing the true meaning of the words in s 1 of the Criminal Attempts Act 1981, and previous common law tests were irrelevant. In this case, D had not 'embarked upon the crime proper', since his weapon was an imitation, he made no attempt to remove it from his pocket, he was not wearing a disguise and he had not entered the post office. His acts were merely preparatory and therefore he was not guilty of attempted robbery.

AG's Reference (No 1 of 1992) (1992): Attempted penetration not necessary for attempted rape
Facts
D attempted to have sexual intercourse with a girl without her consent, whilst in an intoxicated state. He pulled her behind a hedge, forced her to the ground, lay on top of her, lowered his trousers and interfered with her private parts, but was unable to attempt penetration and have sexual intercourse with her. The case was referred to

the Court of Appeal for an opinion as to whether, in order to prove a charge of attempted rape, D had to have attempted penetration of the girl's vagina with his penis.

Decision

The Court of Appeal held that the previous common law tests concerning the *actus reus* of attempts were irrelevant; it was necessary to prove that D had 'embarked on committing the crime itself'. In the case of rape, this did not necessarily mean that D had to have attempted or achieved penetration; other acts, such as forcing the girl to the ground, lowering his trousers and interfering with her private parts could allow the jury to conclude that D committed acts which were more than merely preparatory.

15.3   Abandonment

Haughton v Smith (1975): Abandonment must take place before any act committed

Facts

A man was stopped in his van by the police on a motorway. The police found stolen goods in the van. The man was taken to the police station, but was later allowed to continue on his journey, with two police officers in the van and another following, to the service station where the goods were to be handed over to D and some others. D was arrested and charged with attempting to handle stolen goods.

Decision

The House of Lords ruled that if D changed his mind before committing any act which could amount to an attempt, then he was clearly not guilty of attempting to commit a crime, since there was no *mens rea* at the relevant time. If, however, D changed his mind later, after committing an act which is not merely preparatory, he was guilty of attempting to commit the offence. In this situation, there was no defence of abandonment.

15.4   Impossible attempts at common law

15.4.1   Legal impossibility

Haughton v Smith (1975): No liability where offence is legally impossible

Facts

See 15.3 above.

Decision

The House of Lords held that there could be no liability for attempt in such circumstances. The act of D must 'form part of a series which would constitute the actual commission of the offence if it were not interrupted'. If the series of acts could never constitute a criminal offence, then D could not be guilty of attempt.

15.4.2 Physical impossibility

Partington v Williams (1977): No liability where offence is physically impossible

Facts

D took a wallet from a drawer in her employer's office. She looked to see if it contained any money, intending to steal anything she found. It was empty; D was convicted of attempted theft.

Decision

The Queen's Bench Divisional Court held that there could be no liability for attempted theft in these circumstances, since the substantive offence was impossible.

Nock (1978): Wording of indictment important

Facts

D agreed to produce cocaine by separating it from other substances in a powder which he believed to be a mixture of cocaine and lignocaine. In fact, the powder contained no cocaine and D could not, in these circumstances, have produced any. D was convicted of attempting to produce a prohibited drug.

Decision

The House of Lords argued (*obiter*) that whether there could be liability for an attempt to commit a crime, which was physically or legally impossible to commit, depended on how the indictment was framed. If it was framed specifically, for example, attempting to steal a particular piece of property, there could be no liability according to *Haughton v Smith* (see 15.4.1 above). However, if the indictment was framed more loosely, for example, attempting to steal from V, then there could be liability, since the substantive offence, as loosely defined, was not impossible.

15.4.3 Impossibility due to incapacity

White (1910): Incapacity does not negate liability for attempt

Facts

D tried to kill his mother by poisoning her, but did not use enough poison to successfully cause her death.

Decision

The Court of Appeal upheld D's conviction of attempted murder. *Per* Bray J:

> We are of the opinion that the trial judge's directions are correct and that the completion or attempted completion of a series of acts intended by a man to result in a killing is an attempt to murder, even though this completed act would not, unless followed by other acts, result in killing.

Haughton v Smith (1975): Incapacity does not negate liability for attempt

Facts

See 15.3 above.

Decision

The House of Lords held:

> ... a man may set out to commit a crime with inadequate tools. He finds that he cannot break in because the door is too strong for him. Or he uses poison which is not strong enough. He is certainly guilty of attempt; with better equipment or greater skill, he could have committed the full crime (*per* Lord Reid).

15.5   Impossibility after the Criminal Attempts Act 1981

Anderton v Ryan (1985): Impossibility negates liability for attempt

Facts

D was charged with attempting to handle stolen property, a video recorder. When she had bought the video, she had believed it was stolen but, since no evidence could be found that it was in fact stolen, it had to be assumed that it was not.

Decision

The House of Lords held that if s 1 of the Criminal Attempts Act 1981, which overruled the common law of attempt, creates the offence of attempting a crime which is objectively impossible, simply because D subjectively thinks it is possible to commit, the results would be 'asinine'. Parliament cannot have intended such a result; therefore, s 1(2) and (3) of the Act must be interpreted so as not to convict D of attempt, who mistakenly believes that the substantive offence is possible to commit. D's conviction in this case was quashed.

Shivpuri (1987): Impossibility does not negate liability for attempt

Facts

D was convicted of attempting to deal with and harbour drugs. D believed he was dealing with a prohibited drug such as cannabis or heroin, whereas in fact the substance was harmless vegetable matter.

Decision

The House of Lords in this case overturned its previous decision in *Anderton v Ryan*, and decided that s 1 of the Criminal Attempts Act 1981 must be read as it stands. Any attempt to commit an impossible substantive offence carries liability, provided D intended to carry out the substantive offence and did an act which was more than merely preparatory. The concept of 'objective innocence' in *Anderton v Ryan*, that is, the concept that if the acts were objectively innocent, then no offence is committed, 'is incapable of sensible application in relation to the law of attempts. What turns what would otherwise, from the point of view of the criminal law, be an innocent act into a crime is the intent of the actor to commit an offence ...' (*per* Lord Bridge). Therefore, there can be no such concept of objective innocence in criminal law where the subjective mental state of the accused is crucial in determining whether an offence has been committed.

CHAPTER 16

CONSPIRACY

Introduction

There are offences of conspiracy in statutory form (s 105 of the Criminal Law Act 1977) and at common law. The statutory offence amounts to making an agreement between two or more persons necessarily entailing the commission of a crime provided it is carried out in accordance with their intentions. This means that two or more defendants must agree to or plan to commit a crime. This is an inchoate offence, since a charge of conspiracy may arise even where the substantive crime never happened. Making the agreement with the intention to carry it out is sufficient. A belief that the substantive offence is impossible, as well as the objective fact that the substantive offence is impossible, afford the defendants no defence (*Anderson* (1986)).

The common law offences of conspiracy have been created by the House of Lords in order to deal with the circumstances of particular cases where statutory offences were inadequate to deal with those circumstances. Conspiracy to corrupt public morals and outrage public decency was established as an offence in 1962 in the case of *Shaw v DPP*, and covers an agreement to publish indecent material for consumption by at least some sections of the public. The offence of conspiracy to defraud was established in 1975 in the case of *Scott v Metropolitan Police Commissioner*, and covers an agreement between the defendant and another to dishonestly deprive someone of an entitlement (proprietary or otherwise) (for example, an agreement to obtain National Insurance numbers to sell to illegal immigrants – *Moses and Ansbro* (1991)).

16.1 Statutory conspiracy to commit a criminal offence

16.1.1 An agreement between two or more persons necessarily entailing the commission of a crime

Jackson (1985): Meaning of 'necessarily'

Facts

During the trial of E for burglary, C and D agreed to shoot their friend E in the leg if he was convicted, in order to mitigate E's sentence.

Decision

The Court of Appeal found C, D and E guilty of conspiracy to pervert the course of justice. 'Necessarily' under s 1(1) of the Criminal Law Act 1977, is not to be held to mean that there must inevitably be the carrying out of the offence; it means, if the agreement is carried out in accordance with the plan, that there must be the commission of the offence referred to in the conspiracy count.

Comment

Conspiracy is largely covered by ss 1–5 of the Criminal Law Act 1977, with s 1(1) of the Act being amended by s 5(1) of the the Criminal Attempts Act 1981. The two Acts codify conspiracy offences regarding crimes, corruption of public morals or outraging public decency, or fraud.

Anderson (1986): Agreement need not be carried out

Facts

D agreed, for a fee, to supply diamond wire capable of cutting through metal bars, in order to enable a prisoner to escape. D did not believe the plan would succeed and intended to go abroad after supplying the wire.

Decision

The House of Lords found D guilty of conspiracy to commit the offence:

(1) Conspiracy may be committed even without intending the agreement to be carried out.

(2) An intention to play some part in the agreed course of conduct must be established. *Per* Lord Bridge: 'Neither the fact that he intended to play no further part in attempting to effect the escape, nor that he believed the escape to be impossible would … have afforded him any defence.'

Siracusa (1989): Participation in conspiracy may be active or passive

Facts

An agreement was undertaken among many defendants to import prohibited drugs over a period of time, contrary to customs laws.

Decision

The Court of Appeal found the defendants, including the organisers remaining in the background, were guilty of conspiracy. *Per* O'Connor LJ: 'Participation in a conspiracy is infinitely variable: it can be active or passive.'

Yip Chiu-Cheung (1994): Intention to carry out plan essential

Facts

D met with N, a US undercover policeman, and arranged for N to transport heroin from Hong Kong to Australia.

Decision

The Privy Council found D guilty of conspiracy to traffic in heroin. *Per* Lord Griffiths:

> The crime of conspiracy requires an agreement between two or more persons to commit an unlawful act, with the intention of carrying it out. It is the intention to carry out the crime that constitutes the necessary *mens rea* for the offence. As Lord Bridge pointed out [in *Anderson*, above], an undercover agent who has no intention of committing the crime lacks the necessary *mens rea* to be a conspirator.

However, here, N intended to traffic in drugs by exporting the heroin, albeit for the purpose of combating drug trafficking and with full knowledge of immunity from prosecution.

Ashton (1992): Identical verdicts for all parties not necessary

Facts

D and W were charged with conspiracy to murder. At their trial, the judge directed the jury that they must return the same verdict in respect of the case against both defendants. Both were convicted; D appealed on the ground that there was evidence that he was not guilty, but that the judge had not allowed the jury to consider an alternative verdict in his case.

Decision

The Court of Appeal held that, although it was superficially odd that one person may be convicted of conspiracy with another while that other was acquitted, the common law rule requiring identical verdicts for both parties to a conspiracy had been revoked by s 5 of the Criminal Law Act 1977. Where there was a material difference in the evidence against two alleged conspirators, it was not appropriate to direct the jury to find identical verdicts for each. In this case, there were important differences between the cases of D and W, D's defence being stronger than W's. D's conviction was therefore quashed.

16.1.2 Impossibility

Nock (1978): No liability for conspiracy to commit impossible crime

Facts

D and co-defendants agreed to obtain cocaine from a quantity of powder obtained from co-defendants. D was unaware that the powder contained no cocaine; that is, it was impossible to produce cocaine.

Decision

The House of Lords found D not guilty of conspiracy to produce cocaine. *Per* Lord Diplock:

> … to agree to pursue a course of conduct, which, if carried out in accordance with the intention of those agreeing to it, would not amount to or involve the commission of any offence, would not have amounted to criminal conspiracy at common law, nor does it now constitute an offence of conspiracy under s 1 of the [Criminal Law Act 1977].

Comment

Notwithstanding s 5(1) of the Criminal Attempts Act 1981, the common law position remains true for conspiracy offences not covered by statute; no liability is incurred for a conspiracy to commit the impossible.

Anderson (1986): Belief that crime is impossible affords no defence

See 16.1.1 above.

16.2 Common law conspiracy to corrupt public morals and outrage public decency

16.2.1 Conspiracy to commit non-criminalised acts

Shaw v DPP (1962): Conspiracy to corrupt public morals

Facts

D published a 'Ladies Directory', containing the names and addresses of prostitutes and the services they provided.

Decision

The House of Lords found D guilty of conspiracy to corrupt public morals.

Comment

This common law conspiracy offence of corrupting public morals is now replaced by statute: s 5(3) of the Criminal Law Act 1977.

Knuller v DPP (1973): 'Public' means those influenced by D

Facts

D published a magazine containing advertisements soliciting homosexual acts amongst consenting adults.

Decision

The House of Lords found D guilty of conspiracy to corrupt public morals:

(1) '... conspiracy to corrupt public morals ... really means to corrupt the morals of such members of the public as may be influenced by the matter published' by D, with 'corrupt' being synonymous with 'deprave' (*per* Lord Reid), or amounting to 'conduct which a jury might find to be destructive of the very fabric of society' (*per* Lord Simon).

(2) Regarding the offence of outraging public decency, 'the substantive offence ... must be committed in public', that is, before more than one person. '"Outraging public decency" goes considerably beyond offending the susceptibilities of, or even shocking, reasonable people' (*per* Lord Simon).

16.3   Common law conspiracy to defraud

16.3.1   An agreement to dishonestly deprive someone of an entitlement or to injure someone's property right

Scott v Metropolitan Police Commissioner (1975): Deception not required

Facts

D agreed with employees of cinema owners to remove films from cinemas, temporarily, in order to make copies of them, without the owners' consent, for the purposes of commercial distribution.

Decision

The House of Lords found D guilty of conspiracy to defraud at common law:

(1) *Per* Viscount Dilhorne: '... an agreement between two or more by dishonesty to deprive a person of something which is his or to which he is or would or might be entitled and an agreement by two or more to injure some proprietary right of his, suffices to constitute the offence of conspiracy to defraud.'

(2) Deception is not a requisite element of the offence.

Comment

This common law conspiracy offence is now replaced by statute: s 5(2) of the Criminal Law Act 1977.

16.3.2 Neither deception nor economic loss are requisite elements of fraud

Wai Yu-tsang (1991): Economic loss not required

Facts

D agreed with employees of a bank to conceal in the bank accounts the dishonouring of cheques the bank had purchased, in order to prevent a run on the bank.

Decision

The Privy Council found D guilty of conspiracy to defraud, which is 'not limited to the idea of economic loss, nor the idea of depriving someone of something of value. It extends generally to the purpose of the fraud and deceit ... If anyone may be prejudiced in any way by the fraud, that is enough' (*per* Lord Goff).

Moses and Ansbro (1991): Public officers acting contrary to their duty

Facts

M was a former employee and A an employee of the DHSS. They agreed to obtain National Insurance numbers, by required practice, for immigrants not entitled to such numbers.

Decision

The Court of Appeal found M and A guilty of conspiracy to defraud. *Per* Jowitt J:

> Officers of the department who played a part in the processing of these applications which, on the true facts, ought not to have been processed, were acting contrary to their public duty. The *dictum* of Lord Diplock in his speech in *Scott v Metropolitan Police Commissioner* [16.3.1 above] ... deals with the point: 'Where the intended victim of a "conspiracy to defraud" is a person performing public duties as distinct from a private individual, it is sufficient if the purpose is to cause him to act contrary to his public duty, and the intended means of achieving this purpose, are dishonest. The purpose need not involve causing economic loss to anyone.'

CHAPTER 17

INCITEMENT

Introduction

It is an offence at common law to encourage, persuade or demand another to commit a crime. This offence is known as incitement. The *actus reus* of the offence may be committed verbally, in writing, by publication or by behaviour such as offering a prohibited article for sale (*Invicta Plastics Ltd v Clare* (1976)). In some of these situations the incitement may not even be explicit but implied in the words or behaviour of the defendant, but that does not affect liability. The defendant must actually incite the perpetrator of the offence and cannot incite through a third party (*James and Ashford* (1985)). The inciter must intend that the crime they are inciting is carried out; so they must have *mens rea* in relation to the *actus reus* of the substantive offence (whether or not it is actually ever carried out). Unlike the other inchoate offences of attempt and conspiracy, there can be no liability at all for inciting another to commit a crime which is impossible, regardless of why it is impossible.

17.1 *Actus reus* of incitement

17.1.1 Encouragement, persuasion or command of another to commit an offence

Higgins (1801): An 'act'

Facts
D solicited a servant to steal his master's goods.

Decision
The Court of Appeal held that it is an indictable offence at common law to incite or solicit a person to commit any offence:
(1) '... is there not an act done, when it is charged that the defendant solicited another to commit a felony? The solicitation is an act' (*per* Lord Kenyon CJ).
(2) D may incite by words as well as by acts.

Race Relations Board v Applin (1973): Meaning of 'incitement'

Facts
D distributed a circular complaining of a neighbour's adoption of non-white foster children, for the purposes of having the neighbour adopt white foster children only.

Decision
The Court of Appeal found D guilty of incitement to do an unlawful act contrary to the Race Relations Act 1968. *Per* Lord Denning: '... to "incite" means to urge or spur on by advice, encouragement or persuasions, and not otherwise ... A person may "incite" another to do an act by threatening or by pressure, as well as by persuasion.'

Invicta Plastics Ltd v Clare (1976): Implied incitement

Facts

D advertised for sale a police radar alerting device that was illegal to operate without a licence, albeit not illegal to own.

Decision

The Queen's Bench Divisional Court found D guilty of inciting an unlawful act, by persuading and inciting the use of the device. The *actus reus* may be implied rather than express, incitement being determined by looking at the acts taken 'as a whole' (*per* Park J).

Whitehouse (1977): Incitement and legal impossibility

Facts

D urged his daughter to commit incest with him; she was legally incapable, by her age, of being either a principal or accessory to incest.

Decision

The Court of Appeal found D not guilty of incitement for persuading his daughter to commit an act which was not an offence. *Per* Scarman LJ: '... at common law, the crime of incitement consists of inciting another person to commit a crime ... An inciter is one who reaches and seeks to influence the mind of another to the commission of a crime.'

Comment

It is today an offence, under s 54 of the Criminal Law Act 1977, for a man to incite a female under 16, whom he knows to be his granddaughter, daughter or sister, to have sexual intercourse.

James and Ashford (1985): Incitement of third party

Facts

D manufactured devices used to reverse electricity meters, with the intention to sell them to a third party retailer, who in turn was to sell the boxes to customers who would employ the device illegally.

Decision

The Court of Appeal found D not guilty of incitement because D did not incite the 'middleman' to use the boxes, nor was there evidence that D incited the middleman to incite the ultimate users.

Marlow (1997): Encouragement of criminal behaviour

Facts

D wrote a book on the cultivation and production of cannabis, which was used by customers to commit drug offences.

Decision

The Court of Appeal found D guilty of incitement to commit drug offences. Incitement is established where, '(a) taken as a whole, the words on which the charge is based amount to encouragement or persuasion of a person to whom they are directed to commit a crime, and (b) the author of the words in fact intended to encourage the commission of that crime' (*per* Potter LJ).

Booth (1998): Incitement of multiple offences

Facts

A group of authors allegedly called upon readers to commit offences of criminal damage and economic sabotage in the causes of environmentalism and animal liberation.

Decision

The Court of Appeal found the defendants were not guilty of incitement to commit criminal damage and arson. The jury direction failed to spell out all the elements of all alleged primary offences. *Per* Henry LJ:

> ... where ... a single count charges a conspiracy to commit (or in [this] case, incite) more than one offence, the Crown must probably prove that the conspiracy embraces all the offences alleged in the particulars, or at least that it embraces the offence which is the most serious of those alleged.

17.2   *Mens rea* of incitement

17.2.1   *Intention as to the circumstances surrounding and the result of the actus reus*

Curr (1968): Incitee must know actions are criminal

Facts

D was trafficking in family allowance books; lending money in return for family allowance books containing signed vouchers, which were in turn cashed by agents under D's direction.

Decision

The Court of Appeal found D not guilty of incitement to solicit the agents to commit a summary offence, unless the agents knew their actions to be an offence.

Shaw (1994): Lack of dishonest motive

Facts

D persuaded E to accept bogus invoices and to issue cheques in the customary manner. D knew that E would be acting dishonestly.

Decision

The Court of Appeal found D not guilty of incitement to obtain money by deception. D's motive was to reveal the company's poor accounting systems.

Mason (1998): Subjective test for *mens rea*

Facts

D1, D2 and V lived in the same house. D1 told her brother, D2, that she wanted her lover, V, 'out of my life. I want to get rid of him'. One night, D2 bludgeoned V with a hammer and stabbed him.

Decision

The Court of Appeal found D1 was not guilty of inciting attempted murder, but was guilty of inciting the infliction of grievous bodily harm. The 'correct test' for determining the *mens rea* for incitement is not an objective test, but, *per* Buxton LJ, 'what [the defendant] subjectively herself intended to convey by the use of those words' alleged to be the incitement.

17.3   Impossibility

17.3.1   Impossibility may exculpate an incitement

Fitzmaurice (1983): No liability for inciting an impossible crime

Facts

X asked D to organise the robbery of a woman. But X, unbeknown to D or the other perpetrators, wished to obtain a reward for reporting the robbery of a security van arriving at the same time as the planned but fictional robbery.

Decision

The Court of Appeal found D guilty of inciting a robbery, because its commission ('robbing a woman at Bow') was not impossible at the time of the incitement, regardless of the fact that it ended up being a charade. *Per* Neill J, *obiter*: '... where an offence is *de facto* impossible, D will not be liable for incitement to commit it.'

Comment

Liability is incurred for attempting the impossible and for statutory conspiracies to commit the impossible, leaving incitement as the only inchoate offence where impossibility is relevant.

Whitehouse (1977): Inciting an impossible crime

See 17.1.1 above.

CHAPTER 18

OMISSIONS

Introduction

Most criminal offences occur where the defendant does an act which is prohibited by the criminal law. However, in some situations it may be that the defendant's failure to act produces liability. In these cases, the defendant may be said to have caused the prohibited result and if criminal law were framed in these terms there would be no ideological problem with finding liability for a failure to act. However, since it is not, the courts have been reluctant to establish liability for omissions except in specific circumstances. One way of avoiding their distaste for liability for omissions would be to construe a failure to act as a continuation of an initial act (a failure to stop doing something) which causes the prohibited result. The courts took this approach in *Fagan v Metropolitan Police Commissioner* (1969) and in *Speck* (1977).

The difficulty with extending liability for omissions too far is that it tends to impose unreasonable burdens on persons to act. For example, in this country we do not have any general duty on citizens to rescue others in difficulties. It is for this reason that the courts have developed the case law in such a way that a defendant can only be liable for a failure to act where he is under some sort of legal duty to act, so that his failure to act is a breach of that duty. The duty may arise in a number of circumstances. Some special relationships give rise to a duty of care. A parent has a duty to care for their child provided the child is under 18 or otherwise dependent on them (*Shepherd* (1862)). It is the dependence of the relation on the defendant which creates the duty of care, so the same duty arises between husband and wife (*Smith* (1979)). Other family members may not be owed a duty of care for this reason but, in common with any other person, may be owed a duty arising out of an assumption of responsibility on the part of the defendant. Where the defendant (expressly or impliedly) begins to take care of another, but then fails to continue with that care causing harm to the other, they are deemed to have assumed a responsibility and have a duty to maintain their care (*Stone and Dobinson* (1977); *Wacker* (2003)). It is often the defendant's behaviour which determines their duty to act rather than any voluntary assumption of responsibility (*Singh (Gurphal)* (1999)).

A defendant who creates a dangerous situation and then fails to remedy that situation may be deemed to have a duty to act to alleviate the danger (*Miller* (1983); *R and G* (2003)). In this situation, their failure to act is hardly distinguishable from their original act which created the dangerous situation, and that initial act may be said to continue until such time as the harm is caused. Other duties arise out of a contract where someone is assigned an express or implied duty to act in accordance with the terms of the contract (*Pitwood* (1902)); or the defendant may be under a statutory duty to act (such as a police officer's statutory duty to carry out his duties or a parents statutory duty to care for their child – *Lowe* (1973)).

Failure to act where the defendant is under any sort of duty to do so is not just a breach of that duty of care, possibly giving rise to civil liability, but, with the requisite *mens rea*, can result in criminal charges. The *mens rea* required will depend on the criminal offence that the offender is charged with.

18.1   Special relationship

Shepherd (1862): No duty between parent and independent adult offspring

Facts
D was charged with the murder of her daughter. D was alleged to have purposely neglected to procure a midwife to attend to her daughter when she went into labour. The daughter died in childbirth.

Decision
The Court of Appeal stated that no duty to act exists between a parent and an 18 year old 'entirely emancipated' daughter. There is no expectation of assistance in such a situation as there is with a younger child.

Stone and Dobinson (1977): Assumed responsibility for a relative

Facts
See 18.2 below.

Decision
The Court of Appeal found that there was a blood relationship between one of the defendants and the deceased, but the duty to act arose from an assumed responsibility.

Gibbins and Proctor (1918): Duty of birth parent to child

Facts
A man and a woman lived together with the man's child. The child died of starvation, the man and the woman having withheld food from it. They were both convicted of murder.

Decision
The Court of Appeal held that the man owed a duty to act towards the child as a parent owes a duty to his child. The woman owed a duty arising from the assumption of responsibility.

Smith (1979): Duty between spouses

Facts
V died after childbirth. Her husband, D, had not called a doctor and kept her illness a secret from relatives and the doctor. D wanted to call a doctor, but V refused to allow him because she had a medical condition which gave her an aversion to doctors and medical treatment. D was charged with manslaughter.

Decision
The Crown Court held that spouses owe a duty to act, arising from their relationship towards one another.

18.2   Assumption of responsibility

Instan (1893): Legal duty arises from moral obligation

Facts

D lived with her 73 year old aunt. The aunt developed gangrene in her leg and could not walk or look after herself or call for help. D alone knew of her condition, gave her no food and did not call for medical assistance. The aunt died and D was convicted of manslaughter.

Decision

The Court of Appeal held that: 'It would not be correct to say that every moral obligation involves a legal duty, but every legal duty is founded on a moral obligation. A legal common law duty is nothing else than the enforcing by law of that which is a moral obligation without legal enforcement' (*per* Lord Coleridge CJ). D had assumed responsibility for the aunt. Such a moral obligation gave rise to a legal duty to act, and failure to do so resulted in a rightful conviction for manslaughter.

Stone and Dobinson (1977): Assumption of responsibility

Facts

Two defendants, both of low intelligence and mentally subnormal, lived together with F, D's sister. F was eccentric, anorexic and often stayed in her room for days. Eventually, F became unable to get out of bed. The defendants knew of F's condition and made ineffectual and unsuccessful attempts to summon a doctor. One D washed her once. F was found dead in a terrible state of neglect. Both Ds were convicted of manslaughter.

Decision

The Court of Appeal held that since F had come to live at the Ds' house and since both Ds had made efforts to care for F, the jury were right to conclude that they had assumed the duty to care for her when she became bedridden. Failure to carry out that duty rightly resulted in conviction for manslaughter.

Airedale NHS Trust v Bland (1993): Assumption of responsibility by doctors

Facts

See 13.3.3 above.

Decision

The House of Lords argued that the doctors would not be acting unlawfully by withdrawing life support treatment in these circumstances. Although the doctors had assumed a duty of care towards B, and withdrawal of treatment would ordinarily amount to an omission, it would not, in this case, be an unlawful breach of duty. There was no absolute rule that a patient's life had to be prolonged in all circumstances, and regard could be had to the wishes of the patient and/or those of his family. Doctors should follow the principles set down by the responsible professional body (the Medical Ethics Committee in this case).

Singh (Gurphal) (1999): Proximity and assumption of responsibility

Facts

D helped to maintain properties owned by his father. A lodger in one of the properties complained to D, while he was in charge in his father's absence, that his gas fire was faulty and that he was suffering from headaches. V, another lodger in the same property, died from carbon monoxide poisoning 10 days later. D was convicted of manslaughter by gross negligence, but appealed on the grounds that he owed no duty of care, given that he was merely helping out with the maintenance.

Decision

The Court of Appeal held that the jury had to look at the whole situation in considering whether D owed a duty of care or not. In this case, D possessed enough information to make him aware of a danger of death from the gas fire. Although he did not possess the skill to discover how the danger arose, he was responsible for taking reasonable steps to call in expert help to deal with the situation. There was, therefore, sufficient proximity between the lodgers, on the one hand, and D, on the other, to place a duty of care on D.

Wacker (2003): Assumption of responsibility and duty of care

See 3.3.1 above.

18.3 Duty assumed under a contract

Pitwood (1902): Contractual assumption of responsibility

Facts

D was employed to shut a railway gate across a track when trains passed over the track. A train hit a cart, killing the cart driver, when D forgot to shut the gate.

Decision

D owed a duty to act arising from his contract of employment. The expectations of others, arising from D's assumption of responsibility for shutting the gate, which in turn arises from the terms of the contract, is what gives rise to a legal duty, not the mere existence of the contract itself.

18.4 A duty arising where D creates a dangerous situation

Miller (1983): Failure to remedy consequences of D's actions

Facts

See 13.4.1 above.

Decision

The House of Lords held that: 'If, when [D] does become aware that the [prohibited consequences] have happened as a result of his own act, he does not try to prevent or reduce the risk of damage by his own efforts or, if necessary, by sending for help,' he is under a legal duty to act; failure to carry out that duty amounts to an offence (*per* Lord Diplock).

18.5   Statutory duties

Lowe (1973): No liability for omissions

Facts

D was of subnormal intelligence. His daughter died of dehydration and emaciation when she became ill. D had told his girlfriend to take the child to the doctor, but she had not done so. D was convicted of manslaughter and cruelty by wilful neglect contrary to s 1(1) of the Children and Young Persons Act 1933.

Decision

The Court of Appeal held that:

> We think there is a clear distinction between an act of omission and an act of commission likely to cause harm … If I strike a child in a manner likely to cause harm, it is right that, if the child dies, I may be charged with manslaughter. If, however, I omit to do something, with the result that it suffers injury to health, concluding in its death, we think that a charge of manslaughter should not be an inevitable consequence, even if the omission is deliberate (*per* Phillimore LJ).

Mavji (1987): Liability for breach of statutory duty by omission

Facts

D was the director of a company. He was charged VAT on gold that he dealt in, but he did not account for the tax to Customs and Excise. D was charged with the offence of cheating the public revenue.

Decision

The Court of Appeal held that the common law offence of cheating the public revenue consisted of fraudulent conduct by which money was diverted from the Revenue and the Revenue was deprived of money to which it was entitled. This offence could be committed by omission as well as by the positive act of deceit. D had a statutory duty to pay VAT arising from s 38(1) of the Finance Act 1972, and failure to do so could amount to a criminal omission.

18.6   The distinction between acts and omissions

Fagan v Metropolitan Police Commissioner (1969): A continuing act

Facts

D accidentally drove his car onto a policeman's foot. When told to reverse off, D refused and turned the ignition off. Eventually he reversed off. D was convicted of assaulting a police officer in the execution of his duty. He claimed failure to reverse off the policeman's foot was not an 'act' capable of amounting to an assault.

Decision

The Queen's Bench Divisional Court held that a distinction should be drawn between acts which are complete, and those which are continuing. D's failure to reverse off the policeman's foot was the continuing 'act' of battery in driving onto it.

Speck (1977): Inactivity as an 'invitation' to act

Facts

A girl aged eight went up to D and put her hand on his penis outside his trousers. She left her hand there for about five minutes. As a result of the child touching his penis, D had an erection. D remained inactive throughout and did nothing to encourage the child's act. D was charged with gross indecency with a child. D claimed his inactivity could not amount to an 'act' of gross indecency.

Decision

The Court of Appeal held that inactivity by D was capable of amounting to an invitation to a child to undertake the act done by the child. If the circumstances justified the view that D's inactivity did amount to an invitation to the child to continue to do the act, that constituted sufficient activity on the part of D for a conviction of gross indecency.

Empress Car Co v National Rivers Authority (1984): Failure to prevent

Facts

D maintained a diesel oil tank in its yard, which drained directly into a river. A vandal opened a tap on the tank and the contents flowed into the river. The National Rivers Authority charged D with 'causing' pollution to enter controlled waters. D was convicted and appealed on the ground that the leakage into the river was caused by the vandal, not by D.

Decision

The House of Lords held that a person caused pollution, for the purposes of this offence, where they actively did something to produce the situation where the polluting matter could escape. This was so even where that person was not the immediate cause of the pollution. The act of D in maintaining a diesel oil tank on its land was sufficient to 'cause' the pollution for the purposes of this charge.

CHAPTER 19

RECKLESSNESS

Introduction

Recklessness is a *mens rea* requirement for a number of criminal offences and falls short of direct or oblique intention (see Chapter 1). Recklessness is proved where, although the defendant did not intend for the result to happen, he may have foreseen it as a consequence of his actions. Note that the degree of probability of a risk for recklessness falls short of that required for oblique intention (foresight of highly probable or virtually certain consequence). Recklessness on the part of the defendant is assessed subjectively; that is, by looking at the defendant's state of mind at the time of the offence and what he actually foresaw. If he foresaw a risk but went on to take it, then he is reckless. If he failed to foresee the risk for whatever reason, then he does not have the requisite *mens rea* for the offence (*Cunningham* (1957)).

This subjective test caused problems for the courts in the case of *Caldwell*, where the defendant caused criminal damage by setting fire to a hotel but was incapable of foreseeing the risk that people's lives may be endangered by his actions because he was drunk at the time. Consequently, the House of Lords in that case introduced an objective test of recklessness, whereby the defendant may additionally be found to have the requisite *mens rea* if he failed to give any thought to the existence of a risk that would have been obvious to the ordinary reasonable (sober) person. Whilst this would have ensured that *Caldwell* himself was convicted, it had the unfortunate effect of convicting other defendants who failed to recognise an obvious risk due to their own incapacity. A young child or a person with learning difficulties may not recognise a risk that would have been obvious to an ordinary reasonable adult, but this was through no fault of their own. The *Caldwell* judgment attracted a great deal of criticism as a result of the injustice it was causing in other cases. In 2003, the House of Lords had the opportunity to revisit the issue when two juvenile defendants had been convicted of criminal damage having failed to recognise the obvious risk their actions caused on account of their youth. The House of Lords decided that the *Caldwell* judgment did indeed cause injustice and was manifestly wrong, and consequently overruled it. We are therefore now in a position that, where recklessness suffices for the *mens rea* for any crime, it must bear its subjective meaning as laid down in *Cunningham* (1957).

19.1   Subjective recklessness

Cunningham (1957): Meaning of 'maliciously'

Facts

D stole a gas meter and its contents from a house and in doing so fractured a gas pipe. Gas escaped into a bedroom and V, who was asleep in the bedroom, inhaled a large quantity of gas. D was charged under s 23 of the Offences Against the Person Act 1861, causing V to take a noxious thing maliciously and unlawfully.

Decision
The Court of Appeal held that the word 'maliciously' meant foresight of the consequence. D must have foreseen a risk and recklessly gone ahead and taken it.

Parker (1977): Closing mind to an obvious risk

Facts
D ineffectually tried to make a telephone call in a public telephone kiosk. He lost his temper and slammed the receiver down. The telephone was made of breakable material and was damaged by D's actions.

Decision
The Court of Appeal held that:

> If the defendant did not know that there was some risk of damage, he was, in effect, deliberately closing his mind to the obvious – the obvious being that damage in these circumstances was inevitable. In the view of this court, that type of action, that type of deliberate closing of the mind, is the equivalent of knowledge (*per* Lane LJ).

Stephenson (1979): D must foresee risk

Facts
D crawled into a haystack to sleep. To keep warm he lit a fire, which destroyed the haystack. D was known to be suffering from schizophrenia. D was convicted of criminal damage.

Decision
The Court of Appeal held that the word 'reckless' required that D must actually have foreseen the risk of damage resulting from his actions and, nevertheless, ran the risk. D, through no fault of his own, was incapable of appreciating the risk because of his mental condition. D was therefore entitled to be acquitted.

19.2   Objective recklessness

Caldwell (1982): Lack of foresight of an obvious risk

Facts
D worked at a hotel. After a quarrel with his employer, D got drunk and set fire to the hotel. He was charged with causing criminal damage with intent to endanger life or being reckless as to whether life was endangered. D pleaded not guilty on the ground that, being intoxicated, he was unable to appreciate the risk.

Decision
The House of Lords held that in order to establish that D was reckless in a charge of criminal damage, the jury must consider a two part test:

(1)   Did D commit an act which created an obvious risk that property would be damaged?; and
(2)   When D committed the act, did he either give no thought to the possibility of there being a risk or, having recognised the risk, did he go on to take it (*per* Lord Diplock)?

G & R (2003): *Caldwell* overruled

Facts

G and R (aged 11 and 12 respectively) went camping without their parents' permission. They set fire to some newspapers in the yard at the back of a shop and threw the lit newspapers under a wheelie bin. They left the yard without putting the fire out. The fire spread to the bin and the shop causing around £1 million worth of damage. At their trial for arson, G and R argued that they thought the newspapers would burn themselves out on the concrete floor of the yard, and that they did not appreciate the risk of fire spreading as it did. The trial judge directed the jury to consider recklessness according to the objective test laid down in *Caldwell*. G and R were convicted and appealed.

Decision

The House of Lords held that according to various Law Commission Reports preceding the enactment of the Criminal Damage Act 1971, Parliament clearly intended recklessness in relation to the offence of criminal damage to hold its subjective meaning as laid down in *Cunningham* (1957). The House of Lords in *Caldwell* had misconstrued s 1 of the Criminal Damage Act 1971, and the model direction in *Caldwell* was capable of producing obvious unfairness. It was not moral or just to convict a child on the basis of what an ordinary reasonable adult would have foreseen, even if D himself had not foreseen the risk. Not only had the decision in *Caldwell* been subject to rigorous academic and judicial criticism, but it was also offensive to principle and apt to cause injustice. *Caldwell* was overruled.

Comment

The House of Lords in this case finally overruled *Caldwell*, and the objective test of recklessness has been abolished. The objective test, in their view, caused manifestly unjust results, especially in a case such as *G & R* where the defendants were children who were less capable of appreciating a risk that may have been obvious to the ordinary reasonable adult. The test for recklessness in a case of criminal damage is now a subjective test as laid down in *Cunningham* (1957).

INDEX